The Christian's Hope
The Anchor of the Soul

The Christian's Hope
The Anchor of the Soul

What the Bible Really Says About Death, Judgment, Rewards, Heaven, and the Future Life on a Restored Earth

JOHN W. SCHOENHEIT

ISBN#0-9628971-6-7

Christian Educational Services
2144 E. 52nd St.
Indianapolis, IN 46205
Phone: (317) 255-6189
Fax: (317) 255-6249
E-mail: jesusces@aol.com
Website: Christianeducational.org

Note: Most Scriptures quoted in this book are from The New International Version (NIV). References taken from other translations or versions are noted as such, e.g., King James Version = (KJV), New American Standard Bible = (NASB), etc. In verses or quotations from other authors, words in bold print have been emphasized by the author and words inside brackets have been added by the author.

Contents

Acknowledgements

First and foremost I would like to acknowledge my Heavenly Father and my Lord Jesus Christ. Of a truth, they "open the eyes of the blind so that they may see." I have vivid memories of the time in my life when I was "blind" to the truths and facts contained in this book and did not have a good understanding of the Hope and my everlasting future. I am grateful for the gift of the life I am living now and the everlasting life that has been promised to me in the future. I am also extremely thankful for the privilege of knowing about the wonderful hope that lies in store, not only for me, but also for all those who call upon the name of the Lord Jesus.

It is often said that no man is an island, and that certainly is the case when it comes to writing a book. I did not ferret out all the material in this book simply by reading the text of the Bible. Other godly men and women have gone before me and placed their works and their lives like stepping stones so that I might proceed. Some of these works are footnoted in the text or are mentioned in the books that are footnoted in the text.

A special thanks is due my family, especially my wife Jenivee, my loving companion, faithful friend, and prayer partner. Her love and support helps keep me strong in my work. Special thanks are also due to Mark Graeser, who has spent hours discussing these issues with me. He is an expansive thinker and philosopher, and my discussions with him have helped clarify many issues. John Lynn has also discussed these issues with me and tirelessly edited the manuscript. I seem to be blind to my own grammatical errors, and John has not only edited manuscript after manuscript for punctuation and proper grammar, but he can also turn a phrase with the best of them and his comments have greatly improved this work. Judy Dupuis, Ken Schleimer, Cindy Freeman, Mike Colombaro, and Dr. Shawnee Vickery have also returned multiple revisions to me and made helpful suggestions. Eddie DeBruhl has been a constant source of insight and inspiration through the entire time I have been writing this book, and for years before, because we have discussed the Hope for decades now. His insights are keen, his suggestions thoughtful, and his friendship invaluable. His insights contributed greatly to the understanding of John 3, which is expounded in Appendix H. Thanks also to Sharon Whitaker and Robin Lawrence, who spent hours working on the maps and graphs, which make the work much easier to understand. My thanks to Elizabeth Boyle for a great cover design.

Christian Educational Services has many research-minded associates who have read and made comments on this book, and I want to make special mention of them and give them my thanks and appreciation. God placed Christians into a family and the family works together for the blessing of all. If this book is a blessing, it is because the family of God came together to make it so.

John W. Schoenheit

Prayer

Although diligent study is important to the understanding of Scripture, the value of prayer cannot be overstated. Scripture says, "Ask and you will receive." Many people read the Bible without asking for understanding and then go away frustrated when they do not have it.

James wrote: "You do not have because you do not ask God" (James 4:2). Truly the Lord opens our blind eyes so that we may see and opens our hearts so we can understand both the meaning and value of the timeless Word of God. My prayer, for myself and for you as you read this book, is not original. It was in the heart of the apostle Paul and penned to the church at Ephesus almost 2000 years ago.

> **Ephesians 1:18**
> I pray also that the eyes of your heart may be enlightened in order that you may know the Hope to which he has called you, the riches of his glorious inheritance in the saints.

May we all understand the Hope the Lord has set before us.

Introduction

"You go to heaven when you die." This statement, it seems, is almost universally accepted and believed by Christians (and even many non-Christians) today. It is asserted boldly at funerals, in movies, and nearly everywhere people offer an opinion about the future beyond death. But is this really a true statement? And is "heaven" the everlasting destiny of the Christian? What is heaven and what will it be like? Is the moment of one's death really the "gateway" to heaven? Certainly these are important questions, and we should have solid answers to them. But, sad to say, most Christians have a very vague conception of the future because there is such a lack of clear-cut teaching on this subject. Ironically, the Bible is full of insight about a marvelous future on a restored earth which is promised to those who are saved, but this has been lost on most Christians who have been taught to expect a heavenly destiny about which little is known.

Like a beautiful diamond, the Christian hope is many faceted and very bright. It includes seeing the Lord Jesus face to face when he returns. It also includes everlasting life in a new and glorious body and living forever on a wonderful, recreated earth where there is justice, peace, safety, plenty of food for everyone, and lots of laughter and joy.

Unfortunately, through the centuries, the truth that the saved will live forever on the earth has been replaced by the concept that "heaven," a place in the air, is the eternal dwelling place of those who are saved.1 This book will establish from the Word of God that the everlasting home of the saved is on earth, even as the Lord Jesus said, "The meek will inherit **the earth**."

---

[1] It is common to hear Christians speak of "eternal life," meaning the life that they will spend forever with the Lord. Technically, "eternal" means no beginning and no end. God is "eternal," but the life that we will spend with Him is "everlasting," meaning it has no end. It is profitable for accuracy's sake to begin to use "eternal" and "everlasting" properly, and I have attempted to do that in this book.

The Lord Jesus Christ preached "the good news of **the Kingdom**" (Matt. 4:23; 9:35). The prophets had spoken about it before Jesus (Dan. 7:14) and Paul spoke about it after him (Acts 28:23).[2] "The Kingdom" is so central to the message of Jesus Christ that unless one understands it, he cannot really understand what Jesus was saying. It is mentioned 50 times in Matthew, 15 times in Mark, 39 times in Luke, and 4 times in John for a total of 108 times. In spite of the fact that the message of the Kingdom is central to the Four Gospels and, indeed, to the Bible as a whole, it has been obscured today to the point that the average Christian cannot begin to say what it is.

This book will show that the Kingdom of which Jesus Christ, John the Baptist, the prophets, and the New Testament writers spoke is the Kingdom that Christ will set up on the earth and over which he will rule as King. It will also show what the Bible says the earth will be like in the future. It will examine verses in both the Old and New Testaments that speak of the future life on earth that those who are saved will enjoy. The Bible has much to say about various aspects of this future life, such as the work that men and women will do. It says each person will have the position that he deserves based on what he did in this life. At the Judgment, the Lord will richly reward believers who lived godly lives, while those who ignored God's commands will receive less. This book will also examine how it came to be that orthodox Christianity accepted heaven instead of the earth as the future dwelling place of saved individuals. And most importantly, this book makes it clear that Jesus Christ truly is "the Way" to Paradise and "the Door" through which men enter into it.

It is my contention that without an accurate understanding of the Hope, it is extremely difficult for a Christian to stand strong and anchored in the faith when the storms of temptation and doubt assail. It is vitally important that the vague misconceptions of traditional

---

[2] There are many more times the Kingdom is mentioned than the example verses given, and they can be found by looking up "kingdom" in any exhaustive concordance.

teaching be replaced with the concrete and vivid images of the future life that are so abundantly portrayed in Scripture. If the believer's vision of the future is clear and certain, he has a much better chance of standing like a rock and working tirelessly in service to the Lord until the day of his death or the Day of Christ's appearing, whichever comes first. Without such vision, it is almost inevitable that burnout, discouragement, and succumbing to the temptations or cares of this world will prevail. The more serious the worker, the more important is the knowledge contained in this book.

CHAPTER 1

Our Valuable Anchor

A Biblical Look at "Hope"

In order to properly understand the Christian's hope, it is important to examine the exact meaning of the word "hope." "Hope" means "a desire for, or an expectation of, good, especially when there is some confidence of fulfillment." It is used that way both in common English and in the Bible. However, the Bible often uses the word "hope" in another way—to refer to the special expectation of good that God has in store for each Christian in the future. This includes the "Rapture," receiving a new, glorified body, and living forever in Paradise. Today, the ordinary use of "hope" allows for the possibility that what is hoped for will not come to pass.[1] However, when the Bible uses the word

---

[1] It is due to the fallen nature of man that the meanings of words degenerate over time. E. W. Bullinger was a wonderful biblical scholar and fluent in Greek, Hebrew, Aramaic, Latin, and other languages. His study of language led him to this interesting conclusion: "It is a strange commentary on fallen human nature to see words thus changing their usage; for this change is uniformly in one direction; it is *always a change for the worse.* We never find a word acquiring a higher meaning! It is always down, down, down, like fallen and falling man himself, who thus drags down with him the meanings of the words he uses. How, for example, did the change in the usage of this word "prevent" come about? [Bullinger had been writing of the word "prevent" and how in earlier English usage it used to mean "precede, go in front of, go before"]. It was because whenever one man got before another, it was generally for his own advantage, and to the hindrance, hurt, and loss of the other; hence the word came to have this new and lower meaning. The same may be seen in *apology*, which was used of a *defense*, as in Jewel's *Apology* (i.e., *Defense*) *of the Reformation.* But, because man's defenses of himself are usually so poor, the word has come to mean a mere *excuse.* Our word *censure* was used simply of *judgment*, which

(continued)

"hope" to refer to things that God has promised, the meaning of "hope" shifts from that which has a *reasonable chance* of coming to pass to that which will *absolutely* come to pass. To be a useful *anchor*, hope must hold fast.

A biblical occurrence of "hope" as "an expectation of good" can be found in Acts 27:20. Paul was on a ship bound for Rome. A storm came up and raged for many days, such that "we gave up all **hope** of being saved." Another example is in 3 John 14 where the apostle John wrote to his friend Gaius and said, "I **hope** to see you soon, and we will talk face to face." These are examples of the Bible using the word "hope" in the way it is used in everyday language, such as when someone says, "I hope it rains this week," or "I hope you feel better." There are also many biblical examples of the word "hope" referring to everlasting life and the blessings associated with it. Colossians 1:23 mentions "the **hope** held out in the gospel," i.e., "the expectation of future good presented in the gospel."

It is unfortunate that the word "hope" has come to be used in common English as a synonym for "wish." In the sentence, "I *hope* it will rain this week," the word "hope," if properly used, implies a certainty or confidence that it will, in fact, rain. If there is no such confidence, then it would be more proper to say, "I *wish* it would rain this week.

---

might be favorable or otherwise; but, inasmuch as such judgments have generally proved to be unfavorable, the word is used today only of blame. Our word *story* was originally short for *history*, but because so many histories and stories are what they are [i.e., made up or embellished], the word has come to mean that which is not true. *Cunning* meant merely *knowing*; but because knowing people generally know too much, or use their knowledge to a bad purpose, it has come to have its present usage. *Villain* meant a servant of a villa, or of a country or farm-house. The house has kept its good meaning, but the man has lost it." E. W. Bullinger, *How to Enjoy the Bible* (Samuel Bagster and Sons, Ltd., London, reprinted 1970), p. 230. The meaning of hope has degenerated also. From meaning something that was likely to occur, the modern English usage of "hope" actually implies that what is hoped for is very likely not to occur. For instance, one might say "I hope to go to the store today" when there is doubt that he actually may do so.

The Christian's Hope

As noted above, when the Bible uses the word "hope" in reference to events in the future, there is no doubt at all that the events will occur. The book of Titus contains a usage of "hope" referring to the believer's expectation of eternal life:

Titus 1:1,2
(1) Paul, a servant of God and an apostle of Jesus Christ for the faith of God's elect and the knowledge of the truth that leads to godliness—
(2) a faith and knowledge resting on the hope of eternal life, which God, who does not lie, promised before the beginning of time.

This is a good example of the word "hope" referring to our expectation of everlasting life. In this case, it implies more than just a desire or a wish. It is an expectation of the future that will absolutely come to pass. God, "who does not lie," made many promises about the future everlasting life of the believer. Although we may not know *when* He will fulfill those promises, we can be absolutely certain that *He will fulfill them*.

The Anchor of the Soul

The Bible has a great deal to say about the future life in Paradise that saved people will enjoy. God speaks about the future for a reason: He wants each and every Christian to make up his mind to obey Him and to be committed to Him in good times and in bad times. History and experience both show that it is difficult to make and keep a Christian commitment. Many people commit to the Lord for a while, but then, for various reasons, abandon their commitment. Many once-dedicated Christians have stopped praying, reading the Bible, fellowshipping with other Christians, etc., for all sorts of reasons. God speaks about the future to provide hope so that believers will have an anchor for their souls; an anchor to hold them steadfast to Him. Hebrews 6:19 says, "We have this hope as an anchor for the soul, firm and secure."

God's use of the anchor to represent the believer's Hope is appropriate and poignant. An anchor keeps a boat from drifting away with the currents or being blown away in a storm. Thus, using an anchor to describe the purpose of the Christian Hope makes perfect sense. When a Christian has a clear picture of what he is hoping for in the future, especially the rewards that the Lord will give to those who have earned them, it helps to keep him from "drifting away" from his commitment and becoming involved with the sinful pleasures and abundant temptations offered by the world. It also helps to prevent him from being "blown away" from God during the storms of life.

Because the Hope was referred to as an "anchor," the anchor was the earliest known Christian symbol. It was used to represent the Hope of resurrection unto everlasting life. At Pompeii, the Roman city buried by lava in 79 AD when Mt. Vesuvius erupted, a ring was discovered with a beautiful image of an anchor and the Greek word *elpis*, "hope," inscribed on it.[2] Some of the earliest Christian graves have an anchor carved into the rock next to them.[3] Christians today use a cross as their common symbol, but there is no reference to the cross being a revered Christian image until after the Roman Empire became Christian. The cross was so abhorred as an instrument of torture that no early Christians venerated it. Historically, the first interest in the image of the cross came after Queen Helena, the mother of the Roman Emperor Constantine, reportedly found the "true cross" on her trip to Israel in 326 AD.[4] Before that time, the anchor was the symbol that the early

---

[2] E. M. Blaiklock and R. K. Harrison, eds., *The New International Dictionary of Biblical Archaeology* (Regency Reference Library, Grand Rapids, MI, 1983), p. 28.

[3] The earliest Christian graves are not in graveyards with a tombstone but are either in caves or catacombs with the actual grave being dug into the rock. Often an anchor would be carved into the rock next to the grave.

[4] Blaiklock and Harrison, op. cit., *Dictionary of Biblical Archaeology*, p. 141.

Christians used to show their hope of resurrection and a wonderful, everlasting future.[5]

The Psychological Value of Hope

The Adversary has made a concerted attack on the subject of the Hope because of the value that it has to anchor people to godliness and truth. An accurate knowledge of the Hope will anchor Christians by energizing and strengthening them to endure pressures and pleasures in a way that nothing else is able to do. People without hope become defeated, broken, and unable to cope with adversity. Hopeless people give up. If Christians are going to stay energized and motivated to do the work of the Lord day in and day out, putting up with all the trouble that the Devil and people put them through, it is vital to have a hope that is real, alive, and vivid.

The strengthening and energizing value of hope shows up in many ways in everyday life. When a mother tells her hungry family that dinner will be ready in ten minutes, she gets a totally different response than if she says she does not know when it will be ready. The hope of eating soon gives the family the energy to hold on a little longer. Having hope is vital in the medical field. Modern medicine acknowledges the healing value of hope because hopeful people have more strength and endurance. A mother will tell a sick child that the medicine will make him feel better "soon" because that helps the child stay positive and endure the pain.

---

[5] The fish was also an early symbol used in Christianity, but it did not represent the hope. The origins of the fish symbol are obscure as to who started using it and when. It is not referred to in the New Testament as is the anchor. Apparently the reason that the fish came to be used to identify Christians is that the Greek word *ichthus*, "fish," is the word spelled by the first letters of the phrase "Jesus Christ, God's Son, Savior" when that phrase is written in Greek. Leland Ryken, James C. Wilhoit and Tremper Longman III, eds., *Dictionary of Biblical Imagery* (Intervarsity Press, Downers Grove, IL, 1998), pp. 290–91; F. L. Cross and E. A. Livingstone, eds., *The Oxford Dictionary of the Christian Church* (Oxford University Press, New York, 1974), p. 514.

Having a hope in the form of a visible goal is also important in athletic performance. Every coach knows the value of yelling, "Last lap!" to the runner or swimmer whose muscles are already screaming from fatigue. Hearing "One more lap!" causes the athlete to reach deep and find the energy to push through to the end. Runners, skiers, skaters, rowers, and other athletes know that muscles that seem to be just holding on somehow come to life and have extra strength when the finish line comes into sight. The hope that the race will soon be over infuses the body with energy that seems to come from nowhere. There is no question that having hope anchors a person to his goal and gives him energy and strength to go on.

Just as hope energizes and strengthens, it is also true that being without hope drains one's strength. The feeling of being "hopeless" is devastating. A person with no hope, with no expectation of good, often sinks into depression and despair and may even commit suicide. The effects of being hopeless are well documented. People who have no hope of everlasting life grieve over death in ways that Christians who are confident of everlasting life do not. Paul wrote to the Thessalonians and told them that the dead Christians would be raised to life when Christ comes "down from heaven, with a loud command, with the voice of the archangel, and the trumpet call of God" (1 Thess. 4:16). Paul knew that when they really had hope in the raising of the dead, they would not "grieve like the rest of men, who have no hope" (1 Thess. 4:13).

Christian work can be difficult. It is often under-financed and under-appreciated, many times involving endless hours of work in poor conditions for unthankful people. Furthermore, Christians are still human, and so, although it should not be this way, Christian work is often accompanied by envy and jealousy, power struggles, distrust, personal agendas, cliques, backbiting, and other less than desirable things. Why would anyone work—often on a volunteer basis—in those conditions? One answer is that many people start out being very idealistic, but idealism usually does not last long in the

The Christian's Hope

"real" world. Without a vivid hope to sustain them, they eventually burn out. Having a vivid hope, however, gives people strength and energy to press on. The mistreatment and lack of appreciation can be dealt with when one realizes that there will be rewards that he or she will receive at the Judgment. Paul wrote about this very thing:

1 Corinthians 15:58
Therefore, my dear brothers, stand firm. Let nothing move you. Always give yourselves fully to the work of the Lord, because you know that your labor in the Lord is not in vain.

Unfortunately, too many Christians do not "know" that their "labor in the Lord is not in vain." Many have been taught that salvation is the "be all, end all" for the Christian. They have not been taught that an important part of their hope is the *rewards* they will receive for their work in this life. Thus, as they look around and see other "saved" Christians doing much less work, they lose their energy and strength and become discouraged. If these people really knew the rewards their efforts were earning, they would have the strength to go on. Because accurately teaching the Hope has the effect of strengthening and invigorating Christians, the Adversary has launched a powerful attack on it. To date, the attack has been very successful. Nevertheless, the scriptures concerning the Hope stand clear. It is therefore the purpose of this book to present those scriptures so that Christians will become knowledgeable of the Hope and benefit from the application of that knowledge, for truly, a vital hope is the anchor of the soul.

CHAPTER 2

The Hope of Israel

This chapter will show that the Hope of the historical nation of Israel is that its righteous people will be raised from the dead and live on a wonderful, recreated earth.[1] It is important for Christians to understand this hope for several reasons. First, it is the foundation for understanding many verses in the Bible that would otherwise remain unclear. Furthermore, when the saved of Israel are with their Messiah, Jesus

---

[1] Although reference is made to "the Hope of Israel," other people besides Israelites are included in the Hope of everlasting life on a regenerated earth. There was no "Israel" until God changed Jacob's name to "Israel" (Gen. 32:28), and it was many years later that "Israel" became a nation. Thus, chronologically, for more than one-half of the Old Testament there was no "Israel." Noah, Abraham, Sarah, and others were certainly "believers" but they were not "Israel." They were "Gentiles." Furthermore, even after Israel became a nation, there were many Gentiles who lived righteous lives and to whom the Lord God will grant everlasting life, even though they were not from the ancestry of Israel.

It may seem strange to say that chronologically more than half of the Old Testament was already completed by the time of Jacob, but it is true. Conservative scholars studying the chronological information given in the Old Testament have long seen that the creation of Adam was somewhere in the neighborhood of 4,000 years before Christ, and Jacob was born about 1800 BC. Bishop Ussher, whose dates appear in the margins of many older King James Versions, calculated the creation of Adam at 4004 BC. See also: Martin Anstey, *Chronology of the Old Testament* (Kregel Publications, Grand Rapids, MI, 1973), pp. 8, 149; E. W. Bullinger, *The Companion Bible* (Zondervan Bible Publishers, Grand Rapids, MI, reprinted 1964), Appendix 50; Ivan Panin, *Bible Chronology* (The Association of the Covenant People, Vancouver, BC), p. 143; H. B. Hackett, ed., *Smith's Dictionary of the Bible* (Baker Book House, Grand Rapids, MI, reprinted 1981), Vol. 1, pp. 432–51. Christian Educational Services, using its own unpublished chronology of the Old Testament, has calculated a date of 3961 BC for the creation of Adam and 1794/1793 BC for the birth of Jacob.

Christ, Christians will also be there with him. Thus, the Hope of Israel both grounds and illuminates the Hope of Christians. Ephesians teaches that in Christ, Christians have become "heirs together with Israel" (Eph. 3:6). Christ will reign on the earth in the future, and the Bible says that Christians will be with him on earth, as will the saved of Israel.

Everlasting Life for Israel on a Recreated Earth

The Hope of Israel is plainly stated many times in the Old Testament: the righteous will be raised from the dead and live on a wonderful, recreated earth where justice and peace will prevail. There will be no sickness or hunger, and even the lion and the lamb will live together peacefully. The traditional picture is "the lion and the lamb" even though that exact phrase never occurs in Scripture. The actual wording is "the wolf will live with the lamb" (Isa. 11:6) and "the wolf and the lamb will feed together" (Isa. 65:25). The context of these phrases, however, makes it clear that the wolf, lamb, leopard, goat, calf, and lion will all feed together and also that "the lion will eat straw like the ox." So the mental picture of the lion and lamb feeding together and lying down together is correct, even if the exact phrase does not occur in the Bible.

In the "Sermon on the Mount," Christ spoke very plainly to the crowd concerning life on a renewed earth. One of the first things he said was, "The meek shall inherit **the earth**" (Matt. 5:5). Jesus meant exactly what he said, and he was not teaching new doctrine. He was simply confirming the teaching of the Old Testament: that God will destroy the wicked, but the righteous will inherit the earth.

> **Psalm 37:9–11**
> (9) For evil men will be cut off, but those who hope in the LORD will **inherit the land**.
> (10) A little while, and the wicked will be no more; though you look for them, they will not be found.

(11) But **the meek will inherit the land** and enjoy great peace.

Isaiah 57:13c
The man who makes me his refuge will **inherit the land.**

Ezekiel 37:12
Therefore prophesy and say to them: "This is what the Sovereign LORD says: O my people, I am going to open your graves and bring you up from them; **I will bring you back to the land of Israel**."

Revelation 5:9,10
(9) And they sang a new song: "You are worthy to take the scroll and to open its seals, because you were slain, and with your blood you purchased men for God from every tribe and language and people and nation.
(10) You have made them to be a kingdom and priests to serve our God, and **they will reign on the earth**."[2]

These verses are a small sampling from among the many verses in the Bible that indicate the everlasting home of Israel will be the earth.[3]

---

[2] This verse from the book of Revelation refers to Israel, not the Christian Church. E. W. Bullinger, *Commentary on Revelation* (Kregel Publications, Grand Rapids, MI, 1984), p. 3.

[3] These come in many forms. Some mention the earth specifically, such as Psalm 37:9,11,29. Others are wishes for the future, such as the psalmist's cry, "May sinners vanish from the earth and the wicked be no more" (Ps. 104:35), which will in fact be the case in Christ's Kingdom because the earth will indeed be freed from the grip of wicked men, and in the Eternal Kingdom they will be gone altogether. Some verses mention the attributes of the future earth, such as Isaiah 41:18, which speaks of the deserts having springs and pools of water. Others speak specifically of the Kingdom on earth, such as Daniel's interpretation of Nebuchadnezzar's dream. In the dream, the rock that smashed all the other kingdoms will "fill the whole earth" (Dan. 2:35). Prophecies of the future speak of each person having his own vine and fig tree and of swords being made into plows (Mic. 4:3,4). These are all visions and prophecies of the earth, not of "heaven." There are no visions of "living in heaven" in the Bible.

God promised Abraham and his descendants the land, not "heaven." Through the years, as a result of erroneous theological teaching, "heaven" came to replace "earth" as the home of the saved. But this is not what the Bible says nor what Christ taught. How people came to believe that "heaven" is the final destination of those who are saved will be covered in Chapter 7. Now, however, it is important to concentrate on the scriptures that clearly state that the earth is man's final destination.

God blessed Abraham by promising him that his descendants would get the land forever. In fact, the reason that Israel is commonly called "the promised land" is that God promised it to Abraham and his descendants.

Genesis 13:15
All the **land** that you see I will give to you [Abraham] and your offspring forever.

Genesis 15:18
On that day the LORD made a covenant with Abram and said, "To your descendants I give this **land**, from the river of Egypt to the great river, the Euphrates."

Genesis 17:8
The whole **land** of Canaan, where you [Abraham] are now an alien, I will give as an everlasting possession to you and your descendants after you; and I will be their God.

Abraham never saw the fulfillment of God's promise. He never received the land. Stephen made that very clear when he spoke to the Sanhedrin, who were the leaders of the Jewish nation. He said:

Acts 7:4,5
(4) So he [Abraham] left the land of the Chaldeans and settled in Haran. After the death of his father [Terah], God sent him to this **land** where you are now living.

(5) He gave him **no inheritance here**, not even a foot of ground. But God promised him that he and his descendants after him would possess the **land**.

Not only did Abraham never actually possess the land promised to him, the Israelites never inherited the full extent of the land promised to them. Although God plainly stated that He wanted Israel to conquer and possess the land, they were only partially successful and never conquered all the land promised to them.

Deuteronomy 1:8

See, I have given you this **land**. Go in and take possession of the **land** that the LORD swore he would give to your fathers—to Abraham, Isaac and Jacob—and to their descendants after them.

In spite of what God said, Israel never fully possessed the land that God offered them. Judges 1:19–36 speaks of the failure of the Israelites to conquer the land. The closest they came was during the days of David and Solomon. Even then, the full extent of the promise God made to Abraham was never realized. God cannot lie (Titus 1:2), so one day His promises must be fulfilled. Since Abraham is dead, the only way that God's promise to him and his descendants can be fulfilled is that God will give the Promised Land to them *after they are resurrected.*

Up from the Grave and Back to the Land

The truth that the land will be given to Israel after the Resurrection is clearly portrayed in Scripture.[4] Ezekiel has a vivid description of graves being opened and the believers of Israel being raised from the dead and brought back to the land of Israel.

---

[4] For a chart of the order of the comings of Christ, the Rapture, Armageddon, and other events of the last times with short explanations, see Appendix A.

Ezekiel 37:12–14

(12) Therefore prophesy and say to them: "This is what the Sovereign LORD says: 'O my people, I am going to open your graves and bring you up from them; I will bring you back to the **land** of Israel.

(13) Then you, my people, will know that I am the LORD, when I open your graves and bring you up from them.

(14) I will put my Spirit in you and you will live, and I will settle you in your own **land**. Then you will know that I the LORD have spoken, and I have done it, declares the LORD.'"

These verses are clear. God will open the graves of the people of Israel and bring them back to their land. This is how God will fulfill His promise of giving the land to Israel. Abraham did not receive his inheritance in his first life, but he will one day receive it in full just as God promised. It is important to note that when the graves are opened and the people come out, the Bible says God will "**bring** you into the land of Israel." Israelites who died outside the land of Israel will not be raised from the dead inside the country of Israel. They will be resurrected from where they were buried, and then travel into the land of Israel. This is an important point to keep in mind because it will make other promises God made to Israel easier to understand. This point will be expanded upon later in this chapter.

Since Israel was divided into tribes, after the resurrection a portion of land will be given to each tribe.

Ezekiel 47:13,14

(13) This is what the Sovereign LORD says: "These are the boundaries by which you are to divide the **land** for an inheritance among the twelve tribes of Israel, with two portions for Joseph.

(14) You are to divide it equally among them. Because I swore with uplifted hand to give it to your forefathers, this **land** will become your inheritance."

These verses state that the land will be divided among "the twelve tribes of Israel." The reader who is not familiar with the history of Israel may be confused by the fact that "Joseph shall have two portions." This is because Joseph had two sons, Ephraim and Manasseh, whose descendants became tribes in Israel just like the descendants of Jacob's other sons, Reuben, Simeon, Judah, Dan, etc. When Joshua conquered the land, he gave both Ephraim and Manasseh tribal areas, so "Joseph" was actually given two tribal areas. This will also be the case in the Millennial Kingdom.[5]

At the time Ezekiel was prophesying (c. 590–570 BC), the tribes of Israel had split into two kingdoms, "Israel" in the north and "Judah" in the south, but the northern kingdom, Israel, had been taken away from their land.[6] The Assyrians conquered Israel and scattered the people by deporting them to other nations they had conquered. Then, they brought people from these other foreign nations and placed them in the land of Israel. For God to fulfill His promise to give the land to "the twelve tribes," Israel and Judah would have to become one kingdom again. This was impossible during Ezekiel's day, but it will happen after the Resurrection. Righteous Israelites from each of the twelve tribes will be raised from the dead so that Israel will again be

---

[5] This is the first mention of the Millennial Kingdom in this book. It will be handled in detail in Chapter 4.

[6] The names "Israel" and "Judah" can be confusing, and the Bible student must understand them. After the death of Solomon, the twelve tribes (a United Kingdom) divided into two kingdoms. The northern kingdom, consisting of ten of the twelve tribes, was called "Israel." The southern kingdom, consisting of two tribes, was called "Judah." Before the two kingdoms were formed, "Israel" referred to all the tribes, but once the separate kingdoms were formed, "Israel" usually meant the northern kingdom. Before the kingdoms were formed, "Judah" referred to the individual tribe of Judah, but later it referred to the southern kingdom. To confuse the situation even more, the word "Israel" was still used to refer to all the tribes even after the United Kingdom split up, and "Judah" is still used to refer to the tribe of Judah. Therefore, the exact meaning of "Israel" and "Judah" must always be determined from the context. Bromiley, op. cit., *Bible Encyclopedia*, Vol. 2, pp. 907–8, 1143–48.

a complete nation, and they will settle in the land God promised them. Several other chapters in Ezekiel also speak of Israel and Judah returning to the land of Israel. Ezekiel 11:15 mentions the whole house of Israel, and then goes on to say how they will come back from the countries where they were scattered and will return to the land of Israel.

Ezekiel 11:15–20

(15) Son of man, your brothers—your brothers who are your blood relatives and the whole house of Israel—are those of whom the people of Jerusalem have said, "They are far away from the LORD; this land was given to us as our possession."

(16) Therefore say: "This is what the Sovereign LORD says: Although I sent them far away among the nations and scattered them among the countries, yet for a little while I have been a sanctuary for them in the countries where they have gone."

(17) Therefore say: "This is what the Sovereign LORD says: I will gather you from the nations and bring you back from the countries where you have been scattered, and I will give you back the land of Israel again."

(18) They will return to it and remove all its vile images and detestable idols.

(19) I will give them an undivided heart and put a new spirit in them; I will remove from them their heart of stone and give them a heart of flesh.

(20) Then they will follow my decrees and be careful to keep my laws. They will be my people, and I will be their God.

Although some theologians have thought that these verses apply to Judah's return from Babylon, there are several reasons why this cannot be the case. "Judah" was not "the whole house of Israel" (v. 15) and even when Judah returned from Babylon, the people did not have an "undivided heart" or a "new spirit" (v. 19). They certainly were not "careful" to keep the Law (v. 20). Thus, the content of this section of Scripture shows that these verses in Ezekiel refer to believers from all twelve tribes returning to Israel after the Resurrection, when people from all the tribes will return to Israel with a new heart and new spirit and will be careful to obey the Lord. Other Old Testament books besides Ezekiel foretell Israel's return to the land. For example:

Jeremiah 3:18 (KJV)
In those days the house of Judah shall walk with the house of Israel; and they shall come together out of the land of the north, to the land which I caused your fathers to inherit.

It is comforting to know that, in the future, Judah and Israel will "walk" together, a custom signifying that they would be united. Amos 3:3 says, "Can two walk together except they be agreed?" The statement that Judah and Israel will walk together beautifully portrays the fact that part of the future hope for the Jews is that they will once again enjoy an undivided nation. This is especially significant because history reveals that Israel and Judah never truly "walked together" even before Israel was carried away by the Assyrians. When Jeroboam split the ten northern tribes off from the United Kingdom of Israel ruled by Solomon's son Rehoboam, Rehoboam would have gone to war if a prophet had not intervened and called for peace (2 Chron. 11:2–4). That tenuous peace, however, came to an end during the reign of Rehoboam's son and successor, Abijah (2 Chron. 13:2). The hostility and differences between the kingdoms of Israel and Judah continued with only a few short interruptions during the approximately 220-year existence of the northern kingdom of Israel.

According to Amos' prophecy, after they are resurrected, the people of Judah and Israel will be united and will walk together from the land of the north to Israel. "The land of the north" is specifically designated because both the northern kingdom of Israel and the southern kingdom of Judah were taken captive to the north. Israel was taken to Assyria and Judah was taken to Babylon. So, there are many believers' graves in the north. Those people, though dead now, will come back to the Promised Land from the north after the Resurrection.

Isaiah also mentions the people of Israel coming back to the land. He actually states that it is the people of the nations (Gentiles) who will bring the people of Israel back when they come to see the glory of God:

Isaiah 66:18–20

(18) "And I, because of their actions and their imaginations, am about to come and gather all nations and tongues, and they will come and see my glory.

(19) I will set a sign among them, and I will send some of those who survive to the nations—to Tarshish, to the Libyans and Lydians (famous as archers), to Tubal and Greece, and to the distant islands that have not heard of my fame or seen my glory. They will proclaim my glory among the nations.

(20) And they will bring all your brothers, from all the nations, to my holy mountain in Jerusalem as an offering to the LORD—on horses, in chariots and wagons, and on mules and camels," says the LORD. "They will bring them, as the Israelites bring their grain offerings, to the temple of the LORD in ceremonially clean vessels."

There are many other verses stating that, in the future, God's people will be gathered to Israel. These include Isaiah 11:10–16; Jeremiah 23:3–8; 30:3; 31:8–11; 33:7; Ezekiel 28:25; 37:15–28, and Hosea 1:10,11. Resurrected believers will again inhabit the land. Then, what both the Psalmist and Christ said will be fulfilled: "The meek will inherit **the earth**."

Prophecies of Restoration

Another reason to believe that everlasting life will be on earth is that all the prophecies relating to the activities of Israel in the future are tied specifically to the earth. These include:

> The wolf lying down with the lamb and the lion eating grass like cattle (Isa. 11:6–9; 65:25).
>
> The land healed and the deserts blooming (Isa. 32:15; 35:1,2,7; 51:3).
>
> Israel becoming the glory of the earth (Isa. 60).
>
> The country of Israel being divided among the 12 tribes (Ezek. 47:13–48:29).
>
> The Messiah getting his own land area (Ezek. 45:7; 48:21,22).
>
> A new temple built in Jerusalem (Ezek. 40–44).
>
> A river flowing out of the Temple and healing the land (Ezek. 47:8–10).
>
> The law going forth from Jerusalem (Isa. 2:1–3; Mic. 4:1,2).
>
> People living in secure homes (Isa. 32:18).
>
> Each family having its own vine and fig tree (Mic. 4:4).

The nations of the earth are mentioned in many different contexts.

> They will be ruled over (Ps. 2:9; Dan. 7:27; Rev. 2:27).
>
> They will come to worship (Zech. 8:20–23).
>
> The fortunes of many destroyed nations will be restored: Egypt (Isa. 19:18–25; Jer. 46:26); Assyria (Isa. 19:23–25); Moab (Jer. 48:47); Ammon (Jer. 49:6); Elam (Jer. 49:39). These nations once existed on the earth, and they will be restored.[7]

---

[7] The extent of the restoration is not clearly stated and whether the ancient names will be used is not known.

It is hard to see how anyone reading the prophecies of the land being healed, the nations being restored, and the wolf and lion living peacefully together with domestic animals could conclude that this is somehow going to happen in the air.[8] No, these prophecies will be fulfilled on the earth. The earth is going to be healed from the curse placed on it in Genesis and will become a wonderful place, just as God originally intended when He made the Garden of Eden.

Not only is the earth going to be the home of believers, it is going to be their home *forever*. Many teach that believers will be in heaven forever, but there is no verse in the Bible that says so. There are some verses that have occasionally been misunderstood to imply that heaven will be the home of the saved, and these are covered in Appendix B. However, these verses do not actually say that the believer's everlasting home is heaven. Here is what the Bible does clearly, plainly, and unmistakably say:

Psalm 37:29
The righteous will inherit the land and dwell in it forever.

---

[8] I do not mean to set up a straw man here. There are many Christians who assume that heaven has firm turf to walk on. However, it must be noted that there is no verse that actually says that. There are many Christians who believe that the "floor" of heaven is clouds or cloud-like and that the saved will simply have bodies that can walk there without "falling through" to the earth. There is also a plethora of religious art that shows people in the air or in the clouds.

CHAPTER 3

The Christian's Hope

This chapter will show that all Christians will eventually reside on the earth where they will live everlastingly, just as will the believers of Israel.[1] Christians will be with Christ on earth during his Millennial Kingdom and in the Everlasting Kingdom. But unlike Israel, Christians will be taken to heaven for a short while where they will be with Christ before returning to earth with him.

The Rapture and Seven Years in Heaven—A Major Distinction Between Israel and the Christian Church

It is vitally important for the serious Bible student to recognize that Israel and the Christian Church are two separate entities. They have different origins, different promises, and different purposes. Although it is sometimes taught that Israel "became" the Church, this is an unfortunate misunderstanding.[2] One of the major distinctions between the saved people of the Old Testament and the saved people of the Christian Church is that there is no prophecy or verse that says the saved people of Israel will spend any time in heaven or be in the air at any time. As Ezekiel made clear, the saved of the Old Testament get resurrected and go directly into the land, i.e., the Kingdom that Christ

---

[1] Christians are those from Pentecost (Acts 2) to the "Rapture" (1 Thess. 4:17) who have confessed Jesus as Lord and believe that God raised him from the dead (Rom. 10:9,10), and have thereby been "born again." For more information, see Appendix C.

[2] For more information on the differences between Israel and the Church see Appendix C.

will set up on earth.[3] As for those righteous Israelites (and Gentiles) who survive the Tribulation and Armageddon, Matthew 25:31–46 says that after Christ comes to the earth, he will gather them together and will judge them. Those people who are judged as righteous will enter immediately into his Kingdom. Thus, the righteous people of Israel who are dead will be resurrected directly into the Kingdom while people judged to be righteous who are still alive after Armageddon will also enter directly into it. Neither the dead who are resurrected nor the living who are judged righteous go into the air to meet Christ.

In contrast to Israel, 1 Thessalonians says that Christians will be raised from the earth and meet the Lord in the air.

1 Thessalonians 4:16,17

(16) For the Lord himself will come down from heaven, with a loud command, with the voice of the archangel and with the trumpet call of God, and the dead in Christ will rise first.

(17) After that, we who are still alive and are left will be caught up together with them in the clouds to meet the Lord in the air. And so we will be with the Lord forever.

This meeting of the Lord "in the air" is generally known as "the Rapture." From this, many have concluded that Christians will *remain* in the air, or "in heaven." But the end of the verse says that we will be with the Lord "forever," and Scripture is clear that the Lord will come down from heaven to the earth. Thus, the biblical evidence is that Christians eventually end up on the earth where they will live everlastingly, just as the believers of Israel will. The saved of Israel and the

---

[3] The only exceptions to this are the two witnesses of Revelation 11:3–12. These two men are resurrected into the air just as are Christians. Even so, there are some differences between them and the Church. Christians are raptured instantaneously ("in a flash, in the twinkling of an eye"—1 Cor. 15:52) and are just "missing," but the two witnesses ascend while their murderers watch in horror.

Christian Church share a common destiny: earth. For the Church, there will be an interim stop in "heaven" during the Tribulation period.

In contrast to Israel, Christians will be raised (if dead) or caught up together (if alive) and be with Christ in heaven for the duration of the Tribulation. The Tribulation is a seven-year period starting after the Rapture and ending with the battle of Armageddon.[4] Christ will come in the clouds and rapture (take up) both the dead and the living Christians from the earth prior to the Tribulation.[5]

It is crucial to understand and separate the different comings of Christ. At his *First Coming* to the earth to Israel, he was crucified. At the *Rapture* of the Christian Church, often referred to in Scripture as his "appearing," Christ never actually arrives on earth. He comes for Christians only and they meet him in the air. At his *Second Coming*, Christ again comes to the earth to Israel.[6] He rides a white horse (Rev. 19:11ff) down to earth from heaven, sets up his throne, and

---

[4] Arnold Fruchtenbaum, *In the Footsteps of the Messiah* (Ariel Ministries Press, Tustin, CA, 1982), p. 121. Paul Lee Tan, *A Pictorial Guide to Bible Prophecy* (Bible Communications, Inc., Garland, TX, 1991), pp. 77–82.

[5] CES believes in, and teaches, a pre-Tribulation Rapture. However, we are well aware that some people reading this book believe in a mid-Tribulation, pre-Wrath, or post-Tribulation Rapture. Disputing the timing of the Rapture should not distract us from the point being made here, namely, that the Christian Church is raptured into the air and the saved of Israel are not. For more information on the timing of the Rapture, refer to *23 Reasons to Believe in a Rapture Before the Great Tribulation* (Christian Educational Services, Indianapolis, IN), and the audiotape seminar, *The Book of Revelation.*

[6] The biblical vocabulary used to describe the coming of Christ can be very confusing. For example, the word "coming" is used both of Christ's coming for Israel and for the Church (cp. Matt. 24:27 and 1 Thess. 4:15) and both Israel and the Church are "gathered" or "gathered together" (Isa. 56:8; Ezek. 11:17; and Matt. 25:23 all refer to Israel, while 2 Thess. 2:1 refers to Christians). It is common for the Bible to use the same word to refer to different things. Context is always the key to properly understanding any particular verse. If Christians have an agreed-upon vocabulary, it helps to keep misunderstandings from developing. In this book, the author uses the word "Rapture" to describe Christ's coming in the air to gather together the Christian Church and the words "Second Coming" to refer to Christ's coming back to the earth to fight the battle of Armageddon and then reign as King.

gathers the nations before him. Many scriptures testify of Christ setting foot upon the earth, including Zechariah 14:4, which states that he will stand on the Mount of Olives.

In Acts 3, Peter was talking to a crowd of Jews who had gathered around him after he and John had healed a man who had been lame for more than forty years. Peter knew that Jesus would one day come back to earth and restore it, and he also knew that the crowd of Jews to whom he was speaking could not comprehend Christ's ascension because it was not a part of their standard teaching about the Messiah. The crowd expected a Messiah who would restore the earth as the Old Testament prophets had said. They did not believe Jesus was that Messiah nor did they understand that the Messiah would have to die and then ascend to heaven prior to conquering the earth.[7] The Jews wondered why, if Jesus were the Messiah, he did not restore the earth like the Old Testament prophecies said he would. Peter assured them that God would send Christ back from heaven but that "He must remain in heaven until the time comes for God to restore everything as He promised long ago through his holy prophets" (Acts 3:21). Peter would never have said, "He must remain in heaven **until**," unless there was a time when Christ will come back from heaven. When he does, all Christians, who were previously raptured to meet him in the air, will come back with him. As 1 Thessalonians 4:17 says, each Christian will be "with the Lord," who will then be on the earth.

Understanding this vital difference between the saved of Israel and the saved of the Christian Church answers a frequently asked question: "When are the saved people from the Old Testament, such as Ruth and Esther, raised from the dead?" It is common to hear discussions about whether they will be raised with Christians at the Rapture or later, at the First Resurrection, the Resurrection of the Just, which occurs

---

[7] For the beliefs that the Jews held about their Messiah, see: Graeser, Lynn, and Schoenheit, *One God & One Lord* (Christian Educational Services, Indianapolis, IN, 2000), Chapter 5, *The Messiah the Jews Expected*, pp. 98–132.

shortly after Christ's Second Coming when he fights the battle of Armageddon. The prophecies to Israel, which were covered in the last chapter, all say that Israel will come up from the grave and go to the land. There is not one scripture saying that they will be raptured into the air with the Christian Church. The saved of Israel will not get up at the Rapture but will await the First Resurrection.[8] Their graves will be opened and they will go to the land of Israel.

Israel Is Not Raptured

The Rapture is part of the "mystery," better translated "secret," of the Administration of God's Grace (Eph. 3:2).[9] It is part of the revelation of the Church Epistles and is not found in the Old Testament or the Gospels.[10] Israel will not be raptured, as we have already covered in this book. Nevertheless, some Christians are confused about the Rapture being only for the Church and not Israel. Much of this confusion comes from the fact that many Christian teachers and preachers misunderstand Matthew 24:37–41 and Luke 17:26–35, which refer specifically to Israel, not to Christians. In particular, they believe that these sections of Scripture make reference to the Rapture, which is not so.

---

[8] Some Bible commentators believe that the phrase "the dead in Christ" in 1 Thessalonians 4:16 includes those Old Testament saints who died looking forward to Christ's coming. However, the phrase "in Christ" occurs only in the writings to the Christian Church, and it refers to Christians. One reason Christians are said to be "in Christ" is that we are part of the Body of Christ (Eph. 1:23), while Old Testament believers were not. For more information see Appendix C.

[9] For more information about the Administration of the Secret, see Appendix C.

[10] The revelation that is addressed specifically *to* the Christian Church is written in the seven epistles (letters) of Paul to the Church, known theologically as the "Church Epistles." The fact that these seven epistles (Romans through Thessalonians) are especially important to the Christian Church is not often taught, yet it is of vital importance. A short overview is provided in Graeser, Lynn, and Schoenheit, op. cit., *One God & One Lord*, Appendix J, but a full treatment of the subject is provided by E. W. Bullinger, *The Church Epistles* (Eyre and Spottiswoode, England, 1905), now available through *Truth for Today*, *Inc.*, in Lafayette, Indiana.

An unfortunate consequence of believing that Matthew 24 and Luke 17 refer to the Rapture is that it shatters the uniqueness of the Christian Church, which had a distinct beginning on the Day of Pentecost and will have a sudden end at the Rapture. The Rapture is part of the "secret" that was hidden in God and first revealed to the apostle Paul (Eph. 3). It is not mentioned outside of the Church Epistles. To understand one record is to understand both, so only Matthew will be explained.

Matthew 24:37–41
(37) As it was in the days of Noah, so it will be at the coming of the Son of Man.

(38) For in the days before the flood, people were eating and drinking, marrying and giving in marriage, up to the day Noah entered the ark;

(39) and they knew nothing about what would happen until the flood came and took them all away. That is how it will be at the coming of the Son of Man.

(40) Two men will be in the field; one will be taken and the other left.

(41) Two women will be grinding with a hand mill; one will be taken and the other left.

Although some people say this section of Scripture refers to the Rapture, it does not. It cannot be wrested from its context, which is Jesus Christ's *Second Coming*, when he comes in judgment to the earth. Matthew 24:30 says the nations will see the Messiah as he comes in power and glory, and that they will "mourn." After some parables about anticipating his coming, Matthew 25:31–33 speaks of the coming of the Messiah and notes that Christ will "sit on his throne" and "all the nations will be gathered before him." These things are not associated with the Rapture of the Christian Church. At the Rapture, the Church meets the Lord in the *air* (1 Thess. 4:17). He never comes all the way to the earth. Those left on earth will be confused about the disappearance of the Christians. They will not know where the Christians went. At the Rapture, the nations do not see Christ nor do they "mourn." So, the contextual evidence shows that Matthew 24 and Luke 17 are speaking of the Second Coming of Christ to the earth to Israel when he fights at Armageddon, judges, and sets up his Kingdom.

The meaning of "one shall be taken and the other left" is made clear by the context and the scope of Scripture. The time of Christ's coming in judgment will be similar to the time of the judgment in the days of Noah when the flood came and "took" people away. Note that Matthew 24:39 specifically says that the flood "took" the *unrighteous*. The righteous, Noah and his family, were "left" after the flood while all the others were no more. In Matthew, the ones who are "taken" are taken for judgment, not blessing. At the Sheep and Goat Judgment, the unrighteous are *taken* to the flames (Matt. 25:46), while the righteous are *left* on the earth and inherit the Kingdom. Spiros Zodhiates writes:

> In Matt. 24:40,41; Luke 17:34,35, *paralambano* in the passive form is used as the opposite of *aphiemi*, "to let be." In these verses, those who are taken are not to be misconstrued as those whom the Lord favors, as if they were the same saints spoken of in 1 Thess. 4:17 who will be raptured (*harpazo*, "to seize, catch away, as if by force") to meet the Lord in the clouds. The verb *paralambano* in most cases indicates a demonstration in favor of the one taken, but not always. In Matt. 4:5,8, it is used of Satan "taking" Jesus up to tempt him. In John 19:16 it is used of "taking" Jesus to lead him to the cross.
>
> It is used to refer to those in the days of Noah who were taken away, not being favored but being punished, while Noah and his family were "left" intact. Therefore, in this passage in Matthew and the parallel passage in Luke, *paralambano* must not be equated to the believers who are to be raptured at the coming of the Lord for his saints. It refers rather to those who, as in the days of Noah, are taken to destruction. The others are left alone (*aphiemi*) for the purpose of entering into the blessings of Christ's

kingdom (identified by some as the Millennium) and the righteous rule of Christ upon earth.[11]

Robert Mounce comments:

> The man working in the field (v. 40) and the woman grinding meal (verse 41) will be taken away in judgment (not to safety; cf. parallel in v. 39 with those "taken away" by the flood).[12]

Of course there are Christians who say that the scholars quoted above are wrong and that "take" refers to those who are taken for a blessing and "left" refers to those who are left for judgment. Even though this interpretation seems to ignore the context, there is another, more valuable point that needs to be made. The context of Matthew and Luke are crystal clear about the circumstances of Christ's coming, and it is plainly his Second Coming and not the Rapture. Therefore, no matter which group is blessed and which group is judged, *neither group is raptured*. One is blessed and left on earth to enter the Kingdom (Matt. 25:34) while the other is judged and taken away (Matt. 25:41).

The Church's Final Destination: Earth

It is commonly believed that Christians will spend eternity in "heaven," but that is not what the Bible says. Ephesians clearly sets forth that both Jews and Gentiles are made "one" in Christ (Eph. 2:15), and that, as Christians, Gentiles are "heirs together with Israel" (Eph. 3:6). If Christians are to be "heirs," it makes sense to ask what they are going to inherit. Since Christians are heirs *together with Israel*, it is quite clear that they are going to inherit the earth, just as will Israel.

---

[11] Spiros Zodhiates, *The Complete Word Study Dictionary New Testament* (AMG Publishers, Chattanooga, TN, 1992), p. 1108.

[12] Robert H. Mounce, *New International Biblical Commentary: Matthew* (Hendrickson Publishers, Peabody, MA, 1985), p. 229.

There is not a single verse in the Bible that says Christians will spend eternity in "heaven," and none that in any way describes what Christians would be doing there for that long. The Word of God teaches that Christians will spend eternity with the Lord Jesus Christ, who will come from heaven to earth and rule it, first, during the Millennial Kingdom from Jerusalem and then, in the Everlasting Kingdom, from the New Jerusalem. If Christ is to rule the earth from Jerusalem, and if Christians are promised to be with him forever, then they also must be on the earth. Jesus Christ is in heaven now, and he will not come down to earth until he comes to fight the battle of Armageddon, conquer the earth, and set up his Kingdom. Christians will be raptured into heaven before the Tribulation, and they will be with Christ until he comes back down to earth. When Christ does come down from heaven to the earth, Christians will come down with him. He will not leave them up in heaven. Scriptures saying that Christians will be with the Lord Jesus Christ forever will be fulfilled, and they will be where he is—on earth.

1 Thessalonians 4:17 says that Christians will be "caught up" into the air to be with Christ. In the Latin version, the words "caught up" are *rapere*, pronounced "rah-pair-a" (the final "a" is long). The English transliteration, "rapture," thus became the theological word for the event. The Rapture refers to Christians being "caught up" from the earth into the air where they meet the Lord and then are with him in heaven for a short while. After that, they return with Christ to the earth to fight the battle of Armageddon. This, in part, explains why Revelation 19:14 mentions the "armies," not "army," of heaven coming down with Christ to fight—Christians are included with the angelic host.

The fact that Christians are going to come back to the earth is contained in 1 Thessalonians 4:17, but unfortunately that truth is usually lost in translation.

1 Thessalonians 4:17
After that, we who are still alive and are left will be caught up together with them in the clouds to meet *[apantesis]*

the Lord in the air. And so we will be with the Lord forever.

Note that the word "meet" in the above verse is the Greek word *apantesis*. An *apantesis* was a meeting, but an *apantesis* also included additional activities. In the ancient world there were no reliable city maps, street names, or house numbers. If a friend who had never been to your town were coming to visit you, the way to be sure that he arrived safely at your house was an *apantesis*. You would leave your house and go out to a well-known place, meet him, and travel back with him. If a dignitary or important person were coming to town, even if he knew the correct directions, he was often honored by an *apantesis*. The people of the town would show their love and respect by traveling out and meeting the person, then escorting him back. This going out, meeting, and coming back was an *apantesis*.

> When a dignitary paid an official visit (*parousia*) to a city in Hellenistic times, the action of the leading citizens in going out to meet him and escort him back on the final stage of his journey was called the *apantesis*. So Cicero, describing Julius Caesar's progress through Italy in 49 B.C., says, "Just imagine what *apanteseis* he is receiving from the towns, what honors are being paid to him![13]

We Christians will have the honor of having an *apantesis* with the Lord Jesus Christ. We will go up to him, spend a little time with him (the seven years of the Tribulation), and then accompany him back to earth. Of course, it is always appropriate for the approaching dignitary to spend some time celebrating and exchanging niceties with those who have come to meet him before continuing the journey. Recognizing the effort of those who traveled to make the *apantesis* possible is part of the event. So, it would not be inconsistent with the meaning of

---

[13] F. F. Bruce, *Word Biblical Commentary: 1 & 2 Thessalonians* (Word Books Publisher, Dallas, TX, 1990), p. 102.

The Christian's Hope

apantesis to conclude that the Christian Church will spend some time with the Lord in heaven before coming back with him.

The word *apantesis* occurs four times in the Greek New Testament. The first three uses clearly corroborate its meaning as a going out, a meeting, and then escorting back. At the beginning of Matthew 25 is the "Parable of the Ten Virgins." The first and second use of the word *apantesis* are in this parable. The word is used in reference to ten virgins who were to have an *apantesis* ("meeting") with a Bridegroom. As the parable unfolds, the ten virgins were to go out to meet the Bridegroom and then to travel back with him to the waiting Bride (Matt. 25:1,6). Five of the virgins were wise and brought extra oil, while the other five were foolish and did not. Since the Bridegroom was late in arriving, the foolish virgins were away trying to buy more oil while the wise virgins met him and then traveled back with him to the Bride, who was at the banquet. This parable makes the use of *apantesis* very clear: the virgins went out to a place on the road where the Bridegroom would pass, met him, and then escorted him back to the Bride.

The third use of *apantesis* is in Acts 28:15. The apostle Paul was being taken prisoner to the city of Rome. The believers in Rome heard about it and set out for an *apantesis* with him. They left Rome and came to the Forum of Appius (43 miles from Rome) and the Three Taverns (33 miles from Rome), waited until Paul arrived, and then traveled back with him to Rome. This clearly shows the full meaning of *apantesis*. These believers so respected the apostle Paul that they went out more than a day's journey from Rome, met him, and then traveled back with him to Rome.

The fourth and last use of *apantesis* is in 1 Thessalonians 4:17, which we are discussing. This verse says that Christians have an *apantesis* with the Lord, i.e., they go up into the air to him, meet him (and are with him in heaven through the Tribulation period), and then travel back with him to the earth. From our study of the word *apantesis* we conclude that Christians will come back to earth to live with Christ.

More evidence that Christians have to come back to earth is that they must return if they are to receive "the blessing given to Abraham." Christians are promised that blessing, and it includes the land.

Galatians 3:14

He redeemed us in order that **the blessing given to Abraham** might come to the Gentiles through Christ Jesus, so that by faith we might receive the promise of the Spirit.[14]

God also gave the "blessing given to Abraham" to Jacob, long before Galatians was written. Isaac, Jacob's father, prophesied to him and said:

Genesis 28:4

May he [God] give you and your descendants **the blessing given to Abraham**, so that you may take possession of the land where you now live as an alien, the land God gave to Abraham.

As is clear in the above verse, the blessing given to Abraham included the land of Israel.[15] As we saw in the previous chapter, God made a covenant with Abraham and promised him the land (Gen. 13:15; 15:18; 17:8). The fact that Galatians specifically says that the blessing given to Abraham will be given to the Gentiles, who are now part of the Church, is one more proof that the Church will come

---

[14] At first, reading this verse makes it seem like the blessing given to Abraham was holy spirit, but that is not the case. A thorough reading of Genesis will show that God never promised holy spirit to Abraham. The promise of the spirit was given years later to Abraham's seed, and Galatians 3:29a says, "If you belong to Christ, then you are Abraham's seed." The promise of the land, not the spirit, was "the blessing given to Abraham."

[15] Nahum M. Sarna, *The JPS Torah Commentary: Genesis* (The Jewish Publication Society, New York, 1989), p. 196. S. R. Driver, *The Book of Genesis* (Methuen & Co., London, 1904), pp. 186, 263.

back to earth with Christ. If the Church's final destination is not the earth, it cannot be blessed with the blessing of Abraham.

Another verse that shows that Christians are going to come back to the earth is in Corinthians.

1 Corinthians 6:2
Do you not know that the saints will judge the world? And if you are to judge the world, are you not competent to judge trivial cases?

While it is true that Christians will participate in God's judgment of the world and fight at Armageddon, there is a greater truth in this verse. The Greek word translated "judge" can also refer to "administration" or "management" if the judging goes on day after day. The "judges" of Israel not only "judged" by fighting wars, they also made decisions for the people of Israel, settled disputes, and helped to administer the affairs of Israel on a day-to-day basis. Thus, James Moffatt translates the verse as follows:

1 Corinthians 6:2 (Moffatt)
Do you not know that the saints are to manage the world? If the world is to come under your jurisdiction, are you incompetent to adjudicate upon trifles?

The sense of "judge" as "administer" is also picked up in The Amplified Bible:

1 Corinthians 6:2 (AMP) (parenthesis and brackets are theirs)
Do you not know that the saints (the believers) will [one day] judge *and* govern the world? And if the world [itself] is to be judged *and* ruled by you, are you unworthy *and* incompetent to try [such petty matters] of the smallest courts of justice?

These verses are clear. We Christians will help administer and govern the world to come, i.e., the earth. In contrast, there are no verses that indicate we will somehow help rule "heaven." The biblical evidence is indisputable: We Christians will be with the Lord forever as he rules the earth.[16] We will be raptured into heaven to be with him there for a short while, but then we will come back with him and live on earth. Thus, "the meek (which includes Christians) will inherit **the earth**." Looking forward to a wonderful, everlasting life on a renewed earth is an important and motivating aspect of our hope as Christians.

---

[16] Christ clearly rules in his Millennial Kingdom. However, the superiority of God in the Everlasting Kingdom is made plain in 1 Corinthians 15:25–28, which says that when every enemy, including death, is destroyed, then Christ will be subject to the Father.

CHAPTER 4 — *The Two Future Kingdoms on Earth*

The Millennial and Eternal Kingdoms

The Bible indicates that there will be two kingdoms on earth in the future, one following the other. The first kingdom will last 1,000 years and is therefore referred to as the "Millennial Kingdom" (from *mil*, one thousand, and *annus*, year). The second kingdom is referred to by the author as the "Everlasting Kingdom."[1] In the Millennial Kingdom, Jesus Christ will rule as King after he fights and wins the battle of Armageddon at the close of the Tribulation (Rev. 19).[2] The Everlasting Kingdom will begin after the close of the Millennial Kingdom when the Devil and his demons are destroyed and the Final Judgment has taken place (Rev. 21).[3] The sequential order of these two kingdoms is

---

[1] For a depiction of these two kingdoms chronologically on a chart, see Appendix A.

[2] The battle of Armageddon ends the reign of the Antichrist and the Tribulation period. The details of the book of Revelation, such as the seals, trumpets, vials, and the reign and identity of the Antichrist are outside the scope of this book and so will not be covered. A wonderful source for this information is Bullinger, op. cit., *Commentary on Revelation*.

[3] It is sometimes taught that the battle of Armageddon is the "final battle," but this is not the case, as a reading of Revelation 19 and 20 will show. Revelation 19:11–21 says that Christ and his armies come down from heaven and fight the beast, the false prophet, the kings of the earth, and their armies. That is the battle of Armageddon. Then, in Chapter 20, Christ sets up his kingdom for 1,000 years, at the end of which there is another war, the final war in the Bible. It is brief—fire comes from heaven and destroys Christ's enemies. There is no record of either Christ or Christians fighting in this final battle. See Appendix A, events 8 and 12.

apparent through a reading of Revelation 19–22. Following is a brief summary of the events recorded in these chapters.

At the end of the seven-year Tribulation period, Jesus Christ, followed by his armies, rides a white horse down out of heaven to fight the battle of Armageddon. He wins the battle and conquers the earth (Rev. 19). After the battle, the Devil is "chained" and the "First Resurrection" occurs (Rev. 20). The First Resurrection includes the following people: *a)* believers, saved individuals, who lived in Old Testament times and died before the Day of Pentecost recorded in Acts 2; and *b)* believers, saved individuals, who lived and died during the seven-year period of the Tribulation. The people in both these categories are brought back to life and reign with Christ for 1,000 years (Rev. 20:4–7) together with the previously raptured Christians. After the 1,000-year reign of Christ, the Devil is loosed from his "chains" and gathers another army to fight against God's people. This time, instead of Christ fighting and winning the battle, the Devil's army is destroyed by fire from heaven (Rev. 20:7–10). Following the victory, the Second Resurrection and the Final Judgment take place. After the Final Judgment, God sets up the Kingdom that will last forever, the Everlasting Kingdom.

Throughout the Bible there are prophecies concerning both kingdoms, but God does not label the prophecies as "Millennial Kingdom" or "Everlasting Kingdom." The only way to determine which kingdom is the subject of the prophecy is by studying the prophecy in detail, keeping in mind that the Bible cannot contradict itself. For example, some prophecies concerning a future kingdom refer to a temple (Ezek. 40–48), while other prophecies concerning a future kingdom indicate that there will not be a temple (Rev. 21:22). In regard to the Temple, it is relatively easy because Revelation 21, which indicates there will not be a temple, is describing a kingdom that exists *after* the 1,000-year reign of Christ. The only kingdom after the 1,000-year reign of Christ is the Everlasting Kingdom. So, the prophecy in Revelation 21 applies to the Everlasting Kingdom. Ezekiel's prophecy, which describes the Temple in great detail, applies to the Millennial Kingdom.

Another example of an apparent contradiction involves prophecies concerning death. According to some prophecies, there is death in a future kingdom (Isa. 65:20, "He who dies at 100 will be thought a mere youth") while other prophecies indicate there will be no death (Rev. 21:4, "There will be no more death"). One key to resolving the apparent contradiction is knowing that "death" and "Hades" (the grave) are destroyed *after* the Millennial Kingdom ends and *shortly* before the Everlasting Kingdom begins (Rev. 20:14). Another key to resolving the apparent contradiction is determining who is present in each kingdom.

The Millennial Kingdom will be populated by three "groups" of people: *a)* Christians who were transformed and made immortal at the Rapture; *b)* believers who were resurrected and made immortal during the First Resurrection, and *c)* believers who survive the Tribulation and are allowed to enter the kingdom because they are judged righteous. The last "group" will enter the kingdom as mortals and will, therefore, eventually die. Furthermore, they will have children who, like all mortals, will be subject to death. In contrast, the Everlasting Kingdom will be populated only by immortals, namely: *a)* those who were already immortals during the Millennial Kingdom; *b)* believers brought back to life and transformed into immortals during the Second Resurrection, which occurs at the conclusion of the Millennial Kingdom; and *c)* mortal believers who are alive at the beginning of the Everlasting Kingdom who are judged righteous and who will be transformed into immortals.[4] Therefore, because mortals will be present

---

[4] The Bible does not specifically mention this group. However, it must be the case. There is no evidence that the Devil will deceive every natural person in the Millennial Kingdom. He has never been able to do that. Even during the Tribulation there are people from both Israel and the nations who are saved. Thus there will be "natural people" who enter the Everlasting Kingdom, just as there are natural people who enter the Millennial Kingdom. However, since death is part of the Millennial

(continued)

in the Millennial Kingdom, there will be death, but because only immortals will be present in the Everlasting Kingdom, there will be no death.

Attributes of the Millennial Kingdom— The 1,000-year Reign of Christ

The Millennial Kingdom is described in great detail throughout the Bible. This should not be surprising because many of the promises made to Israel will be fulfilled during that time. Some of the significant attributes of the Millennial Kingdom are described below.

The Millennial Kingdom takes place in "a new heaven and new earth" (Isa. 65:17; 66:22).[5]

The fact that the Millennial Kingdom is called "a new heaven and a new earth" can be confusing because the Everlasting Kingdom also takes place in "a new heaven and earth" (Rev. 21:1). Upon reflection, it is easy to see why both kingdoms will require a new heaven and earth. Mankind has polluted and ruined much of the earth. In many places the water is not fit to drink nor the air fit to breathe. Many species of plants and animals are now extinct and more are dying off every day. During the Tribulation and the battle of Armageddon, even more of the wildlife and habitat will be destroyed and the world will generally be unfit for life. Therefore, after the battle of Armageddon, the earth will be anything but "Paradise." The fact that the Millennial Kingdom is also called "Paradise" indicates that a renewal will take

---

Kingdom the natural people will age and die. That will not be the case in the Everlasting Kingdom. Everyone will be immortal.

[5] The words "new heaven" do not refer to the dwelling place of God as if that needs to be remade. The word "heaven" in this phrase refers to what we call the "atmosphere." It is used that way in phrases such as "the birds of heaven" and "the rain from heaven" (Job 35:11; Deut. 11:11—sometimes the translators use "air" instead of "heaven"). Humans have ruined the atmosphere and today much of the air we breathe is polluted and occasionally even toxic. In the Millennial Kingdom, even the air will be remade and will once again be fresh.

place. This is why Christ spoke of "the renewal of all things" (Matt. 19:28). Christ will not set up his Kingdom on a wasted planet but will restore the earth. The deserts will bloom, thirsty ground will become bubbling springs (Isa. 35), polluted water will be healed (Ezek. 47), and the air will be fresh and clean. After this renewal there will be Paradise—"a new heaven and a new earth." At the end of the Millennial Kingdom, this renewed world will be completely destroyed by fire and then the heavens and earth will be totally re-created.[6] Thus, the Everlasting Kingdom is also called "a new heaven and earth" (Rev. 21:1).

The Millennial Kingdom will be a *kingdom* and Christ will reign as King.

Old Testament prophecies foretold that the Messiah would be a king (Gen. 49:10; Num. 24:17–19; Ps. 2; Ps. 110; Dan. 2:44; 7:14) and a descendant of King David (Isa. 9:6,7). While he was on earth 2,000 years ago, Christ, the King himself, spoke of his coming Kingdom (Matt. 16:28; John 18:33–38, etc.). The Book of Revelation also says that Christ will rule over a kingdom (Rev. 11:15). It is clear that the future government will be a kingdom—not a democracy, republic, dictatorship, oligarchy, etc.

Christ will rule his Kingdom with the help of those who were faithful to God in their first life. Ruling with Christ is part of the believer's reward and should "anchor" each believer to righteousness in his day-to-day living. Not every believer will receive the same reward. Believers who have been faithful to God and Christ will receive a greater reward, including greater authority to help Christ rule. Judges and counselors will be restored (Isa. 1:26); "rulers will rule with justice" (Isa. 32:1); and shepherds with the heart of the Lord will lead the

---

[6] The Bible is silent about where all the saved people in the Millennial Kingdom will go when the earth is destroyed by fire. Although "heaven" seems a logical place, there is no way to know. This is a secret still hidden with God.

people with knowledge and understanding (Jer. 3:15). Ruling with Christ is promised to both Israel and the Church.

The following promise in the Book of Revelation is to both the people of Israel and to the believers who will be alive during the Tribulation.[7]

Revelation 2:26,27

(26) To him who overcomes and does my will to the end, I will give authority over the nations—

(27) "He will rule them with an iron scepter; he will dash them to pieces like pottery"—just as I have received authority from my Father.

The same promise is made to the Christian Church, i.e., any Christian who stays faithful and obedient will reign with Christ.

2 Timothy 2:11,12

(11) Here is a trustworthy saying: If we died with him, we will also live with him;

(12) if we endure, we will also reign with him. If we disown him, he will also disown us.

Not every believer will have the same standing in the future Kingdom. Those who endure now and remain faithful and obedient in their Christian walk will reign over the nations with Christ. Any one who disowns him (many versions have "deny him") by acting like an unbeliever will be denied the privilege of reigning with him and will have lesser assignments in the Kingdom. This is very sobering and should help every believer stay "anchored" to Christ and to a Christian lifestyle.[8]

---

[7] For extensive documentation concerning to whom the Book of Revelation is addressed, refer to Bullinger, op. cit., *Commentary on Revelation,* pp. 1–114.

[8] The believer's reward or loss of reward will be developed in Chapter 6.

The Millennial Kingdom will be populated by three "categories" or "types" of people.

a) Christians raptured into the air at the close of the Church Age who then return to earth with Christ during his Second Coming to fight the battle of Armageddon. They will remain on earth and enter the Millennial Kingdom. Each Christian will have a glorious new body fashioned after Jesus' resurrected body (Phil. 3:21).

b) Believers (both Jew and Gentile) who died before the day of Pentecost (Acts 2) and believers who will die during the Tribulation. These believers will be resurrected and transformed into immortals during the First Resurrection, which occurs after the battle of Armageddon (Ezek. 37:12–14; Rev. 20:4–6). This category includes believers such as Abraham and Sarah, Moses and Miriam, Joshua, Ruth, Samuel, David, Esther, Daniel, and those murdered during the Tribulation for their refusal to worship the Beast (Rev. 13:15).

c) "Natural" or mortal believers who survive the Tribulation and the battle of Armageddon and are judged "righteous" (Matt. 25:31–46). This category will include both Jews and Gentiles. The term "natural" is used to provide a distinction between these people, who are mortals, and the people who are no longer "natural" but immortal, namely, those in categories *a* and *b*. These "natural" people will experience the same life cycle of all mortals. They will grow, mature, marry, procreate, age, and die (Isa. 65:20–25).

The Bible makes it clear that there will be survivors after the Tribulation and the battle of Armageddon, and some of them will be judged righteous and allowed to enter Christ's Kingdom. This point must be understood because some Christians teach that after the battle of Armageddon no one will be alive on earth. This is clearly not the case. Yes, the majority of the people of earth will be dead, but as Isaiah 13:12 and 24:6 say, there will be survivors, "very few," but there will be survivors. There are more than six billion people on earth at this time, so "very few" could easily mean a few million or more. Matthew 25:31–46 implies that there will be a significant number because the "nations" will be brought before Christ at the start of his 1,000-year reign.

Because there will be no war and plenty of food, these survivors will multiply rapidly and will repopulate the earth. In fact, they will multiply to such a degree that by the end of the 1,000 years they will be as numerous "as the sand on the seashore" (Rev. 20:8). This growth in population should not be surprising. In the Old Testament, Israel entered Egypt as a group of seventy people (Gen. 46:27). When they came out they numbered about three million. This significant increase in population occurred under horrible conditions. If a few million are present at the beginning of the Millennial Kingdom, imagine the growth potential when the prevailing conditions are peace and prosperity!

As mentioned earlier, it will be the "natural" people who will make up the nations. Because they will still be "natural," they will be subject to the weaknesses of a mortal body and will still be prone to sin. Therefore, even though they are living in Paradise, they will need to be ruled "with an iron scepter." Christ will not be cruel or mean, but he will "rule with an iron scepter" by enforcing the laws so that there is no crime, and people can live in safety and security. In the King James Version, these words are translated as the familiar phrase, "rod of iron." The phrase "iron scepter," or "rod of iron," occurs in four verses: Psalm 2:9; Revelation 2:27; 12:5; 19:15. The application of the iron scepter can be seen in the following verses: Isaiah 11:4; 14:2; 49:22,23; 60:10–14; 61:5,6; 66:12; Micah 7:14–17; and Zechariah 14:16–19.

Prophecies of Christ ruling with an iron scepter are strong evidence that there will be a Millennial Kingdom populated at least in part by unsaved, mortal people. In addition, it should be obvious that these prophecies must apply to the future because they were not fulfilled during Christ's first coming. In spite of the many clear verses on this subject, there are some people who do not believe that the 1,000-year reign of Christ on earth is *literal*, and others who do not believe the

Kingdom is coming *in the future*.[9] If either of these beliefs were correct, then the only people available for Christ to rule with an iron scepter would be the saved believers in the Everlasting Kingdom. Being ruled with an iron scepter is not the way most Christians envision everlasting life. Thankfully, that is not how the Bible portrays it either. It is the unregenerate, "natural" people alive during the Millennial Kingdom who will need to be ruled with an iron scepter.[10]

The need for the iron scepter is due to the fact that these "natural people" still have a sin nature and are therefore prone to be selfish and sinful. Although they will live in Paradise, surrounded by bounty, many of them will still find reasons to complain. That is not unusual. Both history and the Bible teach that there are many times when people who should be happy because they are healthy, well fed, and financially secure still are unhappy and find reasons to complain constantly. The presence of these "natural" people in the Millennial Kingdom explains in large part why there will be disputes in the Millennial Kingdom (Isa. 2:4; Mic. 4:3). The Book of Zechariah says that if any nation selfishly decides not to go and worship in Jerusalem, then that nation will have no rain (Zech. 14:17). This is an example of the natural selfishness and "can't be bothered" attitude prevalent among "natural" people. It is also an example of how Christ will wield the iron scepter. At the end of the 1,000-year period Satan is loosed, and he will deceive many of these "natural" people and incite them to rebel against God and His people. Their rebellion will fail when they are destroyed by fire from heaven (Rev. 20:7–9).

The presence of these natural people in the Millennial Kingdom also helps explain why there will be priests (Ezek. 42:13,14; 44:15–31;

---

[9] Some people erroneously believe that the 1,000-year reign of Christ on earth is happening now in a "spiritual sense." Robert Clouse, ed., *The Meaning of the Millennium* (InterVarsity Press, Downers Grove, IL, 1977), pp. 155–87.

[10] The fact that Satan, when he is loosed at the end of the Millennium, is able to corral an army of disgruntled rebels is evidence enough that unregenerate mankind will be a part of the Millennial Kingdom.

Rev. 5:10). A priest, by definition, is someone who intercedes or mediates between God and another person. Aaron was a priest because he stood between God and Israel. If everyone in the Millennial Kingdom has a new, everlasting, regenerated body and an intimate relationship with God, there would be no need for priests. Since there will be many "natural" people in the Millennial Kingdom, priests will be important.

Some Christians do not believe there will be two literal and distinct kingdoms in the future because, to them, it does not seem possible to have "natural" people (mortals), and immortals alive on the earth at the same time. So they take verses like those cited above and "spiritualize" them by saying they are figurative and not literal. There is no justification for handling these verses in that manner. They are written very clearly and do not have any of the aspects of figurative language. Just because something God says about the future is hard to believe or hard to understand does not mean it is not literal and true.

The Millennial Kingdom will last 1,000 years (Rev. 20:1–4).

Revelation 20:1–4

(1) And I saw an angel coming down out of heaven, having the key to the Abyss and holding in his hand a great chain.

(2) He seized the dragon, that ancient serpent, who is the devil, or Satan, and bound him for **a thousand years**.

(3) He threw him into the Abyss, and locked and sealed it over him, to keep him from deceiving the nations anymore until **the thousand years** were ended. After that, he must be set free for a short time.

(4) I saw thrones on which were seated those who had been given authority to judge. And I saw the souls of those who had been beheaded because of their testimony for Jesus and because of the word of God. They had not worshiped the beast or his image and had not received his

mark on their foreheads or their hands. They came to life
and reigned with Christ **a thousand years**.

The Millennial Kingdom will start after Christ fights the battle of
Armageddon and conquers the earth at his Second Coming and will
end when the earth is destroyed by fire from heaven, after which God
again creates "a new heaven and a new earth" as described in Revelation 21.

**The Millennial Kingdom will be a time of unprecedented joy,
peace, and prosperity.**

The people will "be glad and rejoice" forever (Isa. 65:18) because of
the wonderful life in the Kingdom. There are many reasons why this
will be a time of great joy, including the fact that the Devil will be
chained the entire time and not free to afflict people (Isa. 24:21,22;
Dan. 7:12; Rev. 20:2).

Christ will be both the King and the High Priest during the Millennial Kingdom, fulfilling the prophecies of the Old Testament.

One clear scripture that says that Christ will be both King and High
Priest is in Zechariah:

> **Zechariah 6:12,13**
> (12) Then say to him, "Thus says the LORD of hosts,
> 'Behold, a man whose name is Branch, for He will branch
> out from where He is; and He will build the temple of the
> LORD.
> (13) Yes, it is He who will build the temple of the LORD,
> and He who will bear the honor and sit and rule on His
> throne. Thus, He will be a priest on His throne, and the
> counsel of peace will be between the two offices.'"

It is typical of the character of the Millennial Kingdom that the
Word says there will be "peace" between the office of Priest and King.
Historians know how rare that is. The rivalry between the political
sector and the religious sector is well known and has been almost

continuous throughout history. For example, the rivalry between the Roman Catholic Church (represented by Cardinal Richelieu) and the Crown (represented by Louis XIII) is the background for *The Three Musketeers*. The political versus religious rivalry has had a profound impact on society. In the Millennial Kingdom that rivalry will cease and there will be "*Shalom*" (peace, prosperity, well-being) between the Crown and the Priesthood.

Because of the reference to a temple, these verses further document that there will be two separate and distinct kingdoms in the future. As previously mentioned, there is no temple in the Everlasting Kingdom. Therefore, this prophecy must apply to a kingdom that has a temple, i.e., the Millennial Kingdom. It is interesting to note that while many Christians would say that the throne in the above verses is literal, they do not support the idea of a literal temple. According to their view, the Temple is "spiritual" (meaning figurative) and *represents* the Church. This view is based on scriptures in the New Testament in which the Church, a body of believers, is called a temple. The fact that a group of people is referred to as a temple is no reason to conclude that Ezekiel's Temple is spiritual and not literal any more than it would be a reason to conclude that Solomon's Temple was spiritual simply because it was called a temple. Other scriptural evidence clearly shows that Christ will build a *literal* temple in the Millennial Kingdom and that he will *literally* be both King and High Priest.

In the Millennial Kingdom, the tribes of Israel will each receive a special land area just as they did when Joshua divided up the land.

In the Old Testament, Joshua divided the Promised Land among the tribes of Israel. In the Millennial Kingdom, the land will again be divided among the tribes, but with some important differences. When Joshua divided up the land, the tribal areas were uneven in size and shape. In contrast, the Promised Land in the Millennial Kingdom will be divided into strips of land going lengthwise from east to west with the width of each strip being equal (Ezek. 47:14–48:29). The exact width of the tribal areas is not given in Scripture, but based on the overall boundaries of Israel an estimate can be made. Appendix D contains a map depicting the divisions by Joshua, as well as a map depicting the divisions in the Millennial Kingdom.

In the Millennial Kingdom there will be a rectangular shaped area of land between the tribal areas of Judah and Benjamin that God calls His "special gift" and in the center of this area there will be a "sacred portion" (Ezek. 48:8–10).

This "special gift" land area will run lengthwise from east to west just as will the other tribal areas, but it is specifically said to be 25,000 cubits "wide" (i.e., from north to south).[11] This "special gift" area will have specific areas for the priests, the Levites, the Temple, Jerusalem, and the Messiah himself (Ezek. 45:1–7; 48:8–22). Inside the "special gift" area is a "sacred portion" of land that is laid out in a square, 25,000 cubits wide by 25,000 cubits long—about 8 miles square (Ezek. 45:1–6, 48:8–15). This "sacred portion" will be divided into three parts. The Levites will receive the northern portion measuring 25,000 cubits east to west by 10,000 cubits north to south—about 8 miles by 3 miles (Ezek. 45:5; 48:13,14). The priests will receive the middle portion, which will also measure 25,000 cubits by 10,000 cubits. The Temple will be situated in this area (Ezek. 45:5; 48:13,14). The city of Jerusalem will be situated in the southern portion, which will measure 25,000 cubits by 5,000 cubits—just over 8 miles by 1½ miles (Ezek. 45:6). The city itself will measure 4,500 cubits square— about 1½ miles square (Ezek. 48:16).

---

[11] The cubits used in Ezekiel are the large or "royal" cubits, which are a cubit and a handbreadth (Ezek. 40:5). The exact equivalent of this measure is not known, but most scholars estimate somewhere between 20.4 to 20.7 inches. If we take the cubit as 20.5 inches, 25,000 cubits = 512,500 inches or slightly more than 8 miles (8.09 mi.). 10,000 cubits = 205,000 inches or just over 3 miles (3.2 mi.). 5,000 cubits = 102,500 inches or just over 1½ miles (1.6 mi.). 4,500 cubits = 92,250 inches or just under 1½ miles (1.46 mi.). 500 cubits = 10,250 inches or 854 feet. Bromiley, op. cit., *Bible Encyclopedia*, Vol. 4, pp. 1046–55.

Detail of the "Special Gift" Area

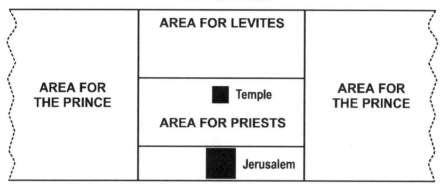

Tribal Area of Judah

AREA FOR LEVITES

AREA FOR THE PRINCE

Temple

AREA FOR PRIESTS

AREA FOR THE PRINCE

Jerusalem

Tribal Area of Benjamin

The relative position of these areas can be determined from the fact that the Temple, the sanctuary, will be in the middle of the "sacred portion" (Ezek. 48:8) and that it is in the section belonging to the priests (Ezek. 48:10). Since the city is on the south side (Ezek. 40:2), the Levites must have the portion on the north side. The land in the "special gift" area that is east and west of this 25,000 cubits square "sacred portion" will be given to "the Prince," who is the Messiah, Jesus Christ (Ezek. 45:7,8; 48:21,22).

That God would allot special areas for the priests, the Levites, and the Prince is reminiscent of what happened in the days of Joshua. When Joshua divided the land, the tribe of Levi did not receive a tribal area of its own. They ministered to Israel from forty-eight Levitical sites (Num. 35:1–8; Josh. 21). In the Millennial Kingdom, part of the "sacred portion" will be set aside for the Levites. Once again, they will not have a tribal area like the other tribes but will have a designated area from which they can minister to the Lord and to the people (Ezek. 45:5). The priests will also have their own section of the "sacred portion," just as under Joshua, when they were given their own cities (Josh. 21:19, Ezek. 45:3,4; 48:9–12). When Canaan was conquered by Israel, the conquering general (Joshua) was given his own inheritance (Josh. 19:49,50). Similarly, the conquering general,

The Christian's Hope

i.e., "the Prince," Jesus Christ, will receive his own portion (Ezek. 45:7; 48:21,22).

By the beginning of the Millennial Kingdom, the physical features of the country of Israel and of the earth in general will be radically altered.

In the Millennial Kingdom, many of the physical features of the earth will be altered from what they are today. In Israel, for example, an earthquake will split the Mount of Olives in two. The northern half will move north, the southern half will move south, resulting in an east-west valley leading down from Jerusalem to the Dead Sea. At the same time, the area of Jerusalem will be lifted up and will become a high mountain—the highest in Israel and perhaps the highest in the world (Isa. 2:2; Ezek. 20:40; 40:2; Mic. 4:1). At first this would seem both unlikely and undesirable. Who would want the highest mountain in the world in Palestine? Who would enjoy climbing it, even to visit the Temple of God? What about oxygen (Mount Everest is more than 29,000 feet and most people cannot survive at the top without supplemental oxygen)? These concerns, however, are not actually valid. Scripture says that during the Tribulation there will be earthquakes and disasters that level (or reduce the height of) the high mountains existing today (Isa. 40:4; 54:10; Rev. 6:14; 16:18–20). Thus the Mountain of the Lord in Jerusalem could be the highest in the world and still be of very modest height by today's standards. In any case, the height of the Mountain of the Lord will not deter people from climbing it.

> **Isaiah 2:3a**
> Many peoples will come and say, "Come, let us go up to the mountain of the LORD, to the house of the God of Jacob."

The Mountain of the Lord will be in the "sacred portion" of Israel. The Temple will sit on top of the Mountain of the Lord, and the city of Jerusalem will be situated on the south side of the mountain (Ezek. 40:2). The river of life will flow out of the Temple of the Lord and down the mountain to the Dead Sea on the east and to the Mediterranean Sea on the west (Ezek. 47:1; Zech. 14:8).

In the Millennial Kingdom, the Temple will be on the top of the Mountain of the Lord (Ezek. 40–44).

The Temple will measure 500 cubits square—about 850 feet square (Ezek. 42:15–20; 45:2). As has been stated before, the presence of a temple in the Millennial Kingdom is proof that there will be two separate and distinct kingdoms in the future because, according to Revelation 21:22, no temple will be present in the Everlasting Kingdom. The detailed description of the Temple provided in Ezekiel makes it evident that it is, in fact, a literal temple. It is true that at times the Church is called a "temple," but in these instances the figure of speech *Metaphor*, a comparison by representation, is being employed.[12] The Church can metaphorically be called a temple because both the Church and the literal Temple are the dwelling place of God. Ezekiel, however, does not simply use the *word* "temple" as does the New Testament. He *describes* it in great detail, including the people who will work there. The description of the Temple in Ezekiel is so detailed that many Study Bibles and Bible Dictionaries have drawings of what it will look like. It is so complete that it is difficult to see how any unbiased person who reads the chapters on the Temple (Ezek. 40–44, 46) could say they refer to anything other than a literal building. The Temple in Ezekiel is

---

[12] Figures of speech is one of the areas in biblical studies that requires exacting scholarship. Unfortunately, few Christians have any training in the field. There are more than 200 figures of speech used in the Bible. Although the names of some of them are thrown around loosely in our vernacular, there are exact definitions for the figures. For example, a *Simile* is a comparison by resemblance ("You eat **like** a pig!"), a *Metaphor* is a comparison by representation ("You **are** a pig!"), and a *Hypocatastasis* is a comparison by implication ("**Pig!**"). When Scripture says that the Church **is** a temple, that is a *Metaphor* (Eph. 2:21). Note that there is no *description* of the Church as a temple with doors, walls, gates, an altar, etc. Only the word "temple" is used. For much more on *Simile*, *Metaphor*, and some 200 other figures of speech used in the Bible, see E. W. Bullinger, *Figures of Speech Used in the Bible* (Baker Book House, Grand Rapids, MI, reprinted 1968).

not a *Metaphor*. It is a literal description of the future Temple that Christ will preside over as High Priest.[13]

There is no teaching that this author is aware of propounding that the Tabernacle or Solomon's Temple are *Metaphors*. Everyone accepts without question that they are actual buildings, and with good reason. Beyond the fact that they were literal buildings, the Bible goes to great lengths to describe the physical details of the buildings and their services. Exodus has twelve chapters on the Tabernacle and its services (Exod. 25–31; 35–39). 2 Chronicles has three chapters on Solomon's Temple (2 Chron. 3–5). When it comes to the Millennial Temple, Ezekiel has six chapters on the Temple and its services (Ezek. 40–44, 46). The volume and detail of these records is in stark contrast to the absence of detail in the verses in the New Testament where the Church is metaphorically *called* a temple. The detailed description of Ezekiel's Temple will someday be realized in a literal temple, built to the specifications and measurements given in Ezekiel, and Jesus Christ will minister there as the High Priest.

There are many conservative Christian scholars who recognize that the Temple in the Book of Ezekiel is described in such a way that it must refer to a literal building. Nevertheless, they do not realize that it is a future temple and state that, for a variety of reasons, it was simply never built. Most of these scholars think that Ezekiel was writing to encourage the people of Judah who had been taken captive to Babylon.

---

[13] Unfortunately, the Temple in Ezekiel is not the only thing in the Old Testament concerning the Millennial Kingdom that is "spiritualized" by many Christians. Often, the entire point of a prophecy concerning the Millennial Kingdom is lost because it is "spiritualized." This leads to some of the following errors: saying that the wealth brought to Israel in the future is the wealth of the Christian Church now, the joy and peace of the Millennium becoming the joy that Christians have in the Lord now, the future rulership of Israel over the world becoming a time when the Church will rule the world, and so on. People who spiritualize prophecy this way usually refer to the Christian Church as "spiritual Israel." Although the phrase is often heard in evangelical circles, it is not used in Scripture. While it is true that the Church is a "joint heir" of the promises, Israel and the Church are two separate things, and what God promised to Israel, He will literally fulfill for them.

These captive Judeans were heartsick that Solomon's Temple had been burned to the ground. Some scholars propose that Ezekiel's vision of a new and grand temple was meant to encourage the captives. The *New Bible Dictionary* states this view well:

> The exiles were heartened in their grief by the vision granted to Ezekiel. More details are given of this [temple] than of Solomon's structure, although it was never built.[14]

Smith's Dictionary of the Bible agrees that the Temple was never built, but goes even further:

> It is not a description of a Temple that ever was built or ever could be erected at Jerusalem.[15]

The idea that God gave the captives in Babylon a vision of a temple that He knew would never be built is preposterous. In fact, the idea that God gave a false vision at all is a stab at the very character of God. The vision of Ezekiel covers nine chapters and gives many details. Can the God who "cannot lie" give such a vision and then it simply not come to pass? That would contradict the nature of God.

It is true that Ezekiel's Temple has not yet been built, but it will be, and it will be the centerpiece of the Millennial Kingdom. Therefore, the minute description of the Temple is very appropriate because it will be the center of attention of the entire world for a thousand years and will play a major role in the life of every single person on earth. The following aspects of the Temple are described in Scripture in detail: location (Ezek. 45:3,4; 48:9,10); size and shape (Ezek. 42:15–20; 45:2); walls, alcoves, rooms, doors, porticos, gates, steps, courtyards, decorations, slaughtering tables, the holy place, the most holy place, altars, and the clothing of the priests (Ezek. 40–44). Interestingly, there will not be an Ark of the Covenant in the Temple (Jer. 3:16). This is understandable because in the Old Testament, the

---

[14] Howard Marshal, ed., *New Bible Dictionary* (Intervarsity Press, Downers Grove, IL, 3rd edition, 1996), pp. 1157–58.

[15] Hackett, op. cit., *Smith's Dictionary of the Bible*, Vol. 4, p. 3202.

Ark of the Covenant, along with the mercy seat, was where God dwelt and where He met His people. In the Millennial Kingdom, God will meet His people through Jesus Christ.

The mention of sacrifices and offerings is one of the reasons that some Christians say that Ezekiel's Temple must be figurative and not literal. They say that the sacrifices have been done away and therefore will not be reinstated in the future. This position assumes that the "new" sacrifices would be identical and serve the same purposes as the "old" sacrifices. Note that nowhere does Scripture say that these "new" sacrifices will be a way to salvation. The book of Hebrews makes it clear that Jesus Christ is the one time sacrifice for sin. The future sacrifices may be memorial offerings similar to the Old Testament Jewish feasts such as Passover, which memorialized a past event. They may also be a means to prove the sincerity of people who are asking for forgiveness for their actions. In any case, the offerings will provide food for the priests and Levites just as they did in the Old Testament.

> **Ezekiel 44:28–30**
> (28) I [God] am to be the only inheritance the priests have. You are to give them no possession in Israel; I will be their possession.
> (29) They will eat the grain offerings, the sin offerings and the guilt offerings; and everything in Israel devoted to the LORD will belong to them.
> (30) The best of all the firstfruits and of all your special gifts will belong to the priests. You are to give them the first portion of your ground meal so that a blessing may rest on your household.

Just because the book of Ezekiel mentions offerings and sacrifices is no reason to dismiss it as a "spiritual temple" or figure of speech. The prophecy that Christ will be both King and High Priest will be fulfilled literally.

In the Millennial Kingdom, Jerusalem will be the capital of the world (Isa. 62:1–7).

Jerusalem will be located in the southern part of the "sacred portion" between the tribe of Judah to the north and the tribe of Benjamin to the south (Ezek. 48:7–23). It will be situated on the southern slope of the Mountain of the Lord (Ezek. 40:2) and will measure 4,500 cubits square— just less than 1½ miles square (Ezek. 48:16). It will be a beautiful city and will be the praise of the earth (Isa. 62:7).

The Millennial Kingdom is still future.

In what is known as "The Lord's Prayer," which is the best-known prayer in Christendom, Jesus instructed people to pray, "Thy Kingdom come" (Matt. 6:10; Luke 11:2). He would not have prayed that prayer, or asked others to pray it, if the Kingdom were already here. Today, some 2,000 years after Christ gave that prayer to his disciples, people still recite it, asking for the Kingdom to come because it has not come yet.

After his resurrection, Jesus' disciples asked him if he was going to set up the Kingdom (Acts 1:6). They wanted the Kingdom to come, and probably not just because they wanted the pain and suffering of this life to come to an end. Jesus had told them that when he set up his Kingdom they would all sit on thrones and judge the tribes of Israel (Matt. 19:28). Jesus politely answered the disciples' question by saying that it was not for them to know the times or dates when the Father would set up the Kingdom (Acts 1:7). As is evident, it was not set up during Christ's life on earth, nor between his resurrection and ascension, nor has it been set up since then.

Christ will set up his Kingdom when he comes back to earth and, when it is here, it will be very obvious. He will be ruling the earth from Jerusalem and "He will proclaim peace to the nations. His rule will extend from sea to sea and from the River to the ends of the earth" (Zech. 9:10). The prophecies and promises of joy, peace, food, and health will all be fulfilled. The blind and the lame will all be healed. There will be justice on earth. The deserts will bloom and a river of life will flow from Jerusalem down the Mountain of the Lord into the

The Christian's Hope

Rift Valley and the Dead Sea will be healed. When the Kingdom finally comes, no one will miss it.

Occasionally, people become confused about whether the Kingdom is already here or if it is still future. This usually occurs for one of two reasons. First, they are confused by the verse that in some versions reads, "the kingdom of God is within you." Second, they are confused by verses that seem to say that believers are already part of the Kingdom. Each of these must be considered. In many versions, Luke 17:21 is translated, "the kingdom of God is within you," and it is often quoted as if it were the only clear verse on the subject of the Kingdom of God and absolutely self-explanatory. Ironically, it is perhaps the most obscure verse on the subject. The hundreds of other verses on the subject, including the Lord's Prayer, make it clear that the Kingdom of God is not "in" anyone, and both the Bible and personal experience testify to the fact that it has not yet been established on this earth. Furthermore, when Christ said, "the kingdom of God is within you," he was speaking to the Pharisees, who opposed both Jesus and his Father. It was to them that he said, "You do not know me or my father" (John 8:19). The Kingdom was certainly not within *them*—they were even in danger of being excluded from it altogether (Matt. 21:23–31, especially verse 31).

It is important to note that the context of Luke 17:21 shows conclusively that the Kingdom is future, alerting the reader to the mistranslation.

Luke 17:20,21

(20) Once, having been asked by the Pharisees when the kingdom of God would come, Jesus replied, "The kingdom of God does not come with your careful observation,
(21) nor will people say, 'Here it is,' or 'There it is,' because the kingdom of God is within you."

The Pharisees knew the Kingdom was future and were asking when it would come. Of course, one might contend that the Pharisees were wrong and the Kingdom was there at the time, but that possibility is excluded when the entire answer that Jesus gave is read and understood. Jesus told his audience that they would not need to search for the Kingdom (v. 23) because, when it does come, it will be like lightning that lights up the entire sky—everyone will see it (v. 24). Jesus went on to say that as it *was* (in the past) in the time of Noah, so it *will be* (in the future) in the "day the Son of Man is revealed" (vs. 26 and 30). This discourse by Christ clearly indicates that his Kingdom is future.

The word "within" in many versions is better translated as "among" or "in your midst." Sadly, much of orthodox Christianity takes this one mistranslated phrase, "the kingdom of God is within you," and then asserts that each person has the Kingdom of God within himself.[16] This teaching misses the mark because it fails to observe two key points of biblical interpretation: *a)* failure to identify *to whom* Christ was speaking and *b)* failure to consider the *context* of the verse. As previously noted, Jesus was speaking to the Pharisees, enemies of God, and the context clearly indicates that the Kingdom is still future.

Then what did Jesus mean when he said, "the kingdom of God is within you"? Besides recognizing that he was speaking to the Pharisees, it is also important to recognize that the Pharisees were challenging him, testing him, trying to prove he was a fraud. They were arrogantly "demanding" (KJV) to know when the Kingdom of God would come. They were aware that some of the people believed Jesus was the Christ—the Messiah, the King—and they wanted to discredit him. Therefore, they brought up what they thought was a good challenge to his credibility, namely, "If you are the King, where's your Kingdom." Of course, Jesus felt no obligation to respond to the challenge, at least not in the way the Pharisees were expecting. Jesus could have answered them plainly. He knew the answer to their question. He had plainly told his disciples that only God knows when the Kingdom will come.

---

[16] Christians do have the powerful gift of holy spirit sealed within them, which Colossians 1:27 calls, "Christ in you," but that is not the Kingdom.

Matthew 24:36

No one knows about that day or hour, not even the angels in heaven, nor the Son, but only the Father.[17]

Jesus told his disciples that he did not know when the Kingdom would come, but he did not answer the arrogant and unbelieving Pharisees as clearly. He answered them, as he often did, somewhat enigmatically. The Greek word translated "within" can also be translated "among" or, perhaps even better, "in your midst." Christ knew he was the King, even though his Kingdom would not be physically manifested until later, so he told the Pharisees, "The kingdom of God is *among* you," i.e., in the person of Christ himself. Although the translation "among" is represented in many versions, Christians generally do not recognize or quote it. This is a result of mainline Christian thinking that perceives the Kingdom as a figurative kingdom that is somehow inside each Christian and not as a literal kingdom.[18] In making the Kingdom figurative, the force of Christ's powerful statement is lost.[19]

---

[17] This verse has caused problems for many theologians who could not imagine that there was something Jesus did not know. So, as the manuscripts were copied, the phrase "nor the Son" was dropped from many of them. This fact is discussed in many books on the history of the text. See Bart D. Ehrman, *The Orthodox Corruption of Scripture* (Oxford University Press, New York, 1993) pp. 91–92; Bruce Metzger, *A Textual Commentary on the Greek New Testament* (Deutsche Bibelgesellschaft/German Bible Society, Stuttgart, 1994), pp. 51–52; Bruce Metzger, *The Text of the New Testament: Its Transmission, Corruption and Restoration* (Oxford University Press, New York, 1992), p. 202. For more information on why Jesus did not know this information, see Graeser, Lynn, and Schoenheit, op. cit., *One God & One Lord*.

[18] Changing the kingdom from the literal Kingdom of Christ on earth to a figurative kingdom has resulted in a murky and mystical theology. Christians who say that the kingdom is inside them usually only have a vague idea of what that means.

[19] It is important to understand that, although the Kingdom is literally in the future, the presence of the King meant that the Kingdom was occasionally spoken of as if it were already present. That is why there are verses, such as Matthew 12:28: "But if I drive out demons by the Spirit of God, then the kingdom of God has come upon you," that indicate the Kingdom is present. Christ's presence foreshadowed the coming of the Kingdom. In a similar way, things that will be experienced in fullness

(continued)

He subtly derided the arrogance of the Pharisees because they failed to acknowledge that the King was in their midst. They did not recognize him. They not only failed to understand that the King was in their midst, but they also had him crucified as a blasphemer.

In spite of the fact that most Christians quote the verse using "within" instead of "among," there is an impressive list of versions that read "among" or "in your midst." These include: the New American Standard Bible, International Standard Bible, The New English Bible, The Jerusalem Bible, The Revised Standard Version, The Emphasized Bible (by J. B. Rotherham), The Bible: James Moffatt Translation, Complete Jewish Bible (by David Stern), God's New Covenant (by Heinz Cassirer), and the acclaimed translation in contemporary idiom, The Message (by Eugene Peterson).

Another reason people believe that the Kingdom is here now is that there are a few verses that seem to say that Christians are already part of the Kingdom. For example, Colossians 1:13 says Christians "have been brought into the kingdom of the Son," making it sound like they are already part of it. The answer to this apparent contradiction lies in understanding a common Hebrew and Greek idiom called the "prophetic perfect." In the use of the prophetic perfect, when something is

---

when the Kingdom comes are experienced in part now. Throughout history, there have been, and continue to be, some healings, some miracles, food occasionally multiplied so that the people present are not hungry, etc. These "glimpses" of the Kingdom are wonderful, but they are certainly not proof that the Kingdom is here now. However, when the King is present, then there is a sense in which the Kingdom can be spoken of as being present. Bullinger writes: "The kingdom depends on the PERSON of the King. It is the king that makes a kingdom, and not the kingdom the king. It is king-dom, the termination *dom* denoting jurisdiction. *Dom* is an abbreviation of *doom* or judgment. Hence it denotes the *sphere* in which anything is exercised, as an earl-dom, wis-dom, Christen-dom. Hence a king-dom is the sphere where a king exercises his rule and jurisdiction. In his absence, therefore, there can be no kingdom. When the Lord said to His enemies, 'The kingdom of God is among you' (Luke xvii. 21, margin), He meant in the person of the king. He could not mean it was "within" the hearts of His enemies, who rejected the King and sought His life." Bullinger, op. cit., *Figures of Speech Used in the Bible*, p. 991.

absolutely going to occur in the future, it is spoken of as having already happened. Thus, the Bible says that Christians are *now* part of Christ's Kingdom because they *absolutely will be* part of it when it does come. The "prophetic perfect" is an idiom used in both the Hebrew and Greek texts of the Bible. Because the impact of the prophetic perfect on both theology and the proper understanding of the Bible is very significant, this idiom is covered in detail in Appendix E.

Biblical Names of the Millennial Kingdom

The Millennial Kingdom is referred to by many different names in Scripture. This should not be considered unusual. Throughout Scripture, a person or place may be called by several different names. For example, Jerusalem is called "the city of David" (2 Sam. 5:7,9), "the city of God" (Ps. 46:4), "Salem" (Ps. 76:2), "Zion" (Ps. 76:2), "the Lord our Righteousness" (Jer. 33:16), "Sodom" (Ezek. 16:46), "the city of the great king" (Ps. 48:2; Matt. 5:35), "Ariel" (Isa. 29:1,2,7, which means "Lion of God" or "Hearth of God"), "the City of Truth" (Zech. 8:3), and others. It is evident from the context of each name that it refers to the city of Jerusalem. The same practice is evident in our culture: New York City is called "the Big Apple" and Chicago is called "the Windy City." Although it can be very confusing to the new student of the Bible when a person or place has different names, this is something that every serious student of the Bible studies and eventually learns.[20] Likewise, the Millennial Kingdom is called by many names and people should not let that fact confuse them. Below are many of the names by which this future Kingdom is known in Scripture. A study of these names in their contexts shows that they all refer to the same Kingdom.

---

[20] Not only can one thing have many names, but also different things can have the same name. We are used to that with people, but in the Bible it is true of cities also. Bethlehem and Jerusalem were both called "the city of David" (Luke 2:4,11; 2 Sam. 5:9), David was born in Bethlehem, but conquered Jerusalem and moved there.

The kingdom of God (Mark 1:15).[21]

The kingdom of heaven (Matt. 4:17).[22]

Your [God's] kingdom (Matt. 6:10 in "The Lord's Prayer").

The kingdom of their Father (Matt. 13:43; "their" being the righteous who will live there).

The kingdom of our father David (Mark 11:10; Christ's Kingdom is recognized as an extension of David's Kingdom and as fulfilling the prophecies that Christ would reign on David's throne).

My kingdom (Luke 22:30; spoken by Jesus who will be King).

Paradise (Luke 23:43; 2 Cor. 12:4; Rev. 2:7; Christ's future Kingdom will be "paradise on earth").[23]

The kingdom of Christ and of God (Eph. 5:5).

---

[21] The list of scriptures is not meant to be exhaustive. A name may be used many times in the Bible even if only one Scripture reference is listed.

[22] "The Kingdom of heaven" could be used because the Kingdom was of heavenly origin or quality. It is also well attested that by the time of Christ the Jews frequently used the word "heaven" as a circumlocution for "God" because they did not like to say the name of God. For example, in what is called "the parable of the prodigal son," the son says to his father, "I have sinned against heaven," i.e., "against God." Even in English we often replace "God" with "heaven." For example, in the phrase, "Heaven knows," what is really intended is "God knows." Thus, "the kingdom of heaven" may simply be a Jewish way of saying "the kingdom of God." Leon Morris, *The Gospel According to Matthew* (William B. Eerdmans Publishing Company, Grand Rapids, MI, 1992), p. 53.

[23] The word "paradise" is used of Christ's future Kingdom on earth in Luke, 2 Corinthians, and Revelation. The Garden of Eden in the Old Testament was also "paradise." The Hebrew word *"eden"* means "delight" or "luxury" and was always translated in the Septuagint by the Greek word *"paradeisos,"* which means "enclosed park or pleasure ground." *Paradeisos* was brought into late Latin as *paradisus* and from there into English as "paradise." By calling the future Kingdom "paradise," Scripture connects the Garden of Eden with the future Kingdom. Both Eden and the future Kingdom are "Paradise." Christ's future kingdom is literally "Paradise regained." In the contexts in which it is used, the word "Paradise" refers to the Millennial Kingdom, but it is clear that the Eternal Kingdom is also "Paradise," so the word can refer to both Kingdoms.

The Christian's Hope

The kingdom of the Son He loves (Col. 1:13).

His heavenly kingdom (2 Tim. 4:18).

The eternal kingdom of our Lord (2 Pet. 1:11).[24]

The Wonderful Qualities of Life Promised in the Millennial Kingdom

Most people who believe that they will live forever want to know what that life will be like. Thankfully, the Bible provides some answers to that question; in fact, many aspects of life in the Millennial Kingdom are described in clear detail. These promises and prophecies of the future are so wonderful that they almost seem "too good to be true." Remember that God cannot lie—these promises will indeed come to pass. The more clearly Christians understand these prophecies, the more each one should be salivating and "champing at the bit" for the Kingdom to come soon.[25] Furthermore, every Christian should be excited enough about the future that he is eager to "spread the word" to those who do not yet know. Some of the wonderful qualities of the Millennial Kingdom are detailed below.

There will be justice on earth.
(Isa. 2:4; 9:6,7; 11:1–5; 32:1,2,5,16,17; 51:5; Jer. 23:5,6; 33:15)

Christ will reign, "establishing and upholding it [his Kingdom] with justice" (Isa. 9:7). Bribery and corruption, bigotry and prejudice,

---

[24] The context of the verse makes it clear that the phrase "eternal kingdom" actually refers to the Millennial Kingdom. "Eternal" is *aionios*, which means "age abiding" or "everlasting." The Millennial Kingdom can be called "eternal" here because the Christians who will enter it will also be part of the Eternal Kingdom, or it could be that "everlasting" is a *Hyperbole* because the Millennial Kingdom lasts 1,000 years.

[25] A number of readers have noticed "champing" and assumed I meant "chomping." I had "chomping" in an earlier version and was corrected by a horse lover. It seems that horses do not "chomp" on the bit because they have no teeth where the bit goes. "Champ" means "to work the jaws and teeth vigorously, to show impatience at being held back or delayed." A horse, excitedly waiting to run but held back by its rider, champs at the bit.

hatred and intolerance have ruined judicial systems since the dawn of man. Through the centuries, the fallen nature of man, combined with self-interest, has often resulted in justice not being served in the courts. In the future Kingdom, there will be many reasons why justice will reign, not the least of which is that Christ, who knows the hearts of all men, will be the "Chief Justice."

There will be no war.
(Isa. 2:4; 9:4–7; 60:18; Hos. 2:18; Mic. 4:3,4; Zech. 9:9,10)

War has been a scourge on mankind since Genesis. There is almost always a war (usually several) somewhere on earth. Furthermore, feuding and "cold wars" have often ruined lives even when there was no overt war. If the money invested in weapons, military training, and maintaining armies were invested in other areas, billions of people could experience a greater quality of life. In Christ's Kingdom, "nation will not take up sword against nation, nor will they train for war anymore." In fact, the weapons that are not destroyed during the Tribulation or the battle of Armageddon will be converted and used as farm implements: "They will beat their swords into plow blades and their spears into pruning hooks" (Isa. 2:4; Mic. 4:3).

The resurrected believers and raptured Christians will enjoy perfect health.
(Isa. 29:18; 32:3,4; 33:24; 35:5,6; 57:19; Jer. 33:6; Mal. 4:2)

Sickness and disease have taken a terrible toll on human life and happiness. What a blessing to know that what medical science has tried and failed to do—cure human sickness—the Lord will do for the resurrected believers and the raptured Christians in his Kingdom. "No one living in Zion will say, 'I am ill'" (Isa. 33:24). At that time the "eyes of the blind will be opened and the ears of the deaf unstopped. Then will the lame leap like a deer, and the mute tongue shout for joy" (Isa. 35:5,6).

Scripture is not as clear about the perfect health of the "natural" people who will be part of the Millennial Kingdom. They will die

(Isa. 65:20; Ezek. 44:25), but whether they will get sick or be healthy until their bodies wear out from old age is not clear. Zechariah 8:4 mentions that people will grow old and need canes to help them walk, but that does not necessarily imply pain and suffering. Of course, since the Devil and his demons are chained during the Millennial Kingdom (Rev. 20:2; Dan. 7:12), any disease that has a spiritual cause will not be present. Note that in the Everlasting Kingdom death and disease will be banished forever and everyone will be perfectly healthy (Rev. 21:4).

Mankind will live safely on the earth.

(Isa. 11:6–9; 32:18; 54:14–17; 60:11,17,18; 65:17–25; Jer. 23:4; 30:10; 33:6; Ezek. 28:26; 34:25–31; Mic. 5:4,5; Zeph. 3:13–17)

Since Adam and Eve were expelled from Paradise, mankind's existence has been a saga of grief and sorrow that is due in large part to a general lack of safety in the world. Unforeseen tragedies constantly ruin lives and destroy families, running the gamut from misfortunes that involve pain and discomfort to those involving broken bones, disfigurement, dismemberment, and even death. These tragedies can be purely accidental, caused by "nature," self-inflicted, or caused by other people. On a daily basis, newspapers record the diverse and seemingly endless array of calamities that plague mankind. Personal safety is a daily cause of concern. Things in the Millennial Kingdom will be different. The wolf will lie down with the lamb. Children will play close to cobras with no fear of harm (Isa. 11:6–8). God promises "abundant peace and security" (Jer. 33:6), a stark contrast from what we have today.

The land will be healed and the deserts will bloom.

(Isa. 32:15; 35:1,2,6,7; 41:18–20; 44:3; 51:3; Ezek. 47:8,9; Hos. 2:21,22; Joel 2:21–23)

Throughout history, deserts and other unusable land have limited mankind's ability to raise crops and to enjoy the earth. Farmers have often struggled just to get meager crops out of the soil. The problem continues to worsen as pollution makes otherwise good land less productive or even unusable. Much of the earth's topsoil has been washed away or depleted and severe weather ruins many crops. The Word of God promises that, in the Messiah's Kingdom, the land will produce bountifully. What a wonderful joy it will be to live when "the desert becomes a fertile field, and the fertile field seems like a forest" (Isa. 32:15). "Water will gush forth in the wilderness and streams in the desert. The burning sand will become a pool, the thirsty ground bubbling springs" (Isa. 35:6,7).

There will be an abundance of food, so starvation and even hunger will be abolished.
(Isa. 25:6; 30:23–26; 32:15; 35:1,6,7; 51:3; Jer. 31:5,11–14; Ezek. 47:1,2,7–12; Joel 2:18–26; 3:18; Amos 9:13)

In the Millennial Kingdom, the land will be healed and the weather will be perfect for farming, so there will be "a feast of rich food for all peoples, a banquet of aged wine—the best of meats and the finest of wines" (Isa. 25:6).[26] Verses such as Jeremiah 31:12 mention flocks and herds. That verse combined with Isaiah 25:6 clearly shows that people will eat meat in the Millennial Kingdom, not just vegetables.[27] Although most people in the United States have never faced starvation, throughout history worldwide hunger and starvation have been a terrible problem and the cause of untold misery. That misery will be abolished in the Messiah's Kingdom because there will be more than

---

[26] Note that this prophecy in Isaiah specifically mentions drinking wine in the Kingdom. Christ knew this scripture and therefore knew that there would be wine in the future Kingdom. In a bold statement at the Last Supper that revealed his love and commitment towards his disciples, he told them that he would not drink wine with them again until he drank it in "my Father's Kingdom" (Matt. 26:29). You can be assured he kept and is keeping his commitment. He drank no wine with them after his resurrection. He is patiently waiting for his Kingdom to come.

[27] Isaiah 25:6 is one verse that makes it plain that we will eat meat in the Millennial Kingdom. The KJV reads, "And in this mountain shall the LORD of hosts make unto all people a feast of fat things, a feast of wines on the lees, of fat things full of marrow, of wines on the lees well refined." The phrase "fat things full of marrow" makes it clear that animals are being referred to.

enough food produced for everyone. Even the animals will have so much food that they will eat "fodder and mash, spread out with fork and shovel" (Isa. 30:24).

Theological arguments and bickering will come to an end.

Everyone "sees through a glass, darkly" today, and there is a lot about God and truth that is not generally agreed upon or known. History, sadly, has been full of religious disagreements and debates that have ended friendships, broken families, and even been the cause of persecution, torture, and religious wars. In the Millennial Kingdom, things will be different. When the Lord rules from Jerusalem, arguments will be easily resolved because people who have questions can go ask him. The house of Israel will know God (Isa. 29:23,24; Jer. 31:33,34; Ezek. 11:18–20), and Christians will "know fully" (1 Cor. 13:12). When Christ rules the earth from Jerusalem, it will be available to know God as never before. Isaiah 11:9 and Habakkuk 2:14 will be fulfilled: "For the earth will be filled with the knowledge of the glory of the LORD, as the waters cover the sea."

The people will be holy and blessed, and there will be joy.
(Isa. 4:2–5; 35:10; 51:3; 60:1–22; 61:4–11; 62:1–12; 65:17–25;
Jer. 30:18,19; 31:4,12–14)

Many verses speak of the blessings and joy in the Millennial Kingdom in general terms. One can easily imagine how much fun life will be when people are healthy and well-fed and there is no fear of war, disaster, or danger of any type. Life will truly be a joy and a blessing to the people who live there. No wonder Scripture tells us that, "From them will come songs of thanksgiving and the sound of rejoicing" (Jer. 30:19).

All believers in the Millennial Kingdom will be given God's promised gift of holy spirit.[28]

(Isa. 32:15; 44:3–5; Ezek. 11:19; Joel 2:28–32; John 7:37–39; 14:16,17; Acts 1:8; 2:16–18,38,39)

In the Old Testament, God made his gift of holy spirit available only to a few people. However, He has promised that there will be a time coming when "all flesh" will receive the holy spirit (Joel 2:28 KJV).[29]

---

[28] God is sometimes called "the Holy Spirit" because He is holy and He is spirit. The gift of God, given to a few people in the Old Testament, and which the Lord Jesus now pours out into each Christian (Acts 2:33), is also holy and it is also spirit, so it is called "the gift of holy spirit" (Acts 2:38). The gift is not a person and should not be capitalized. It is the gift of holy spirit in each believer that gives him or her the ability to manifest the power of God. That is why the spiritually powerful people in the Old Testament were those with the gift of holy spirit, and it is why Christ said to his disciples, "You will receive power when the holy spirit comes upon you" (Acts 1:8). It has caused great confusion in the Christian world that both God and the gift He gives to mankind are called *PNEUMA HAGION* in the ancient Greek texts. The ancient texts were all capital letters, so no spelling distinction was made between the Giver (God, "Holy Spirit") and His gift (His divine nature, "holy spirit"). We, however, must make that distinction because in English we use both capital and lower case letters. For more information on the writing of the early Greek texts, see Graeser, Lynn, and Schoenheit, op. cit., *One God & One Lord*, Appendix A, note on Hebrews 1:8. For more on the difference between God, who is called "the Holy Spirit" and God's gift of holy spirit, see Graeser, Lynn, and Schoenheit, *The Gift of Holy Spirit: Every Christian's Divine Deposit* (Christian Educational Services, Indianapolis, IN, 1995), pp. 17–21, and E. W. Bullinger, *The Giver and His Gifts* (Kregel Publications, Grand Rapids, MI, 1979), pp. 26–41.

[29] It is possible that since Joel was written to Israel, and because Peter was speaking to Jews, that the phrase "all flesh," which is how the Hebrew text reads, refers only to the people of Israel and not to the nations. This interpretation may be true but seems unlikely. The phrase "all flesh" would be God's way of saying "everyone." In this context the phrase "all flesh" is the figure of speech *Hyperbole* or *Exaggeration*. The statement can be understood as an exaggeration and not literal because animals are "flesh" but would not be included. *Hyperbole* is used when God wants to make sure that people expand their thinking. Some examples will help make this clear: Christ said if your hand caused you to sin, "cut it off." Of course, he would be horrified if someone who shoplifted later took a hatchet and cut off his own hand. The use of the exaggeration (*Hyperbole*) was to make the point that we should be very serious about doing what it takes to stop the sin in our lives. Another example of *Hyperbole* occurred when Christ told the disciples to witness to "all creation"

(continued)

Peter understood this and quoted Joel on the Day of Pentecost when holy spirit was first poured out upon the Church (Acts 2:17). Since Peter spoke about the outpouring of holy spirit to the Jews on the Day of Pentecost, it is clear that he did not think that someone had to be raised from the dead at the Resurrection of the Just in order to receive holy spirit from the Lord. This fact should set the standard for Christian thinking about holy spirit being poured out in the Millennial Kingdom. It is not only for those who have been raised from the dead, it is "upon all flesh." The word "all" should be qualified by the context and scope of Scripture to mean "all who believe."[30] That is certainly what happened at Pentecost, and it is in line with what Christ taught about the coming gift of holy spirit:

> **John 7:37–39**
> (37) On the last and greatest day of the Feast, Jesus stood and said in a loud voice, "If anyone is thirsty, let him come to me and drink.
> (38) Whoever believes in me, as the Scripture has said, streams of living water will flow from within him."
> (39) By this he meant the Spirit, whom **those who believed in him were later to receive**. Up to that time the

---

(Mark 16:15). Christ knew that no one would go and tell the good news to animals even though they are part of the "creation." If Christ had spoken literally, he would have said, "all mankind," but the *Hyperbole* was used to emphasize to the disciples that they were to witness to *everyone*. Even so, they missed the point and for a decade or so witnessed to Jews only. It would have been hard for the Jews reading Joel to believe that God would really pour out His spirit on every single Israelite, even the slaves and children. It would have been even harder for them to believe that God would actually give His spirit to the Gentiles. It would appear that God used the *Hyperbole* "all flesh" in an effort to indicate that that is exactly what He intended to do.

[30] A more detailed study of how the word "all" is used in Scripture can be found in Graeser, Lynn, and Schoenheit, op. cit., *One God & One Lord*, Appendix A, Colossians 1:15–20, Numbers 5, pp. 510–11.

Spirit had not been given, since Jesus had not yet been glorified.[31]

As covered earlier, there will be "natural" people in the Millennial Kingdom. Initially, they will all believe to some degree. However, through the years people will be born who will not believe, and from what Scripture says, they will not receive holy spirit. There would be no point in Jesus saying that *those who believed* would later receive the spirit (v. 39) if in fact *every person*, whether he believed or not, were going to receive the spirit.

The Bible student should not be confused by the fact that there will be a need for the "rod of iron" during the Kingdom even though many people will have the spirit of God. The gift of holy spirit does not force a person to obey God. The Old Testament has dozens of examples of people with holy spirit making mistakes, being disobedient, and even openly rebellious towards God. Joshua had holy spirit but made the mistake of making a covenant with the Gibeonites (Josh. 9). Gideon had holy spirit but made an ephod idol that the people of Israel worshipped. King Saul had holy spirit, yet he repeatedly disobeyed God.[32] David had holy spirit, yet he committed adultery with Bathsheba and plotted the death of Uriah. Solomon had holy spirit but "did evil in the eyes of the Lord" (1 Kings 11:6). The New Testament continues the theme. Many Christians, all of whom have the gift of holy spirit, currently live in sin and disobedience. Through the gift of holy spirit the

---

[31] Although most Christians say this prophecy is about the giving of holy spirit on the day of Pentecost, Jesus' Old Testament reference, "as the Scripture has said," is to Isaiah 58:11, which was not about the Christian Church but about the Millennial Kingdom. Christians have "the promised holy spirit" (Eph. 1:13) but that does not mean the prophecy of Christ was specifically addressed *to* us. The Lord gave the holy spirit to the Church because of his love and grace. The prophecy was specifically for the Millennial Kingdom.

[32] Occasionally when someone sinned grievously enough against God, God would remove holy spirit from the person. This happened to Saul (1 Sam. 16:14), but not to every person.

Lord can speak to us, but it is a "still small voice," a gentle guiding. Anyone who makes up his mind to disobey is free to do so.

In the Grace Administration, every person who is saved (every Christian) has God's gift of holy spirit and so, having holy spirit is often equated with being saved. That is not the case however in other administrations. It was not the case in the Old Testament or the Gospels, and it will not be the case in the Millennial Kingdom. The gift of holy spirit enables believers to experience greater communion with God than would otherwise be possible, but it does not take over and control a person's thoughts or actions, nor does it keep a person from sinning.[33] The gift of holy spirit does not make a person obedient to God.

People from other nations will come to Jerusalem to worship, and foreigners will be allowed to sacrifice at the Temple.
(Isa. 2:2,3; 14:1; 19:18–25; 56:4–8; 60:3,9,14; 66:21; Zech. 2:11; 8:20–23; 14:16)

The words of Isaiah, made famous by Christ, "My house will be called a house of prayer for all nations" (Isa. 56:7), will be fulfilled. It may even be the case that some foreigners are made priests and Levites (Isa. 66:21). The Jews thought that the Tabernacle and Temple were exclusively theirs. Foreigners who came into the Temple (and the Jews who brought them there) were executed (Acts 21:27–32). This will change when Christ sits on his throne as King and High Priest. All people will be welcome to worship and pray in the Temple.

---

[33] The difference between holy spirit being "upon" someone before the Day of Pentecost or being "born in" Christians (the Christian Church started on Pentecost) is dealt with in the book by Graeser, Lynn, and Schoenheit, op. cit., *The Gift of Holy Spirit*, pp. 24, 102.

Some nations that are destroyed during the Tribulation and at Armageddon (or before) will be restored.

The Bible foretells the destruction of many nations that have sinned against God. Yet, it also specifically foretells that there will be nations whose fortunes will be restored when Christ sets up his Kingdom. These nations include Egypt (Isa. 19:18–25; Jer. 46:26), Assyria (Isa. 19:23–25), Moab (Jer. 48:47), Ammon (Jer. 49:6), and Elam (Jer. 49:39). Many of the peoples of these nations will love the Lord and will worship him. They may have been enemies of God and idolatrous nations in the past, but the prophecies reveal that they will have a change of heart. The Temple in Jerusalem will become a house of prayer for all nations.

Summary Remarks about the Millennial Kingdom

Several issues should now be clear. First and foremost is the issue of whether the Millennial Kingdom is in the future or the present. It should be clear that the Kingdom is still future because the promises of health, safety, justice, no war, no hunger, and great joy on earth are not yet fulfilled. The religious leaders of Christ's time wrongly assumed that when the Messiah came his Kingdom would come at the same time, and so, when Christ came and the Kingdom did not appear, they crucified him as a blasphemer and imposter. But Scripture indicates that his Kingdom will be established in the future, at his Second Coming, when he comes from heaven and conquers the earth.

The issue of whether the Kingdom is heavenly or earthly is also clear. There is no need to heal the land and have the deserts bloom if no one will be present to farm and to enjoy the land. Why heal the land if no one will be here? Christ and the prophets of old have made it clear that the meek will "inherit the earth," not "go to heaven."

Understanding the Messiah's Kingdom should do another thing—it should produce in each believer a great desire to be a part of it. How could anyone really understand what the Messiah's Kingdom will be like and not want to be part of it? This book has pointed out that the

Hope of a glorious future life is an anchor for the soul. But, the Hope is not only to anchor the life of the believer, the one who has already made a commitment to God; it is also to be a prime motivator for the unbeliever who is considering becoming a Christian. Too often Christians try to "scare people to Christ" by graphically portraying unbelievers suffering in "hell." God never does that.[34] There is absolutely

---

[34] Some people may say Luke 16:19–31, the record of the rich man and Lazarus, portrays suffering, but those verses are a parable, not a literal portrayal of factual events. Jesus spoke the parable to the Pharisees who believed that evil people suffer after death. By wording the parable the way he did, Christ was "becoming a Pharisee to win the Pharisees," (cp. 1 Cor. 9:19–22). He was speaking their language to make the point that even if a person returned from the dead, the hard of heart would not believe. This was shown to be the case when both Lazarus and Christ rose from the dead.

People who assert that the record about Lazarus is actual and not a parable argue that *a)* Jesus did not say it was a parable and *b)* no other parable contains a proper name. In answer to *a)*, note that many parables start without Christ saying that he is speaking a parable. A few examples from Matthew include the parable of the Workers in the Field (20:1–16), the Two Sons (21:28–31), the Wise and Foolish Virgins (25:1–13), and the Talents (25:14–30, which is different from the parable of the Minas in Luke 19:11–27). In Luke 15 and 16 the openings of the parables are very similar. The parable of the Prodigal Son (Luke 15:11–32) opens, "There was a man." The parable of the Shrewd Manager (Luke 16:1–13) opens, "There was a rich man." The parable of Lazarus and the Rich Man opens, "There was a rich man." The similarity of these openings is strong evidence that Jesus was continuing to speak in parables.

In answer to *b)*, note that there is no rule that says a parable cannot have a proper name. Some parables contain very specific details, such as amounts of money or goods, times of the day, and even the specific names of cities. For example, the parable of the Good Samaritan mentions both Jerusalem and Jericho (also, it is not called a parable, and it opens with, "A man"). This author has reviewed commentaries and study Bibles in several theological libraries and found that the majority of conservative and orthodox biblical scholars believe that the record of Lazarus and the rich man is a parable. An exhaustive list would not be appropriate, but the sources are varied and include: Henry Alford, *The Greek Testament*; Geoffrey W. Bromiley, ed., *The International Standard Bible Encyclopedia*; E. W. Bullinger, *The Companion Bible*; Trent Butler, ed., *Holman Bible Dictionary*; F. L. Cross, and E. A. Livingstone, eds., *The Oxford Dictionary of the Christian Church*; Edward Fudge, *The Fire that Consumes*; H. B. Hackett, ed., *Smith's Dictionary of the Bible*; James Hastings, *A Dictionary of the Bible*; R. C. H. Lenski, *The Interpretation of St. Luke's Gospel*; John Lightfoot, *A Commentary on the New Testament from the Talmud and*

(continued)

no biblical basis for the descriptions found in classical literature of people being burned or tortured by demons, placed head-first in boiling mud pools, being stabbed by red-hot pitchforks, or any such thing.

It is very clear in Scripture that God motivates unbelievers with the wonderful attributes of Paradise rather than "scaring them into salvation" by the horrid features of "hell." God shows how wonderful the future life will be for people who believe. And since Christians are to be "imitators of God" (Eph. 5:1), we should imitate how He reaches out to unbelievers with His goodness. Christians need to study and learn about the coming Kingdom of Christ and become experts in presenting it to others in order to bring them to Christ. Each and every Christian should be so excited about the wonderful qualities of the Kingdom and his personal part in it that he works to become knowledgeable to the end he has no difficulty communicating these great truths to others.

The End of the Millennial Kingdom

After 1,000 years, Christ's wonderful Kingdom will come to an end. This end is described in the Book of Revelation:

Talmud and Hebraica; Watson Mills, ed., *Mercer Dictionary of the Bible*; W. R. Nicoll, *The Expositor's Greek New Testament*; Alfred Plummer, *The International Critical Commentary: The Gospel According to S. Luke*; A. T. Robertson, *Word Pictures in the New Testament*; R. C. Trench, *Notes on the Parables of Our Lord,* and Claus Westermann, *The Parables of Jesus in the Light of the Old Testament.*

The Bible portrays a final death for the unsaved. They are thrown into the lake of fire and incinerated, burned to ashes. It is commonly believed that those who are thrown into the lake of fire burn forever, but that is not true. The origin of that belief is a couple difficult verses such as Revelation 20:10. However, if people are alive and burning forever, then they too would have everlasting life. Scripture makes it plain that the only way to have everlasting life is to be saved. There are many verses that indicate that the unsaved will be completely consumed. The unsaved do not live forever anywhere, even Gehenna. Those thrown into the lake of fire are eventually burned up. Graeser, Lynn, and Schoenheit, *Is There Death After Life?* (Christian Educational Services, Indianapolis, IN, 1993), pp. 45–51, 88–91. See also Edward Fudge, *The Fire that Consumes* (Providential Press, Houston, TX, 1982).

Revelation 20:7–10

(7) When the thousand years are over, Satan will be released from his prison

(8) and will go out to deceive the nations in the four corners of the earth—Gog and Magog—to gather them for battle. In number they are like the sand on the seashore.

(9) They marched across the breadth of the earth and surrounded the camp of God's people, the city he loves. But fire came down from heaven and devoured them.

(10) And the Devil, who deceived them, was thrown into the lake of burning sulfur, where the beast and the false prophet had been thrown. They will be tormented day and night forever and ever.

As these scriptures state, at the end of the 1,000 years the Devil will be loosed. He will then deceive the "nations" so that they will come against God's people. The "nations" will be comprised of the "natural" people living in the Kingdom. These rebellious "natural" people will be descendants of the Tribulation survivors who were judged righteous and allowed to enter the Kingdom. Like the Israelites in the Old Testament who forgot the hard lessons learned by their ancestors, these people will have forgotten what their own ancestors had learned during the Tribulation and the battle of Armageddon. This is an interesting commentary on human beings. It seems that every generation needs to discover for itself that rebellion against God ends only in self-destruction.

Although the people in these nations will have a sin nature, the Eden-like conditions on earth and Christ's firm but just hand of rulership will maintain order until, at the end of the 1,000 years, "Satan," i.e., the Devil, and his hordes of demons, are released from prison (Rev. 20:2; Dan. 7:12). The Devil then sows his seeds of discontent, jealousy, greed, and hatred until finally millions of people from the nations band together to attack Israel. They will forge weapons and march on Israel with the intent of destroying it. Their weapons will be primitive by modern standards and will be similar to weapons that existed in biblical times, because the weapons of destruction that exist today will either have been converted for useful purposes (Isa. 2:4; Mic. 4:3), or burned up and destroyed (Isa. 9:5). At the end of the Millennial Kingdom, the rebels will not have developed the weapons of mass destruction that nations have today. Nevertheless, a spear or sword will be as deadly then as it has always been. It is this attack on God's people that is one reason for the well-known verse in Isaiah, "No weapon that is formed against you shall prosper" (Isa. 54:17, NASB). This unbelieving army does not prevail. Their weapons do not "prosper" and they do not win the war. In fact, there is no evidence that a war even begins. When Satan's army surrounds God's people, fire falls from heaven and kills all of them (Rev. 20:9).

It is common to hear Isaiah 54:17 quoted by Christians as if it applied to them. It clearly does not, however, as is evidenced by the fact that Christians die every day by various weapons of unrighteousness. They are shot, stabbed, poisoned, etc., and have been since the inception of Christianity. This is true in wars, in crimes, and in specific acts of hatred against Christians. It is clear from the immediate and remote context that this verse in Isaiah applies to God's people in the Millennial Kingdom and is an absolute promise to those Christians and resurrected believers who will be there. No Christian or resurrected saint from Israel (like Moses or David) or from the Gentiles (like Noah or Abraham) will need to fear a weapon wielded by a malcontent. No weapon formed against *them* will prosper.

The fire from heaven not only destroys the enemies of God, it destroys the earth as well. This fact is elaborated on in the following verses:

2 Peter 3:10–12
(10) But the day of the Lord will come like a thief. The heavens will disappear with a roar; the elements will be destroyed by fire, and the earth and everything in it will be laid bare.

(11) Since everything will be destroyed in this way, what kind of people ought you to be? You ought to live holy and godly lives

(12) as you look forward to the day of God and speed its coming. That day will bring about the destruction of the heavens by fire, and the elements will melt in the heat.

Because the world is destroyed by fire at the end of the Millennial Kingdom, in order for God to put His people back on the earth in the New Jerusalem, He will have to create a new heaven and new earth. This is exactly what Revelation 21:1 says: "Then I saw a new heaven and a new earth, for the first heaven and the first earth had passed away."

Between the Millennial Kingdom and the Everlasting Kingdom

Before the Everlasting Kingdom can start, the "business" of the Millennial Kingdom must be concluded. For one thing, millions of people must be judged. It is between the two Kingdoms that what is known as the "Second Resurrection" or "Resurrection of the Unjust" occurs. It is called the "Second" Resurrection because the "First" Resurrection will have already occurred at the start of the Millennial Kingdom (Rev. 20:4). It is called the "Resurrection of the Unjust" because the vast majority of people who get up will be unjust. This is explained by the fact that all of the righteous people from the time of Adam until the start of the Millennial Kingdom will have already gotten up at either the Rapture or the "Resurrection of the Just" (KJV—Luke 14:14). The only righteous people remaining to be resurrected are those who died during the Millennial Kingdom. The rest of the people who will be resurrected consist of all the unjust and unsaved people who have ever lived. The "Resurrection of the Unjust" is the only time when unbelievers will be raised from the dead. At that time, every unbeliever who ever lived will be raised for judgment.

The judgment associated with the Second Resurrection is known as the "Final Judgment" because it is chronologically the last judgment in

Scripture. It is also known as the "White Throne Judgment" because Jesus Christ will be sitting on a "great white throne."[35]

Revelation 20:11–15

(11) Then I saw a great white throne and him who was seated on it. Earth and sky fled from his presence, and there was no place for them.

(12) And I saw the dead, great and small, standing before the throne, and books were opened. Another book was opened, which is the book of life. The dead were judged according to what they had done as recorded in the books.

(13) The sea gave up the dead that were in it, and death and Hades [the grave] gave up the dead that were in them, and each person was judged according to what he had done.

(14) Then death and Hades were thrown into the lake of fire. The lake of fire is the second death.

(15) If anyone's name was not found written in the book of life, he was thrown into the lake of fire.

The White Throne Judgment clears the way for God's Everlasting Kingdom to begin. Those people whose names are in the Book of Life will be given everlasting life, while those people who are not listed there will be thrown into the lake of fire and incinerated, thus experiencing a "second death."[36] After the White Throne Judgment, death is abolished. In the Everlasting Kingdom, there will be no more death.

---

[35] It is Christ who will be sitting on the throne, not God. Jesus Christ will do the actual judging (John 5:22; Acts 17:31). Many people think that "God" is on the throne because the KJV reads, stand "before God" in verse 12. However, a study of the Greek texts will reveal that the original reading was "throne" and not "God." Because of that, the vast majority of the modern translations read "before the throne."

[36] When verses speak of the "death" of the wicked, it is frequently this second death that is being referred to. For an explanation of an example from Proverbs, see Appendix F.

The Christian's Hope

The Everlasting Kingdom

After the Final Judgment, God will create a new heaven and new earth and set up a new Kingdom. He will rule this Kingdom from a throne in the New Jerusalem along with His Son, Jesus Christ. Although the Bible has no specific name for this kingdom, the "Everlasting Kingdom" is appropriate because this kingdom will last forever. There are many similarities between the Millennial Kingdom and the Everlasting Kingdom, but there are also significant differences—evidence that there are in fact two different kingdoms.

Attributes of the Everlasting Kingdom

Although Scripture provides less detail about the Everlasting Kingdom than the Millennial Kingdom, what is provided is both enlightening and encouraging. The following are some of the distinctive attributes and characteristics of the Everlasting Kingdom.

1) The Kingdom will begin after fire from heaven destroys the earth (2 Pet. 3:10–12; Rev. 20:7–10) and God creates "a new heaven and a new earth" (Rev. 21:1).

2) The Kingdom will last forever (Rev. 22:5).

3) The Devil and his demons will not be present. At the close of the Millennial Kingdom, they are all cast into the lake of burning sulfur (Rev. 20:10).[37]

4) Only believers, the saved, will populate the Kingdom. All unbelievers will have been judged and cast into the lake of fire to be incinerated (Rev. 20:11–15).

---

[37] The KJV reads, "the lake of fire and brimstone." "Brimstone" is an old term for sulfur. Some commentators understand from the Greek construction that the phrase is a *Hendiadys*, the figure of speech in which two words are connected by a conjunction to express a single thought as if one of the words were actually an adjective. Thus, "fire and sulfur" is actually "burning sulfur."

5) There will be no death in this Kingdom. This is in direct contrast to every other kingdom or time period recorded in the Bible from the time Adam and Eve were expelled from the Garden of Eden through the Millennial Kingdom. (Rev. 21:4). The absence of death may also mean that animals will not die either. In the Original Paradise both man and animals ate plants only (Gen. 1:28–30). This may well be the case in the Everlasting Kingdom, but the Bible does not speak specifically about it.

6) God and Christ will live in and rule from the "New Jerusalem" (Rev. 21:2), which will be by far the largest city the world has ever seen. The apostle John saw the city in a vision and described its dimensions: "The city was laid out like a square, as long as it was wide" (Rev. 21:16). The Greek text gives the measurements of the city as "12,000 stadia; the length and the width and the height of it are the same" (Rev. 21:16). A Roman stadia was 625 Roman feet, or 606¾ American feet, which makes the city roughly 1,400 miles on each side.[38] The city is so large that it is quite possible that every saved person from all of time could live in it comfortably.

7) There will not be a temple in the New Jerusalem (Rev. 21:22). This is a key difference between the Everlasting Kingdom and the Millennial Kingdom. Although this may seem to be a minor

---

[38] The fact that the text says that the city will have equal width, length, and height has caused problems for commentators because it seems so unrealistic. However, we must remember that "the old order of things has passed away" (Rev. 21:4). Who would believe that there would be light but no sun (Rev. 21:23; 22:5) and no night at all (Rev. 21:25; 22:5)? Who would believe that the city and its streets would be made of pure gold (Rev. 21:18,21)? Yet these things are clearly stated. It is possible that the city is a cube. It is also possible that the city is a pyramid or that there is a high mountain in the midst of the city, perhaps with the throne of God on top. Scripture does not say if part of the city is 12,000 stadia high or if all of it is that high. It simply states that it is as high as it is wide and long. It seems best to take the testimony of what John saw at face value and not try to make it into "figurative language" simply because we cannot imagine such a structure.

point, it is very significant. The reason given in Revelation 21:22 for the absence of a temple in the Everlasting Kingdom is that, "The Lord God Almighty and the Lamb are its Temple." Understanding the word "temple" is the key to unlocking the significance of this verse. In the first Paradise, Eden, there was no building called a temple that Adam and Eve visited regularly to worship God. Instead, God would appear "in person" to Adam and Eve. He came in a human form so He could fellowship with them intimately. When Adam and Eve disobeyed God, sin entered the world and, therefore, God no longer chose to "reside" in the world. He did on occasion appear in a human form to people throughout the Old Testament, including Abraham (Gen. 12:7; 15:1; 17:1; 18:1), Moses and some elders (Exod. 24:9–11), Samuel (1 Sam. 3:10), Isaiah (Isa. 6:1–5), and Daniel (Dan. 7:9–14).[39] Nevertheless, His personal presence was represented to the people through the temple building.

In the Church Age, there is no temple building. God's gift of holy spirit gives each believer personal access to Him, which is also why the Church is figuratively referred to as a "temple." In the Millennial Kingdom, a temple building will again be present to represent God's presence to the people. He will not be personally present because there will still be sin in the world via the "natural" people inhabiting the Kingdom. But in the Everlasting Kingdom, God Himself will be personally present just as He was in Eden because there will be no more sin in the world. Therefore, there is no need for a temple building because, "The Lord God Almighty and the Lamb are its Temple."

---

[39] It is not generally taught that God Himself occasionally took on human form to fellowship with people. For a much more extensive treatment of this very important subject, see Graeser, Lynn, and Schoenheit, op. cit., *One God & One Lord*, Appendix A, Genesis 18:1,2.

Scripture says of the Everlasting Kingdom, "The dwelling of God is with men, and He will live with them" (Rev. 21:3).

The fact that God will not be personally present in the Millennial Kingdom the same way He will be personally present in the Everlasting Kingdom explains 1 Corinthians 15:24, which says that when the end comes, Christ will hand over the Kingdom to God. During the Millennial Kingdom, Christ will reign in Jerusalem as High Priest and King, and he will worship God in the Temple described in Ezekiel. There will be no throne for God because He will not be personally present yet. But when the Everlasting Kingdom begins, God will take His place on His throne in the presence of all people, and Christ will present Him the Kingdom. There will be no need for a temple because God Himself will be tangibly present.

8) The Tree of Life will grow in the city (Rev. 22:2). This is the first specific mention of the Tree of Life since the Garden of Eden. Ezekiel 47:12, in the context of the Millennial Kingdom, refers to trees with similar qualities and may in fact be the same type of tree, but they are not specifically called "the tree of life."

9) In the Everlasting Kingdom, there will be no sun and no moon, so day and night as they are known today will not exist. Also, there will be no night because God will give the city light (Rev. 21:23,25; 22:5). In the Millennial Kingdom, there will be day and night (Isa. 60:11).

Comparing the Millennial and Everlasting Kingdoms

Comparing some of the aspects of the Millennial Kingdom and the Everlasting Kingdom side by side helps to show the differences between them.

Millennial Kingdom	Everlasting Kingdom
New heaven and earth (old ruined by the Tribulation and Armageddon)	New heaven and earth (old destroyed by fire)
Christ is King	God and Christ are both on the throne and rule
Jerusalem is the capital city	The New Jerusalem is the capital city
Jerusalem is 4,500 cubits square, slightly less than 1½ miles square	New Jerusalem is 12,000 stadia square, slightly less than 1,400 miles square
Lasts 1,000 years	Lasts forever
Ends in a fiery war	Never ends
Devil is bound and locked ("chained") in the Abyss	Devil is thrown in the lake of burning sulfur and destroyed
Populated by: saved and unsaved people, i.e., immortals and mortals	Populated by: saved individuals only, i.e. immortals only
Nations ruled with a "rod of iron"	No need for the "rod of iron"
There will be death	There will be no death
There will be a temple	There will be no temple
Each of the twelve tribes of Israel will receive an area of Israel	Each of the twelve tribes of Israel will have its name written on the gates of the New Jerusalem
Sun, moon, day, and night	No sun, moon, or night

There are literally *hundreds* of verses in the Bible describing these magnificent future kingdoms. It is obvious that God wants to convince people to "choose life" (Deut. 30:19) by showing them how wonderful the future will be. Furthermore, once someone is saved, God wants to "anchor" that person in his or her commitment by promising wonderful rewards to those who are faithful to Him. Because Christians are "ambassadors" for the Lord (2 Cor. 5:20), we should be knowledgeable about the coming kingdoms so we can communicate these truths to others. Christians cannot promise people a problem-free life in the here and now, but each and every one of us can confidently speak the "Good News" and promise people a wonderful life in the future Kingdoms.

CHAPTER 5   *The New Body: Looking Good and Feeling Fine*

Out with the Old and In with the New

Part of the Hope set forth in the Bible is that every saved person will receive a new, glorified body. Probably every person who has lived past the age of 40 has, at one time or another, wanted a "better" body. Every middle-aged person wants fewer aches and pains, more energy, more flexibility, more strength, 20/20 eyesight, better hearing, younger looking skin, fewer sags and wrinkles, and the list goes on and on. For everyone who at anytime has wanted a better body, the Bible has good news. God has promised every saved person a new and very much improved body. Christians will receive their new bodies at the Rapture. The Old Testament believers and the believers who die during the Tribulation period will receive their new bodies when they are raised from the dead at the First Resurrection. People who believed during the Millennial Kingdom and those considered worthy of everlasting life at the White Throne Judgment will receive their new bodies when they are judged righteous at that time, after the Second Resurrection.

The physical bodies we have in this life have been ravaged by sin nature and our own sin and abuse, weakened by improper nourishment and disease, and adversely affected by genetic damage that has occurred in the human race through the years. The Bible describes natural human bodies as "perishable," "mortal," "earthly," "dishonorable," "weak," "lowly," and "natural" (1 Cor. 15:42–44,48,54; Phil. 3:21). In contrast, those same verses describe the new body as "imperishable," "immortal," "of heaven," "glorious," "powerful," and "spiritual." All of these words describing the new body are summed up in the following verse in Philippians.

Philippians 3:21
[Jesus Christ] who, by the power that enables him to bring everything under his control, will transform our lowly bodies so that they will be like his glorious body.

There is no question that our lives on earth would be more joyous if only our bodies stayed youthful, healthy, and energetic. The promise of a new and glorious body that will last forever is something to rejoice about. It is also one more reason to be excited about salvation and about sharing the saving message of Jesus Christ with those who are not yet saved. The Bible says our new bodies will be "spiritual," not "natural." What it means to have a spiritual body is partly clarified in Corinthians.

1 Corinthians 15:45–49
(45) So it is written: "The first man Adam became a living being"; the last Adam, a life-giving spirit.
(46) The spiritual did not come first, but the natural, and after that the spiritual.
(47) The first man was of the dust of the earth, the second man from heaven.
(48) As was the earthly man, so are those who are of the earth; and as is the man from heaven, so also are those who are of heaven.
(49) And just as we have borne the likeness of the earthly man, so shall we bear the likeness of the man from heaven.

The first body is described as "natural" because it came via a natural process and it bears the likeness of the earthly man. The new body is described as "spiritual" because it will come via a supernatural process. Believers will receive their new body from the Lord and it will bear the likeness of his resurrected body. In addition, the new body will be energized (made alive) by "spirit" rather than the force the Bible refers to as "soul." This is made clear in verse 45 above, which, unfortunately, has been so poorly translated in the NIV that much of its truth is unclear. The NASB is more helpful:

1 Corinthians 15:45 (NASB)
So also it is written, "The first MAN, Adam, BECAME A LIVING SOUL." The last Adam *became* a life-giving spirit.

Both the layout and the translation of this verse in the NASB help to make its meaning clear. First, the capitalization is the way the NASB indicates that the section is a quotation from the Old Testament. Second, the word "soul" is more accurate in this context than is "being" that appears in the NIV. Although the words "soul" and "being," or even "person," can be interchangeable in many contexts, interchanging them in this context, when "soul" is specifically being contrasted to "spirit," muddies the waters. The Old Testament quotation is from Genesis 2:7, which speaks of God breathing into Adam's nostrils and Adam becoming a living "soul" (Hebrew *nephesh* = soul). Adam was dead, just a beautiful but lifeless body, until God "breathed" into his nostrils and he came to life.

In contrast to Adam, who became a "soul," Jesus became a life-giving "spirit." The point of the verse is that "soul" was the basis of life for the first Adam, but "spirit" is the basis of life for the last Adam, Jesus. There are two major reasons why this verse cannot be saying that Jesus is a spirit being without a body of flesh and bone. First, it is paralleling Adam and Christ. When the Bible says that Adam became a "soul," it does not mean he had no body. He had a physical body that was *animated* by the life force called "soul." When the Bible says that Jesus became a "life-giving spirit," it does not mean he shed his physical body. He still has a physical body, but it is *animated* by spirit.

Second, Jesus himself told his disciples that he was not a spirit. After his resurrection, he appeared to his disciples who, when they first saw him, thought he was a spirit. Unfortunately, the NIV translates the Greek word *pneuma* as "ghost." The correct translation is "spirit," and Christ plainly said that he was not a spirit being but a human being with flesh and bone. Furthermore, he used the expression, "I myself," not something that he would have said if he were still "I" but somehow not "himself."

Luke 24:39

Look at my hands and my feet. It is I myself! Touch me and see; a ghost [*pneuma* = spirit] does not have flesh and bones, as you see I have.

It is both interesting and noteworthy that Christ did not use the phrase "flesh and blood," a phrase he used in Matthew 16:17 (KJV) referring to human beings. Instead he said, "flesh and bones." From the phrase "flesh and bones," some people have concluded that Jesus' new body does not have blood. This verse does not state that the new body does not have blood, nor does any verse clearly state whether Jesus' new body has blood or not. What is clear from 1 Corinthians is that the life force in his new body is spirit. In the "old" body, the life of the flesh is in the blood (Lev. 17:11). If the new body does have blood, then the blood appears to perform a somewhat different function in the "new" body than it does in the "old" body.

Similarities and Differences between the Old and the New

While there will be significant differences between the new body and the old body, there will also be striking similarities. Christ said he was *flesh and bones*. This is important. Flesh and bone are physical substances with physical properties. Jesus is not a spirit being without a physical body. Nevertheless, as head of all of God's created order who has been given "all authority" (Matt. 28:18), Christ can surely do what angels can do and more. He is not limited to the laws of physics, as we understand them. After the resurrection He appeared inside locked rooms (John 20:19,26), instantaneously moved from one place to another (Luke 24:31), and traveled through the heavens (Acts 1:9; Heb. 4:14). The fact that he could do these things still does not mean that his body was not flesh and bone or was not "physical." Rather it means that Christ could use his authority to do things that would ordinarily be placed in the category of a "miracle."

Since the Bible does not state all the capabilities of the new body, its capabilities cannot be described with absolute certainty. However, based on what is written, it is possible to make some reasonable assumptions. It has already been shown that his body was physical. However, since he could perform supernatural feats, it is reasonable to conclude that he has supernatural abilities. This in no way contradicts anything recorded in the Bible. God has always been able to give human bodies the ability to perform supernatural feats. For example, we read about Christ and Peter walking on water, but do not conclude that they had different, lighter bodies than other humans, or that walking on water is a normal human activity. We read about Philip being moved from his meeting with the Ethiopian eunuch and instantly appearing at Azotus (Acts 8:39,40), but do not conclude that humans can normally "pop around" from one place to another. We read about Shadrach, Meshach, and Abednego staying alive in the burning furnace and know that what they did was not normal for human beings. We realize that there was a miracle, something beyond the ordinary, in these situations. It seems reasonable that the same type of thing will be true for our new bodies. Apparently there will be the way they "usually" respond, and there will also be the power to do more.[1]

---

[1] The exact nature of the "more" that our new bodies can do was the subject of much discussion during the writing of this book. It is possible that the level of power or ability is related to the position that the person will be assigned in the future. Christ, Lord of all, was given "all authority." We see glimpses in Scripture that some angels are more powerful than others (Ezek. 28:12–14; Dan. 10:12–14; Rev. 10:1; 18:21). It is quite possible that the supernatural ability that a person has is somehow related to the tasks he is given to perform. It is also possible that our new bodies will be able to do things that God has not even hinted about in Scripture. God can do "immeasurably

(continued)

That Jesus appeared in a locked room is not a sound basis for concluding that after his resurrection he never used a door. In fact, during the Millennial Kingdom, the exact gate he will use to enter the Temple is specified (Ezek. 46:1–8). The point is that just because Jesus did things after his resurrection that are not normal for humans does not prove that they are "normal" for his body or will be for our bodies.

Many prophecies in the Old Testament describe activities in the future Kingdom that are considered normal activities in this life. The prophecies of the future involve farming, fishing (from the bank of the river, not on top of the water), buildings (with walls, gates, and doors, something seemingly unnecessary if people never actually use them), and other "regular" jobs. People will eat and drink and even sweat in the heat (Ezek. 44:18). There are also indications in Scripture that general obedience to physical laws will continue from the Millennial Kingdom into the Everlasting Kingdom. The New Jerusalem in the Everlasting Kingdom will have walls and gates, even though every person will have a new body. Scripture indicates that people will walk on streets of gold, not float over them.

Another reason to believe our new bodies will be quite similar to the ones we have now is the prophecies of healing for those of us who are not whole now. For example, Isaiah 35:6 promises that in the Kingdom the lame will leap like a deer—a promise that fullness of motion and ability will be restored to those who are crippled now. There is no promise stating, "The lame will fly like a bird." Prophecies state that "the blind will see," which implies that eyes will be useful just as they are today; "the deaf will hear," which implies both the existence of ears and that they will be useful in the future; "the mind of the rash will know and understand" (Isa. 32:4), which implies that people who now have mental problems will be able to think clearly and normally; and "the stammering tongue will be fluent and clear"

---

more than all we ask or imagine" (Eph. 3:20), and it is possible that there is much about the new body that He has not revealed.

(Isa. 32:4), which implies that anyone who has a speech defect will be able to speak normally.

The picture painted by the prophets is a return to normalcy. It is a return to the wonderful, capable physical bodies that God originally created for mankind before the ravages of sin and Satan took their toll. The Bible does specifically promise that flesh and bone bodies will be totally whole and very energetic. The new body will be quite similar to the old body, but with some measure of supernatural ability. People will be immortal, healthy, and strong. After God made Adam and Eve on the sixth day, He saw that what He had made was "very good." God was pleased with the way He had made man. He did not make Adam as a "flesh and bone prototype" just to test His design. No verse of Scripture indicates that God is dissatisfied with His design to the end that in the future He wants to eliminate flesh and bone and make men into spirit beings.

Christians often ask if in our new bodies we will remember this life. The answer to that question is yes, we will. Jesus was still Jesus after he was resurrected and, in his new body, he had full awareness of his earlier life. Since believer's bodies will be made like Christ's new body, believers will also have an awareness of this life. There are many things about both the Millennial Kingdom and the Everlasting Kingdom that indicate we will remember our earlier life. The Millennial Kingdom will have land divisions, the Temple, and other physical features and characteristics that will make no sense if the reasons for them are not known. The foundation of the walls of the New Jerusalem will be labeled with the names of the Twelve Apostles, and the gates will be named after the twelve tribes of Israel (Rev. 21:12–14). All of this would be senseless if no one remembered the Apostles or the tribes of Israel. Furthermore, the Bible says that at the Judgment people will receive what they are due. If people have no awareness of the previous life, rewards would seem to be arbitrarily given. Also, there are verses such as 1 John 2:28 which state that some will feel shame at Christ's coming. No one feels shame unless he can remember what he has done. 1 Corinthians 13:12 states that in the future people will "know fully." This would also seem unfeasible if people cannot remember their former life.

The primary reason for confusion about whether or not people will remember this life is Isaiah 65:17, which says that in the Millennial Kingdom the "former things will not be remembered, neither will they come to mind." The second phrase in the verse explains the first. It is not as if people *cannot* remember the past. It is clear that Christ did, and it is even clear that at the beginning of both the Millennial Kingdom and the Eternal Kingdom there will be some painful memories and tears (Isa. 25:8; Rev. 21:4). However, in the joy and abundance of the Kingdom, the painful past will not come to mind. Anyone who has had a painful experience in his past but has been emotionally healed and is enjoying a wonderful life knows what it means to "forget" the past and not have it come to mind. Isaiah is not referring to actual mental capacity, but to the relation that the person has with past painful memories.

Imagine the joy of having a new and glorious body, alive with energy and youthful vigor. Imagine having that wonderful body and living in a world where people are loving, and where there is peace, safety, and abundant quantities of great food. The God who cannot lie promises this wonderful life to all believers, and it is available to anyone who will come to God through Jesus Christ.

CHAPTER 6

Rewards in the Future Kingdoms

Salvation: The First Step

Before a person can receive a reward in the Kingdom, he or she must first *enter* the Kingdom, which means the person must be "saved."[1] The word "saved" means "rescued," and what each person needs to be rescued from is *death*. According to John 3:16, if a person does not receive everlasting life, he will "perish." Since God wants every person to be "rescued," the subject is frequently presented throughout Scripture. The message is always the same: believe in the Lord Jesus Christ. A very clear verse is in Romans:

> **Romans 10:9**
> That if you confess with your mouth, "Jesus is Lord," and believe in your heart that God raised him from the dead, you will be saved.

Although some people say that getting saved involves a lot of effort and good works, Scripture testifies that salvation is easy. A jailer in the city of Philippi asked Paul and his companion Silas the most important question any man could ask: "Sirs, what must I do to be saved?" The answer was short and simple: "Believe in the Lord Jesus and you will

---

[1] Although salvation and rewards are subjects applicable to every biblical administration throughout history, it is beyond the scope of this present work to handle the subject in detail for every administration. Therefore, this chapter will focus on salvation and rewards as these subjects apply to the current biblical administration, the Church Age.

be saved" (Acts 16:30,31). Getting saved is easy. Furthermore, it is a one-time occurrence and is permanent.[2] It guarantees you entrance into the future Kingdom.[3] Once saved, a Christian never has to fear losing his everlasting life. Although there are people and denominations who teach that Christians can "go to hell" if they do not continue to behave in a Christian manner, this is not what the Bible teaches. The Christian has been bought by the blood of Christ, is a child of God, and has a secure salvation.

Once a person is saved and assured of being in the Kingdom, the next issue that must be considered is this: What position and responsibilities will he or she be given? Christ's Kingdom will be a "kingdom" in the true sense of the word. As with any kingdom, there will be different jobs, some with more honor and authority and some with less. Scripture indicates clearly that the position you will have in the future is related to how well you perform the work Christ gives you to do now.

Receiving What Is Due

It is common to hear Christians talking about "being saved" as if salvation is God's only goal for each person. Of course, having a guarantee of everlasting life is wonderful, but there is more to God's plan. God speaks very clearly that He "wants all men to be saved **and come to a knowledge of the truth**" (1 Tim. 2:4). Obviously, God does not think that salvation is the one and only goal Christians should attain. In addition to being saved, God wants every person to come to a knowledge of the truth. Why? God wants everyone to know the truth because rewards in the future Kingdom will be based on works. When a person

---

[2] For a more in-depth study of the fact that salvation is permanent for the Christian see Appendix C.

[3] If you are not saved, or if you are not sure of your salvation, *please* consider God's gracious offer of everlasting life. If you desire more information than is contained in this book, a small but informative booklet, *Becoming a Christian: Why? What? How?* is available from Christian Educational Services, as well as other materials.

knows the truth, then he knows what God desires for his life. He is in a position to obey the Lord and earn rewards in the Kingdom. It is sad to say that many people are "religious," but, because their religion is based on tradition instead of truth, they are not doing the will of God. There are some traditions that run at cross-purposes to the Bible. Wise Christians make sure that the traditions they follow help reinforce the true teachings of the Bible. Christ specifically said that adherence to manmade tradition can prevent a person from obeying the true commandments in the Word.

Matthew 15:3
Jesus replied, "And why do you break the command of God for the sake of your tradition?"

Tradition is not the only thing that can stand in the way of obedience to the truth. Inaccurate beliefs about what the Bible really says can also cause people to disobey God. The Pharisees would not heal on the Sabbath because they believed it was sin. Their intentions were good, but because their information about the Bible was wrong, they were outside the will of God. Christ warned about doing the wrong thing, even in ignorance.

Luke 12:47,48a
(47) That servant who knows his master's will and does not get ready or does not do what his master wants will be beaten with many blows.
(48a) But the one who does not know and does things deserving punishment will be beaten with few blows.

Christ made it clear that we should check the "light," i.e., the "knowledge," that we have to make sure it is accurate, and that it is not "darkness," i.e., "error."

Luke 11:35
See to it, then, that the light within you is not darkness.

These verses seem quite harsh, but they should serve as a warning to those people who blindly follow tradition or church doctrine, especially if they have a "gut feeling" that what they are doing is somehow wrong. Christians should desire to receive rewards in the future Kingdom, and that means living a godly and obedient lifestyle. It is much easier to do that if you know what the Bible actually says.

Before going any further into the subject of rewards or losses at the Judgment, it should be noted that, although the Bible contains verses that speak of loss, shame, and even punishment at the Judgment, there are far, far more verses that speak of the wonderful life available in the future. God loves people. His desire for each person is obedience to Him because of His kindness and His promises of blessings. The Bible says, "God's kindness leads you toward repentance" (Rom. 2:4). Therefore, God, through the Scriptures, speaks frequently of the blessings that will be awarded to those who are obedient to Him.

When God does speak of losses, He never threatens. He gives factual information so people can make informed choices. God never says anything like, "If you do not do '*x*,' I'll make you the lowest person in the Kingdom." Rather, He honors free will and makes factual statements so people can choose. Regarding rewards, he says things like, "If we endure, we shall also reign with Him; If we deny Him, He also will deny us" (2 Tim. 2:12, NASB). There is no threat, just information that allows people to decide on a path and a future, making each one accountable for his own actions. God is just, and it would not be just or right for God to "surprise" people by waiting until the Judgment to inform them that His judgment is based on their actions.

That a Christian can experience loss of rewards at the Judgment is not commonly taught in Christendom today. If you are hearing about losses at the Judgment for the very first time, you may be shocked at what you read in this chapter, but the verses quoted are in the Word of God. We need to be thankful that God is loving and just and has spoken of these things so that we can make informed choices about our day-to-day behavior now, before we reach the Judgment, because then it will be too late to change.

The Bible repeatedly declares that people will eventually get what they deserve. From the Book of Job, believed to be one of the oldest books in the Bible, to Paul's writings in the New Testament, the theme that God will give to people what they deserve based on their deeds is clearly set forth. The following verse from Jeremiah is a good example.

Jeremiah 17:10
I the LORD search the heart and examine the mind, to reward a man according to his conduct, according to what his deeds deserve.

Other verses that speak the same truth almost word-for-word are: Job 34:11, Psalms 62:12, Proverbs 24:12, Jeremiah 32:19, Ezekiel 33:20, Matthew 16:27, Romans 2:6, and 1 Corinthians 3:8.

A Southern Baptist minister, Rick Howard, writes:

I knew salvation was not attained or affected by good works, but our reward and position in heaven would be. Obviously, all Christians would not have the same station in heaven. When believers stand at the Judgment Seat of Christ at His coming, they will be judged according to their works; according to the fruitfulness of their lives. This judgment will in no way reflect on whether they are saved or lost. The Judgment Seat of Christ determines the reward or loss of reward for the service of each believer. Those standing at the Judgment Seat of Christ are not only saved and safe; they will already be in heaven!

Grace is free, but works are not—and free grace is not cheap. We are born again to have purpose and be useful. God expects certain things from you after you become a Christian. No wonder Paul wrote concerning this judgment, "knowing, therefore, the terror of the Lord, we persuade men..." (2 Cor. 5:11).[4]

Howard is correct when he says that, in the future, not all believers will have the same station. His position is supported by many clear verses that address the future Judgment and the rewards or losses each person will receive. Among those verses are:

Matthew 16:27
For the Son of Man is going to come in his Father's glory with his angels, and then he will reward each person according to what he has done.

Luke 9:26
If anyone is ashamed of me and my words, the Son of Man will be ashamed of him when he comes in his glory and in the glory of the Father and of the holy angels.

2 Corinthians 5:10
For we must all appear before the judgment seat of Christ, that each one may receive what is due him for the things done while in the body, whether good or bad.[5]

---

[4] Rick C. Howard, *The Judgment Seat of Christ* (Naioth Sound and Publishing, Woodside, CA, 94062, 1990), pp. 5, 12–13. Howard makes the statement that Christians will already be in heaven when they stand at the Judgment Seat of Christ. However, as this book has previously documented, Christians will not stay in heaven but will return to earth with the Lord.

[5] The Greek word translated "judgment seat" is *bema*. There are some Christian groups that teach that a *bema* is a place where only rewards are given out. This is incorrect. The *bema* of Christ will be a "judgment seat" in the common sense of the word. Because of the confusion about the *bema*, a quick study of the word is merited. Vine's Greek Lexicon is very helpful in understanding *bema*: "Primarily, a step, a pace (akin to *baino*, to go), as in Acts 7:5, translated 'to set (his foot) on,' lit., 'foot room,' was used to denote a raised place or platform, reached by steps, originally that at Athens in the Pnyx Hill, where was the place of assembly; from the platform, orations were made. The word became used for a tribune, two of which were provided in the law courts of Greece, one for the accuser and one for the defendant; it was applied to the tribunal of a Roman magistrate or ruler." W. E. Vine,

(continued)

Colossians 3:23–25

(23) Whatever you do, work at it with all your heart, as working for the Lord, not for men,

(24) since you know that you will receive an inheritance from the Lord as a reward. It is the Lord Christ you are serving.

(25) Anyone who does wrong will be repaid for his wrong, and there is no favoritism.

1 Thessalonians 4:3–6

(3) It is God's will that you should be sanctified: that you should avoid sexual immorality;

(4) that each of you should learn to control his own body in a way that is holy and honorable,

(5) not in passionate lust like the heathen, who do not know God;

(6) and that in this matter no one should wrong his brother or take advantage of him. The Lord will punish men for all such sins, as we have already told you and warned you.[6]

The Expanded Vine's Expository Dictionary of New Testament Words (Bethany House Publishers, Minneapolis, MN, 1984), p. 612.

The uses of *bema* in the New Testament make its meaning clear: it is used as a place for the foot (Acts 7:5), it is used as a place from which to speak to people (Acts 12:21) and it is used as a judgment seat (Matt. 27:19; John 19:13; Acts 18:12,16,17; 25:6,10,17; Rom. 14:10; 2 Cor. 5:10). The fact that Jesus Christ was sentenced to death from a *bema* and that the Jews brought Paul to Gallio's *bema* for trial (Acts 18:12,16,17) is proof positive that it was not just a place for oration and rewards.

[6] It is sometimes taught that verses that mention punishment or wrath such as this are referring to God's punishment now, not in the future. This is not the case. God is not punishing Christians now. He does "prune," but that is totally different from inflicting loss or punishment on people. The verses quoted in this chapter make it clear that loss, shame, or punishment will be consequences that the disobedient will receive from God at the Judgment. For a more detailed exposition and the explanation of some difficult verses see Appendix G. For more on when God will judge, see

(continued)

These scriptures can be very sobering, even disheartening, to people who are recognizing God's justice for the first time. This recognition may also bring with it a genuine sense of remorse for ungodly behavior. This is to be expected and is an important part of turning around and becoming obedient to God's Word.

The apostle Peter's life provides a good example of turning from sin, repenting, and walking in a godly manner. During Jesus' arrest and trial, Peter denied his Lord. He was well aware of what he had done and wept bitterly when Jesus, already beaten and bloody, looked at him from the High Priest's house. But the important point is that later, with the Lord's help, he was able to "turn around" and overcome his guilt and grief. He "bounced back" to stand strong for the Lord, and at the Judgment he will be able to face the Lord with confidence. In contrast to Peter, some Christians will experience shame for their selfishness when they stand at the Judgment Seat and face the Christ they ignored or denied throughout life. With regard to this, John writes:

1 John 2:28
And now, dear children, continue in him, so that when he appears we may be confident and unashamed before him at his coming.

For most Christians, it is a new concept that some believers will experience shame when Christ comes. Most Christians hear the words of the old song echoing in their mind: "When we all get to heaven, what a day of rejoicing that will be...." While it is true that everyone who has everlasting life will have joy about it, the verses that speak of shame, such as 1 John 2:28 and Luke 9:26, are also true. Scripture is silent on how long the feeling of shame will last, and surely there will be joy and blessings on the future earth. However, there are more

---

Graeser, Lynn, and Schoenheit, op. cit., *Don't Blame God!,* Chapter 7, "The Justice and Judgments of God," pp. 95–106.

The Christian's Hope

verses that mention shame than the two quoted here, so some degree of shame will be a real experience for people who have lived selfish lives. It can be very upsetting to think that carnal and disobedient Christians will be reproved at the Judgment, but it is an undeniable part of Scripture. We should live our lives in such a way that we do not have to feel shame when we give an account of ourselves at the Judgment Seat of Christ. Joseph Dillow noted that it is distasteful to explain the consequence of carnal Christian living.

> Equally distasteful is the task of explaining the consequences of carnality, and they are severe indeed. Once a man is born again in Christ, he is now in God's family, and as any human father would, our divine Father takes a more personal interest in the moral behavior of those who belong to Him than to those who are outside the household of faith.
>
> The practical consequence of carnality is forfeiture of reward.[7]

No tragedy could be greater for someone who is saved than the realization on Judgment Day that selfishness, self-focus, and failure to obey God has resulted in the loss of everlasting rewards and a position of authority in the Kingdom. The Book of Ezekiel contains one of the most graphic portrayals of this kind of loss.

Ezekiel 44:10–16

(10) The Levites who went far from me when Israel went astray and who wandered from me after their idols must bear the consequences of their sin.

(11) They may serve in my sanctuary, having charge of the gates of the temple and serving in it; they may slaughter the burnt offerings and sacrifices for the people and stand before the people and serve them.

---

[7] Dillow, op. cit., *The Reign of the Servant Kings*, pp. 341–44.

(12) But because they served them in the presence of their idols and made the house of Israel fall into sin, therefore I have sworn with uplifted hand that they must bear the consequences of their sin, declares the Sovereign LORD.

(13) They are not to come near to serve me as priests or come near any of my holy things or my most holy offerings; they must bear the shame of their detestable practices.

(14) Yet I will put them in charge of the duties of the temple and all the work that is to be done in it.

(15) But the priests, who are Levites and descendants of Zadok and who faithfully carried out the duties of my sanctuary when the Israelites went astray from me, are to come near to minister before me; they are to stand before me to offer sacrifices of fat and blood, declares the Sovereign LORD.

(16) They alone are to enter my sanctuary; they alone are to come near my table to minister before me and perform my service.

This section of Scripture portrays two categories of Levites and priests: those who were faithful to God in their first life; and those who were not faithful to God but were "carnal," even drifting into idolatry. The Bible makes it very plain that Christ is not interested in ministering together with Levites and priests who were idolaters in their first life.[8] They can do the work in the Temple, but "they must bear the shame of their detestable practices." This record is very sobering and should

---

[8] It should not confuse the reader that some of these priests were idolaters in their first life but still end up saved and in the Millennial Kingdom. They may have, like so many, worshipped God and idols at the same time. Many Christians go to church and worship God, but also check the astrological column in the newspaper for daily guidance. Or they rely on objects such as a rabbit's foot, a "lucky coin" or a "lucky hat" to help them, and when they do, they are practicing idolatry. Physical objects that people look to for "invisible help" are idols.

cause any Christian who is living in sin to wake up and consider the consequences of his actions. The good news is that there is no need for any shame at the Judgment because it can be avoided by dedicating your life to Christ.

Here is another section of Scripture that demonstrates that rewards are earned and can be lost:

1 Corinthians 3:10–17

(10) By the grace God has given me, I laid a foundation as an expert builder, and someone else is building on it. But **each one should be careful how he builds**.

(11) For no one can lay any foundation other than the one already laid, which is Jesus Christ.

(12) If any man builds on this foundation using gold, silver, costly stones, wood, hay or straw,

(13) his work will be shown for what it is, because the Day will bring it to light. It will be revealed with fire, and the fire will **test the quality of each man's work**.

(14) If what he has built survives, he will receive his reward.

(15) If it is burned up, **he will suffer loss; he himself will be saved**, but only as one escaping through the flames.

(16) Don't you [plural = "you all"] know that you [plural] yourselves are God's temple and that God's Spirit lives in you [plural]?

(17) If anyone destroys God's temple, God will destroy him; for God's temple is sacred, and you [plural] are that temple.

Note that in verse 10 God tells Christians to be careful how they build. It is sad to say, but many Christians are not careful. They say and do things that are harmful to the cause of Christ and they spend a lot of time doing what pleases them and not nearly enough time doing what pleases the Lord. Verse 13 says the quality of each man's work will be tested. These are not idle words; they are THE WORDS OF GOD. Verses 14 and 15 are very sobering. People who do good work for the Lord will be rewarded for it and people who do not produce quality work for the Lord will suffer loss. That should be strong motivation to pay attention to the directives in the Word of God and to strive to be obedient. The sobering effect of these words on the wise Christian shows why the Hope is called the "anchor" of the soul. Reminding yourself of what there is to gain or lose by your decisions can influence you to make godly choices.

Verse 15 reiterates the truth that even if a Christian lives in a manner that results in loss and then enters the Millennial Kingdom "as one escaping through the flames," that person will still have everlasting life. This clearly shows that sin does not keep any Christian out of the Kingdom. Sin may result in an extreme loss of reward, but such loss of reward will not include the loss of salvation. Once a Christian has been born into the family of God, that birth cannot be reversed. The Christian is "born again" of God's "incorruptible seed." In that light, verse 17 needs explanation because the word "destroy" gives the wrong impression. As it appears in the NIV and some other versions, it seems to say that a Christian can be "destroyed," i.e., lose his or her salvation. This is not true. The Greek word translated "destroy" is *phtheiro* and means, "corrupt, mar, bring into a worse state, spoil."[9] *Phtheiro* is used in verses such as "Bad company *corrupts* good behavior" (1 Cor. 15:33) and "Put off your old self, which is being *corrupted* by its deceitful desires" (Eph. 4:22). In 1 Corinthians 3:16 and 17 quoted above, the "temple" refers to the whole Church, not an individual.[10]

---

[9] E. W. Bullinger, *A Critical Lexicon and Concordance of the New Testament* (Samuel Bagster and Sons, Ltd., London, 1969), p. 220. The definition is commonly known and can be checked in other lexicons such as *Thayer's Greek Lexicon of the New Testament* and Vine, op. cit., *Dictionary of New Testament Words*, p. 234 ("corrupt").

[10] When I quoted the verse, I indicated that the "you" is plural by placing "plural" in brackets after it. It is sometimes taught from these verses that a person's body is the Temple. Although a person should not mistreat his body, that is not what is being taught in this section of Scripture.

In the context of 1 Corinthians 3, the word *phtheiro* is best understood as "to bring into a worse state" or "to mar." No one can "destroy" the Church. The point of the verse is that if a Christian "brings the Church into a *worse state*," that Christian will be "brought into a *worse state*" by the Lord at the Judgment. In other words, no one mars the Church without personal consequences.

Another great truth contained in 1 Corinthians 3 is in verse 13, which says that God will "test the quality of each man's work." "Quality" is an important word when considering the subject of rewards. Some people have only a short time to serve the Lord. John the Baptist, for example, was active in his ministry for about six months before he was martyred by Herod Antipas, yet Christ said that among all those born of women there was no one greater than John.[11] Some people will live long lives and have more time than others to serve the Lord. The point is not to concentrate on how long you have to serve, but on the quality of your service. Everyone should serve God with all his heart, soul, mind, and strength and seek first the Kingdom of God.

Directly related to quality of service for the Lord is the motivation that each one has for obeying the Scripture. God wants each Christian to serve and obey Him from a godly heart with pure motives. Shortly before he died, David spoke about motives to his son Solomon.

1 Chronicles 28:9a
And you, my son Solomon, acknowledge the God of your father, and serve him with wholehearted devotion and with

---

[11] Matthew 11:11 shows the value of being in the Kingdom. It reads, "I tell you the truth: Among those born of women there has not risen anyone greater than John the Baptist; yet he who is least in the kingdom of heaven is greater than he." Christ was speaking hypothetically to motivate people to live righteous lives and enter the Kingdom. He said that anyone in the Kingdom would be greater than John. John was a powerful prophet, but he was not a part of the Kingdom yet because the Kingdom had not come. The "least" person inside the future Kingdom is greater than a "great" person not yet in the Kingdom.

a willing mind, for the LORD searches every heart and understands every motive behind the thoughts.

Motive is important to God. People who go to church to be approved in the community or make business contacts do not fool God. Like the Pharisees who prayed in the marketplaces just to be heard by men, "they have received their reward in full" (Matt. 6:5). James says to purify the heart (James 4:8).

The following verses in Timothy also show the difference between salvation and rewards:

2 Timothy 2:11–13 (NASB)
(11) It is a trustworthy statement: For if we died with Him, we shall also live with Him;
(12) If we endure, we shall also reign with Him; If we deny Him, He also will deny us;
(13) If we are faithless, He remains faithful; for He cannot deny Himself.

These verses must be read with great care and biblical understanding. As in the verses above from 1 Corinthians, these verses in Timothy show both that rewards are earned and that the New Birth is permanent. Verse 11 refers to the fact that the salvation of the Christian is absolutely secure. The phrase "if we died with him" refers to the Christian's identification with the Lord Jesus Christ. It is similar to the section in Romans 6:3–8, which says that the Christian died with Christ and will, like Christ, be raised from the dead. Each Christian died with Christ (which happens when he gets saved), and therefore he *will live with him*. There is no doubt about it. However, everlasting *life* is not the same as everlasting *rewards*. Everlasting life is by *grace*, while rewards in the Kingdom are *earned*.

Verse 12 begins to address the subject of rewards. Everlasting *life* with Christ does not equal everlasting *reigning* with Christ. Verse 12 says that, "if we endure [in this life], we will reign [in the future life]," but "if we deny him [in this life], he also will deny us [at the judgment for rewards]." Those who have been faithful will reign, while people who have been unfaithful will be denied and thus receive less. To make the truth about salvation clear, however, verse 13 assures the believer that even if he lives without faith, he will enter the Kingdom, because Christ is faithful and will not deny "himself." This verse ties together with other verses that describe each Christian as being a part of Christ's body. Since every Christian is part of Christ's body, he cannot deny any Christian because to do so would be to deny himself.

There is another point that is important to understand when studying the Judgment. The Lord will judge individuals, not groups. It is unwise to feel "safe" about sin or disobedience because "everyone is doing it." Scripture makes it clear that God will judge "everyone." The Old Testament, which spans about four thousand years, details many incidents that serve as examples. 1 Corinthians 10 refers to the Old Testament record of the Israelites wandering in the wilderness after leaving Egypt. After mentioning the fact that they complained, lusted, were involved in sexual immorality, tempted the Lord, and engaged in idolatry, Scripture then says, "their bodies were scattered over the desert" (1 Cor. 10:5). God did not excuse the sin of Israel because "everyone" was sinning. Verse 11 reveals why God wants Christians to know this.

1 Corinthians 10:11
These things happened to them as examples and were written down as **warnings** for us.

Christians need to be warned, especially in light of the ungodliness of the culture in which they live.[12] God's standards do not change just

---

[12] The greater context of 1 Corinthians 10:1–11 indicates that these verses elaborate (by way of an example) on Paul's statements in 1 Corinthians 9:24–27. In 1 Corinthians 9, Paul talks about Christians striving for an incorruptible crown (a reward) and states that he makes his body a slave lest when he has preached to others he himself would be "disqualified for the prize." Some theologians say that 1 Corinthians 10 is referring to the fact that a Christian who does not stay faithful

(continued)

because "everyone" is disobedient. When Israel sinned by worshipping Baal, "everyone" went into captivity (Judg. 3:7,8).

In Genesis 6 "everyone" was sinning—in Genesis 7 their vanity was flooded out. "Everyone" was sinning in Genesis 19—fire and brimstone from heaven fell on everyone. The records in Genesis 6 and 19 are specifically identified as types or foreshadows of the Judgment that will come at the end of the world (2 Pet. 2:5,6). The point is worth repeating: God has never changed His standards just because "everyone" was sinning. Furthermore, there is no reason to expect Him to change in the future. People who want to be disciples need to follow the example of Jeremiah and remove themselves from sin and sinners.

> **Jeremiah 15:17**
> I never sat in the company of revelers, never made merry with them; I sat alone because your hand was on me and you had filled me with indignation.

Sitting alone can be difficult, but it is better to sit alone than to enter into sin with "everyone else." Thankfully, there are a large number of Christians in the world today who do want to obey God. The wise Christian will search for them and then associate with them.

The fact that rewards will be handed out in the future for what one does on earth now is mentioned numerous times in Scripture—far too many times to record in this book. Nevertheless, the following is a partial list:

> **Matthew 5:12**. There will be a reward given for standing against persecution.
>
> **Matthew 5:19**. Obedience to the commandments helps determine your future position.

---

will lose his salvation, but the greater context indicates that the subject is rewards, not salvation.

Matthew 6:1,5. Do not do good deeds and pray so that men will reward you; rather do them in a way that will gain a reward from the Lord.

Matthew 10:41,42. Give hospitality to a prophet and receive a prophet's reward.

Matthew 16:24–27. When Christ comes, he will reward people based on what they deserve.

Matthew 18:1–4 (Mark 9:33–35; Luke 9:46). Who will be greatest (i.e., be assigned the most important position) in the Kingdom?

Matthew 19:29,30. If you have left worldly things, there will be a reward.

Matthew 20:20–26. The mother of James and John asks Christ to let one of her sons sit on his right hand (the most important position in the Kingdom) and the other at his left hand (the second-most important position) in the Kingdom.

Matthew 25:14–29. The parable of the talents shows that faithful people will be rewarded for their faithfulness, while wicked and lazy people will lose even what they have.

1 Corinthians 3:12–15. Christians will be rewarded for how they build on the foundation of Christ.

2 Corinthians 5:9,10. People will receive what they are due, whether good or bad.

Colossians 3:23–25. Christians will be rewarded or repaid for what they had done, and there is no respect of persons with the Lord.

1 Thessalonians 4:3–8. Unconfessed sexual sin will be punished.

1 John 2:28. Continue to obey the Lord so you will not be ashamed when he comes.

2 John 8. Be watchful so that you receive a full reward.

The Bible makes it clear that the bottom line for receiving rewards is obedience to God's commands. In that light, there are certain things clearly commanded in Scripture that every Christian should endeavor to do and even to excel in. For example, prayer is commanded throughout the Bible. Romans 12:12 says, "Be...faithful in prayer," and Colossians 4:2 says, "Devote yourselves to prayer." Do not make excuses if you have a weak or even non-existent prayer life. Learn to pray. Another thing commanded throughout the Bible is giving and generosity. Christ complimented the widow who only threw two "mites" (about one dollar) into the treasury (Mark 12:42).[13] Christ said she had given more than all the others he saw giving that day because she gave even though she herself was in need. Never be discouraged if you do not have much to give. Obey God and He will bless you. Romans 12:13 says, "Share with God's people who are in need."

Obeying God with commitment and diligence promises great reward. On two occasions Christ used the phrase, "Great is your reward in heaven," when he was speaking of people who obeyed God (Matt. 5:12; Luke 6:23,35).[14] Every Christian should desire to obey God in order to receive *great* rewards. This will involve finding out what the Lord wants done and then carrying through with it. This may not be easy; in fact, it may be quite difficult. To *really* obey God may involve significant changes in attitudes and behaviors, but this is why knowing about rewards is helpful. Confronting and overcoming weaknesses and shortcomings is worth it because change carries the promise of *everlasting* rewards. Few people have given up as much as

---

[13] The coin the widow threw into the Temple treasury, which many versions translate as "mite," was the *lepton*, which was worth about 1/128 of a *denarius*, which was a day's wage for a common laborer. If a laborer makes eight dollars per hour and works an eight-hour day, his wages are sixty four dollars and 1/128 of that would be half a dollar. Since the widow threw in two coins, she gave a dollar—hardly enough to run the Temple. However, God does not look on the task to be accomplished, He looks on the heart of the giver. Bromiley, op. cit., *Bible Encyclopedia*, Vol. 1, p. 923.

[14] The reward is actually given out on earth when Christ sets up his Kingdom. See Appendix B, the section, "The Reward in Heaven."

The Christian's Hope

Moses. He was a prince in Egypt. He had attained "the good life," including good food, power, prestige, nice clothes, a couple chariots, slaves. He had a very posh lifestyle but gave it all up. Why? The Bible says he gave it up because he saw the reward in the future.

> **Hebrews 11:24–26**
> (24) By faith Moses, when he had grown up, refused to be known as the son of Pharaoh's daughter.
> (25) He chose to be mistreated along with the people of God rather than to enjoy the pleasures of sin for a short time.
> (26) He regarded disgrace for the sake of Christ as of greater value than the treasures of Egypt, **because he was looking ahead to his reward.**

Moses gave up the good life because he "looked ahead" and saw that he would be rewarded in the Kingdom. Do not be shortsighted. All of us should look ahead to the reward we can have in the future and act in a way that will attain it.

The Fear of the Lord

The phrase "the fear of the Lord" is familiar to almost every Christian. This is understandable because the phrase occurs almost 100 times from Genesis to Revelation.[15] In spite of the pervasiveness of the concept, however, the average Christian cannot seem to grasp what the fear of God is.[16] The reason is simple—too many churchgoers cannot

---

[15] The exact wording differs. Phrases include, "the fear of God," "the fear of the Lord," "fear God," "fear Him," "fear His name," etc.

[16] It is frequently taught that the word "fear" really means "respect" or "awe." This is accurate in some verses, but it would be a mistake to think that "respect" and "awe" can be applied in every case. It is very clear from a study of the Hebrew and Greek vocabulary and from an examination of the contexts of its occurrences that "fear" as it is commonly understood is frequently the intended meaning. Bromiley, op. cit., *Bible Encyclopedia*, Vol. 2, pp. 288–92 and Marshal, op. cit., *New Bible Dictionary*, p. 365.

think of any reason to be afraid of God. They are taught that He is loving, forgiving, merciful, and gracious. Therefore, "God" and "fear" are two words that just do not seem to go together, at least not in modern theology. Nevertheless, the phrase is used throughout the entire Bible. What is the Bible saying? While it is true that God is a God of love and mercy, He is also a God of justice. On Judgment Day, He will give every person what he or she deserves. Like a father who disciplines his children even though it breaks his heart, so God will judge each person. Sadly, the unsaved will not pass muster at all and will be thrown into the lake of fire and burned up.[17] Those who are saved will be granted everlasting life (a wonderful gift in itself!), but of those, the ones who lived selfishly "will suffer loss" and may enter the Kingdom with little or nothing (1 Cor. 3:13–15).

In Scripture, the fear of God is often shown to be the motivation for obedience. Parents understand this concept. As much as parents want their children to obey out of love and common decency, most parents are aware that children often obey because of their fear of conse- quences. So too, the fear of God, meaning the fear of His judgment, can be the reason why a person stops sinning or walks away from sin before getting involved. One of the malefactors hanging on the cross next to Jesus understood this very well. He spoke up when the other malefactor being crucified hurled insults at Jesus. Realizing that his life was coming to an end and that the Judgment loomed ahead, he called out to his fellow malefactor, "Don't you fear God?" (Luke 23:40). The malefactor, though not a good man by any standard, realized that insulting God's Son would only bring wrath at the Judg- ment, and he humbly asked to be "remembered" when Christ came into his Kingdom. With some of the most comforting words ever

---

[17] See Appendix C. Biblically, the word "saved" refers to any person from any administration who is granted everlasting life.

spoken to a dying man, Jesus assured the malefactor that he would one day indeed be with Christ in the Kingdom, Paradise.[18]

Does it really make sense that God will ignore disobedience that has not been confessed and forgiven? Hebrews has more to say about God's Judgment.

Hebrews 10:26,27,31

(26) If we deliberately keep on sinning after we have received the knowledge of the truth, no sacrifice for sins is left,

(27) but only a fearful expectation of judgment and of raging fire that will consume the enemies of God.

(31) It is a dreadful thing to fall into the hands of the living God.[19]

These verses seem so harsh, so hard, and so unloving that they can be unpleasant to read. Yet they were inspired by a loving God and are as much a part of Scripture as the verses that say, "God is love." God *is* love, which is why He will give each person what he or she deserves. He will not "play favorites." Nor will He devalue the good deeds of those who struggled and endured in the faith by giving the same reward to those who did not endure. These emphatic words are given by a loving God to warn people to take their lives seriously and to take obedience seriously. For the person who is undecided about

---

[18] The malefactor did not go to Paradise that day because Paradise, the Kingdom, was not set up then and it is still not set up. When it is, the malefactor will enter it at the Resurrection of the Just. Graeser, Lynn, and Schoenheit, op. cit., *Is There Death After Life?*, p. 91.

[19] Note that verse 27 says the "raging fire that will consume the **enemies of God**." As it states in 1 Corinthians 3:10–17, the "fire" will not consume disobedient Christians, because they are not the enemies of God (Rom. 8:37–39), but it will test the quality of their works. If a believer's work does not "pass muster," it (the work) will be burned up and the believer will suffer loss (of rewards). The believer will be saved but only "as one escaping through the flames" (1 Cor. 3:15). The "enemies of God" who will be consumed in the fire are people who were not saved, the Devil, and demons (Matt. 25:41–46; Rev. 20:10,15).

whether or not to obey God, the fear of God can "tip the scales" towards obedience.

Jay Carty, the founder of Yes! Ministries, teaches about the value of obedience and the consequences of sin. Occasionally, people tell him they do not want to hear about the "fear of God." This is his reply:

> You may be saying, "Jay, I want to hear about the love of God. Don't preach the fear of God to me." Listen carefully. I spend half my time on the road, and there's been an occasion or two when it's just been a solid dose of the fear of God that's kept my nose clean. I have even gotten to the point of being willing to disobey God, but I was afraid of the consequences.[20]

Jay Carty understands what experience teaches so clearly: sometimes it is the fear of God that motivates us to "keep our noses clean." Scripture does make it clear that it is God's primary desire for us to respond to his kindness.

Romans 2:4
Or do you show contempt for the riches of his kindness, tolerance and patience, not realizing that God's kindness leads you toward repentance?

Although God's desire is that everyone would obey Him because of His kindness, gentleness, and love, the fact is that the fear of God is an important motivator in most people's lives because of man's fallen nature.

Jesus taught that the fear of God would help people overcome the fear of man:

Luke 12:4,5
(4) I tell you, my friends, do not be afraid of those who kill the body and after that can do no more.

---

[20] Jay Carty, *Counterattack, Taking Back Ground Lost to Sin* (Multnomah, Portland, OR, 1988), p. 114.

(5) But I will show you whom you should fear: Fear him [God] who, after the killing of the body, has power to throw you into hell [Gehenna]. Yes, I tell you, fear him.[21]

The wise Christian realizes that it's not just the love of God or the fear of God's judgment that keeps us from sinning. Romans 6 and 7 describe the tyrannical rule of sin over the lives of those who do not live according to the standard of God's Word. Romans 6:16 and 17 go so far as to use the phrase "slaves to sin." Anyone who has been in the world for any time knows people who have gotten caught up in the snare of sinful behavior (2 Tim. 2:26). However, the recognition that there is going to be an accounting for sin for which one has not repented helps to anchor the Christian's commitment to holiness in this present life.

Another section of scripture, the "conclusion" to Ecclesiastes, links the fear of the Lord and obedience in this life to the coming Judgment:

Ecclesiastes 12:13,14

(13) Now all has been heard; here is the conclusion of the matter: Fear God and keep his commandments, for this is the whole *duty* of man.

(14) For God will bring every deed into judgment, including every hidden thing, whether it is good or evil.

God's "conclusion" is certainly valid: fear Him and keep His commandments.

The Crowns: God's "Extra Credit" Program

While fear can be a strong motivator, God's primary method of motivation is love. Therefore, God describes ways in which He will reward

---

[21] Jesus was speaking to "a crowd of many thousands" (Luke 12:1), and no doubt many of them were unsaved. Furthermore, this speech took place before the Day of Pentecost when the Christian Church started. No Christian should use this verse to teach that God might throw Christians into Gehenna if they sin.

Christians who go "above and beyond." Every student is familiar with the concept of "extra credit." It is usually a question at the end of an assignment or an exam that is not required but provides the student an opportunity to receive bonus points, usually to make up for other questions that the student might have gotten wrong. Teachers, as well as parents and employers, understand that the promise of reward can be a strong incentive to a better effort. In a sense, God has laid out an "extra credit" program for Christians. God's extra incentives are referred to in Scripture as "crowns." Although the exact nature of these crowns and what they entail is not specifically stated, and the behaviors for which they are credited are elsewhere recommended for all believers, a brief discussion of them is relevant.

The five crowns are:

1) The incorruptible crown: given for exercising self-control and striving to be the best you can be for the Lord (1 Cor. 9:25 KJV).

2) The crown of rejoicing: given for winning others to Christ (1 Thess. 2:19 KJV).

3) The crown of righteousness: given for loving his appearing (2 Tim. 4:8 KJV).

4) The crown of life: given for enduring under trial (James 1:12).

5) The crown of glory: given for eagerly, faithfully, shepherding the flock (1 Pet. 5:4).

The **incorruptible crown** is mentioned in 1 Corinthians 9:25 in the context of athletes who go into "strict training." The NIV says that it is a "crown that will last forever." The Amplified Bible reads: "Every athlete who goes into training conducts himself temperately *and* restricts himself in all things." Athletes train hard to be the best they can be. Good athletes do not settle for "good enough." They endeavor to constantly improve. God wants Christians to have that kind of attitude and behavior. The goal of the Christian should not only be to avoid sin, but to excel in righteousness—to "hit a home run," so to speak. While it is wonderful to live a godly life, it is more wonderful to aggressively seek personal improvement and advance the purposes of God. God has an incorruptible crown for those who endeavor to excel.

The **crown of rejoicing** is for those who win others to Christ. The NIV calls it "the crown in which we will glory." Reaching others with the Word and bringing them to the point of salvation is something that every Christian should want to do. It is an act of compassion because death in the lake of fire is the fate of those who reject God and His Son. If people are going to believe and receive salvation, someone needs to speak:

> **Romans 10:13,14**
> (13) for, "Everyone who calls on the name of the Lord will be saved."
> (14) How, then, can they call on the one they have not believed in? And how can they believe in the one of whom they have not heard? And how can they hear without someone preaching to them?

How will they hear and believe unless someone speaks? Men and women who, without hesitation, would risk their own lives by running into a burning house to save someone are often so intimidated by the fear of rejection, or the uncomfortable feeling of not knowing exactly what to say, that they will not talk to people about Jesus. Yet the end of someone who is not saved is exactly the same as a person trapped in a burning house—death by fire. Although not everyone is called to be an evangelist, everyone is called to "tell the Good News." Witnessing to others can be challenging, intimidating, and occasionally risky because the hearer is not always appreciative. God knows this and rewards those who make the effort to win others to Christ by giving them the crown of rejoicing.

The **crown of righteousness** is given to those who "love his appearing" (KJV). There are Christians who are so well adjusted to this world that it really does not make much of a difference to them when Christ comes back. They are usually healthy and have comfortable lives, and they do not see how the Lord coming back would really help them. There are also Christians who do not have a strong desire to live a godly and obedient lifestyle, perhaps because doing so will bring them persecution ("In fact, everyone who wants to live a godly life in Christ Jesus will be persecuted"—2 Tim. 3:12). Many of these Christians do not want Christ to return because they do not want to quit their sin or face the Judgment. Christians who "long for" (NIV) Christ to return from heaven are not primarily vested in this world and usually have a lifestyle that is godly.

The **crown of life** is given to Christians who endure and stay faithful through trials and temptations. The Bible and history both teach that it is very difficult to remain faithful to a Christian commitment all through one's life. Too frequently, people "on fire" for the Lord "cool off" and abandon their commitment. Unfortunately, the cooling off is often a result of what they see around them in Christianity and the way they are treated by other Christians. It is no secret that many Christians are hypocrites, and this can be very discouraging to those who are sincere in their efforts to live for God. Since the beginning of Christianity some 2,000 years ago, it would not be an exaggeration to say that millions of Christians have backed off from their Christian commitment because of what they have seen in the Church and/or because they were treated badly by fellow Christians. Others have cooled off when faced with trials and temptations. Trials and temptations come in many forms but fall into two broad categories: pressure (persecution) or pleasure (the "pleasures of sin"—Heb. 11:25). One reward for Christians who stay faithful throughout their lives is the crown of life.

The **crown of glory** is given to those who willingly shepherd God's people, not because they are paid for it or because they are "lords" over a group of people, but because they are eager to serve and help people maximize their spiritual potential. Christians can be quite ungrateful and dissatisfied. Almost every leader has at one time or another been at his wit's end as to how to keep people godly and blessed. More than one pastor, elder, or overseer has resigned, not because he or she did not love God, but because it just seemed too difficult to work with people in the Church. There are even Old Testament records of God Himself being disgusted with His people's attitudes and behaviors. At points He was on the verge of abandoning them altogether. God recognizes that it is hard and often thankless work to shepherd people, so He offers a crown to those who will carry out the task in a godly manner.

Working in the Future Kingdom

At one time or another, most orthodox Christians have asked, "What will we be doing forever in heaven?" Peter Kreeft, a Christian writer, exemplifies the orthodox position concerning Christians in heaven in his book, *Every Thing You Ever Wanted to Know About Heaven But Never Dreamed of Asking*. In Chapter 3, titled, "What Will We Do in Heaven," Kreeft comments, "This is the first question most people ask about Heaven."[22] The following quote summarizes his answer.

> The basic idea for my answer to that question comes from Richard Purtill's book, *Thinking About Religion*. In Chapter 10—"Life After Death: What Might It Be Like?"—he postulates three human tasks in Heaven in this order: (1) understanding our earthly life "by Godlight," (2) sharing all other human lives, and (3) exploration into God.[23]

Kreeft's answer is very telling. He does not go to the Bible to find out what the saved will do forever in heaven. Instead, Kreeft quotes the work of another man who "postulates" an answer. To "postulate" is to set forth a possibility or to make an assumption. So Kreeft admits that the best answer he has for what Christians will be doing in heaven is an assumption. What he fails to realize is that there is no biblical

---

[22] Peter Kreeft, *Everything You Ever Wanted to Know About Heaven But Never Dreamed of Asking* (Ignatius Press, San Francisco, 1990), p. 51.
[23] Ibid., p. 52.

answer to this question because the saved will not be in heaven forever! According to Scripture, Christians will be in heaven with Christ for a short period of time and then return with him to earth. Christians will then be involved with the responsibilities of Christ's earthly Kingdom.

In the future Kingdom there will be different positions and responsibilities. At the Judgment, each person will "receive what is due him for the things done while in the body, whether good or bad" (2 Cor. 5:10). Therefore, every person will not receive the same reward or assume the same responsibilities. So, the question is not, "What will we be doing in heaven," but, "What will we be doing in our future life on earth?" The answer to this question can be found in the Word of God.

The Lord is going to make a new earth that will literally be an "Eden" or "Paradise" and, just as God gave Adam and Eve work to do in the original Paradise, there will be work to do in the coming Paradise. In fact, looking back at what God gave Adam and Eve to do in the Garden of Eden provides a prototype or a snapshot of what life will be like in the future Paradise. Genesis 2:15 speaks about two tasks that Adam and Eve had to perform. God put them in Eden "to [1] work it and [2] take care of it." The NASB says, "to cultivate it and keep it." Like any farm or garden, Eden required work or "cultivation." Adam and Eve had to cultivate the garden just as any farmer has to cultivate and work the soil and take care of the plants.

Eden was a garden with wonderful fruits and vegetables, and therefore the second part of Adam and Eve's job was to "take care of" or "keep" it. The Hebrew word translated "take care of" is *shamar*, which means, "oversee, protect, keep, have charge of, tend (for flocks and herds), guard, watch, preserve." The world was full of animals and, in the original Paradise, all of them were plant eaters (Gen. 1:30). Part of Adam and Eve's work was to guard the garden and keep the wild animals from grazing in the Garden of Eden. Imagine Eve looking out the window of her house and shouting; "Adam, the lions are eating my favorite shrubbery. Adam! Get them away from my bushes!" Remember, lions will again eat plants in the future, so you may end up shooing them away from your bushes or your vegetable garden.

God gave Adam and Eve authority and responsibility in the Garden of Eden. He gave them work to do. It should, therefore, be no surprise that various types of work will be part of life on the new earth. The types of work mentioned below are almost always found in the context of the Millennial Kingdom, not the Everlasting Kingdom. Some types of work, like "gravediggers," could not be available in the Everlasting Kingdom because there will be no death. Likewise, because there will not be a temple in the Everlasting Kingdom, all the duties associated with the Temple will be eliminated. Some types of work are clearly stated, while others are only implied. Those that are clearly stated include:

Administration and *rulership* (Isa. 1:26; 32:1; Jer. 3:15; 23:4; Ezek. 44:24; Matt. 19:28; 1 Cor. 6:2,3; 2 Tim. 2:12; Rev. 2:26,27).

Builders (Isa. 54:12; 60:10; 61:4; Jer. 30:18; Ezek. 36:10,33; Amos 9:14).

Cleanup duties (Isa. 9:5; Ezek. 39:14,15).

Farmers (Isa. 30:23,24; 32:20; 61:5; 62:9; Jer. 31:5,12; Ezek. 36:9,34; 47:12; 48:19; Amos 9:13).

Fishermen (Ezek. 47:10).

Gravediggers (Ezek. 39:14,15).

Herdsmen (Isa. 30:23,24; 60:6,7; 61:5; Jer. 31:12).

Landscapers (Isa. 60:13).

Metalworkers (Isa. 2:4; 60:17; Mic. 4:3).

Servants (Isa. 14:2).

Temple duties for those Levites who were not pure-hearted (Ezek. 44:10–14).

Temple duties for those Levites who stayed faithful (Ezek. 44:15,16).

Vinedressers (Isa. 25:6; 62:9; Jer. 31:12; Amos 9:13).

Workers (Ezek. 48:19).

Types of work that are implied but not specifically mentioned include:

Cooks, butchers, and *bakers* (Isa. 25:6).

Musicians. Although everyone will sing and make merry, it seems there will be a need for specialists as there always has been (Isa. 35:10; 65:14; Jer. 30:19; 31:4).

Tentmakers (Isa. 54:2; Jer. 30:18).

Weavers, tailors, and *seamstresses* (clothes are worn in the Kingdom) (Ezek. 44:17–19; Rev. 19:13,14).

The responsibilities described and implied in Scripture provide a general overview of the kinds of work people will be doing. Those doing the work will include everyone in the Kingdom: Christians, resurrected believers, and the "natural" people who are allowed into the Kingdom at the Sheep and Goat Judgment. Although there will be significant differences in the assignments people receive in the Millennial Kingdom, no one will hunger or be in want. Isaiah 14:30 says, "The poorest of the poor will find pasture, and the needy will lie down in safety." The picture painted in Scripture of the future Kingdom is one of people enjoying life. They eat and drink, work and play, sing and dance, and enjoy fellowship with their Lord. The Bible does not give, nor does it need to give, a complete description of all the activities in the future. There will be clothing, so there will be tailors and seamstresses, but there is no specific mention of them in the Bible. There will be pots and containers, but there is no mention of potters. There will no doubt be baskets and rugs, but there is no mention of the weaving trades in verses referring to the future Kingdom.

The point is this: the future life on earth will be one of peace and prosperity in a familiar setting. Most people think that eternity will be vastly different from life now, but God did not make a mistake when He created this world and humans as physical beings on it. In fact, He called it "very good." The Bible describes a future life that will be in many ways very similar to the life that people have lived on earth for centuries—but without disease, war, injustice, hunger, etc. God gives enough information in his Word that people can avoid wild speculation about the future. Bible students can see the future life for what it will be: similar to the way things would have been if Adam and Eve had never sinned and the world had continued to be inhabited by them and their descendants.

When the Kingdom comes and all the saved are in Paradise, will people try to understand their past lives by "Godlight" as Kreeft and other theologians postulate? The biblical evidence suggests they will not. Isaiah 65:17 says, "Behold, I will create new heavens and a new earth. The former things will not be remembered, nor will they come to mind." No one likes to dwell on painful memories. Although remembering things in the past can be a part of forgiveness and heal-ing, once a person is healed and whole, there is no reason to dwell on past hurts and pains. Philippians 4:8 says, "Finally, brothers, whatever is true, whatever is noble, whatever is right, whatever is pure, what-ever is lovely, whatever is admirable—if anything is excellent or praiseworthy—think about such things." Furthermore, Ephesians 5:12 says, "For it is shameful even to mention what the disobedient do in secret." If these are God's commands for Christians who live in the midst of a world of sin, how much more will they be true when life in Paradise is enjoyed apart from all the pain of the past? The secret and sinful activities of people today are not a glory to God, and "every hidden thing" will have already been brought up at the Judgment when sinners will receive what they deserve (Eccles. 12:14). When Chris-tians are whole and in their glorious new bodies living in Paradise, it will not glorify God to dwell on this fallen world.[24]

---

[24] Although we will not want to dwell on the past, we will have some memory of it. See the section, "Similarities Between the Old and the New" in Chapter 5.

When Will Believers Receive Their Rewards?

The Bible promises that those who obey God will be rewarded in the future. However, there is no verse of Scripture that says specifically how or when the rewards will be given. It is very likely that an individual's reward will not be handed out all at once, as if it were a lump-sum cash gift, but rather that it will be given out over time. Since rewards can be positions and assignments in the Kingdom, it is logical that many of the rewards will be "lived out" year after year.

The judgments in the Bible are: the Judgment of Christians associated with the Rapture, the Sheep and Goat Judgment, the Judgment associated with the First Resurrection, and the Judgment associated with the Second Resurrection—the Resurrection of the Unjust (the "White Throne" judgment). Chronologically, the first judgment is the judgment of Christians. This occurs after the Rapture, but how soon after the Rapture is not specified. It seems likely that Christians will stand before the Judgment Seat while in heaven before coming back to earth with Christ. That Christians return with Christ as an army implies that a judgment has taken place and various levels of authority and responsibility have been given out. It seems unlikely that Christians would be raptured and then wait up in heaven through the Tribulation before being judged.

The next two judgments, the Sheep and Goat Judgment and the Judgment associated with the First Resurrection, are very close together or perhaps simultaneous. The "Sheep and Goat Judgment" (Matt. 25:31–46) occurs after Christ fights the battle of Armageddon and conquers the earth. He will gather everyone left alive on earth and judge them. Those people who are judged righteous will enter the Kingdom, while those judged unrighteous will be cast into the lake of fire.

The judgment that is closely associated in time with the Sheep and Goat Judgment occurs just after the First Resurrection, the Resurrection of the Righteous (Luke 14:14). The First Resurrection is when the righteous believers who died before the Day of Pentecost or who lived and died during the Tribulation will be raised from the dead and judged. There are no verses that specifically state if the resurrected believers are judged before or after the Tribulation survivors, or if both groups are judged at the same time. The Bible does, however, indicate how long Christ will be judging people at the start of his Kingdom.

The length of time Christ will be judging at the opening of his Kingdom can be calculated by studying Daniel and Revelation. The Tribulation period lasts seven years. The last half of the Tribulation, three and half years, is known prophetically as "time, times, and half a time" (Dan. 7:25; 12:7; Rev. 12:14), 42 months (Rev. 11:2; 13:5), or 1,260 days (Rev. 12:6). The battle of Armageddon ends the seven years of the Tribulation period. The Book of Daniel, after mentioning the three and a half years that are the last half of the Tribulation, adds the following:

Daniel 12:11,12
(11) From the time that the daily sacrifice is abolished and the abomination that causes desolation is set up, there will be 1,290 days.
(12) Blessed is the one who waits for and reaches the end of the 1,335 days.

The 1,290 days mentioned in Daniel is 30 days longer than the time of 1,260 days specified as the time that the Antichrist will have dominion. That extra 30 days after Armageddon is time for the nations to be gathered together for the Sheep and Goat Judgment. Then Daniel mentions a period of 1,335 days and says that the people who reach the end of that period are "blessed." The difference between the 1,290 days and the 1,335 days is 45 days. It is apparently during that 45-day period that Christ will judge the people before they enter the Millennial Kingdom. Anyone judged righteous at the Sheep and Goat Judgment will be allowed to enter the Millennial Kingdom, and of course all the believers in the Resurrection of the Righteous will enter the Kingdom. No wonder then, that Daniel 12:12 says, "Blessed is the one who waits for and reaches the end of the 1,335 days." Anyone who reaches the end of the 1,335 days will be "blessed" indeed, for that person will have been judged righteous and allowed to enter the Millennial Kingdom.

The last judgment in the Bible is the White Throne Judgment of Revelation 20:11–15. As was discussed earlier in this book, the resurrection preceding this Judgment is called the "Second" Resurrection because the "First" Resurrection will have already occurred at the start of the Millennial Kingdom (Rev. 20:4). It is also known as the "Resurrection of the Unjust" because the vast majority of people who get up will be unjust. All the unsaved people of all time will be raised at this resurrection and stand before the Great White Throne. This judgment will also include any "natural" people alive at the close of the Millennial Kingdom. At this Final Judgment, anyone judged unworthy of everlasting life will be thrown into the lake of fire (Rev. 21:15). Thankfully, there will be some people who are judged worthy of life and allowed into the Everlasting Kingdom.

Every person who has ever lived will be in one of these four judgments just mentioned: the Rapture, the Sheep and Goat Judgment, the Judgment associated with the First Resurrection, or the White Throne Judgment.[25] They will take place at set times, therefore the Bible speaks of a "day of Judgment" (Matt. 10:15; 11:22,24; 12:36; 2 Pet. 2:9; 3:7; 1 John 4:17; Jude 6). People are not judged immediately after they die, as some people teach. Instead they wait "in sleep" until they are raised and judged. Acts 17:31 speaks of "**the day** when He [God] will judge the world with justice by the man he has appointed."

---

[25] The possible exception is the two witnesses of Revelation 11:3–12.

Is It Necessary To Be Motivated by Rewards?

There are many Christians who have never been taught about rewards in the future Kingdom, but who do the will of God for other reasons. Some are so convinced of God's love that they are filled with thanksgiving and are motivated to love and obey God. Others obey God because they are convinced "it is the right thing to do" or "just because He is God" or "because they will be more blessed if they obey." To some people, it seems more pure-hearted to obey God because of love rather than to obey in order to receive rewards in the Kingdom. Certainly love, thankfulness, duty, and being blessed are noble motives, and they *are* valid reasons to obey Him. Christians should love and obey God because He is God and because of all the loving things He has done for them. People are more blessed in this life if they obey God. But one of the goals of this book is to help people see that God does promise rewards to those who obey Him, and those rewards are designed to be a major motivation for godly living.

It also needs to be stated that the things Christians do need to be done in love. It is possible to act out the requirements of the Word without any love in the heart at all. The Pharisees did that quite often. Scripture teaches that people only benefit from their actions when they are done with love (1 Cor. 13:3). It is important to understand, however, that the love of God is not just a "warm fuzzy feeling." It is accompanied by godly action. In fact, a loving action sometimes is accompanied by no actual desire at all, other than the desire to do God's will and bless people. Christ showed supreme love when he went to the cross, even though he had asked his Father repeatedly to take it from him.

People usually appreciate it when they are treated with love and kindness. So too, *God* is appreciative of Christians who express their love for Him through obedience in their daily walk. But Christians cannot ignore the words in the Word. God made the rules and set up the entire system of rewards. Working to receive rewards in the future is not wrong—it is part of obeying God. Rewards in Paradise are designed to be part of the Hope that anchors the Christian's soul.

Knowledge of rewards keeps Christians from being blown outside the will of God by the storms of life or from drifting away from Him, lured by the attractions of the world. It would be nice if love for God kept Christians firmly on course all the time, but experience tells us that the realization of the consequences of disobeying God is often what it takes to help make decisions to stay holy and obedient.

While it is wonderful to obey God simply out of love for Him, it is not wrong to see the value in obeying Him to obtain a reward. God did not have to mention rewards in the Kingdom, but He did. The fact that He speaks of rewards in verse after verse should speak loudly to those who are wise. God wants to reward every believer richly, but He is just, so He will pass out rewards that have been *earned*. It is up to each Christian to be wise in his walk and obey our heavenly Father. Christians can be assured that obedience will be very much "worth it" in the end.

CHAPTER 7   *The Origin of Orthodoxy*

Where Did the Idea Originate That Believers Would Live Forever in Heaven?

The basic teaching of orthodox Christianity concerning what happens after death is that the "souls" or "spirits" of righteous people go either to "heaven" or to some other blissful place. This teaching is in error.[1] It is impossible to understand such false doctrines without understanding their spiritual causes. From as early as the Garden of Eden, the Devil and his demons have been promoting the fact that people do not really die. After God plainly told Adam that he would "surely die" if he partook of the fruit of the tree of good and evil, the Devil lied and said to Eve, "You will **not** surely die" (Gen. 3:4). Ever since that time, the Devil has been actively promoting this same lie wherever and whenever possible. Unfortunately, the idea that people continue living on after they die has found a fertile breeding ground in most religions, including orthodox Christianity.

The vast majority of Christian denominations teach that there is no such thing as death (if "death" is properly defined as "the total absence of life"). Instead, according to their teaching, when the body dies, the "soul," the "real you," goes to heaven or hell and keeps right on living either in bliss or torment. Therefore, most Christians do not believe

---

[1] It should go without saying that an exhaustive treatment of the origin of heaven as the final resting place of the souls of the righteous would fill volumes. This short chapter will only touch on some highlights of the origin of the orthodox belief.

that people actually experience "death" when their body dies.[2] It is common to go to a Christian funeral and hear the minister say, "So and so is now in heaven," even though his dead body is in the open casket in front of the audience.

Since a major part of the Devil's agenda was, and still is, to convince people that "you will not surely die," it is not surprising that most Christians believe that, in some way, "you" go on living even after you die. Whether that "you" is your spirit, your soul, or some other "essence," the bottom line is always the same—"you" are fully conscious after death and not, in fact, "dead" (i.e., without life). This belief has no basis in Scripture. God designed humans as integrated beings with a body, soul, and spirit that together make a whole individual. Adam's body was fully formed, but just "dust" until God breathed life into it (Gen. 2:7). Adam's "life" (whether it be called "soul" or "spirit") had no consciousness or life of its own apart from his body. The idea that the soul or spirit is like a ghost that can separate from the body and still have consciousness and movement without the body was introduced into Judaism after the Babylonian captivity and came from there and other religions into Christianity.[3] The idea of a disembodied living soul did not come from the text of Scripture.

---

[2] This very important point is given much more attention in Graeser, Lynn, and Schoenheit, op. cit., *Is There Death After Life?*, pp. 3–15. Other works that discuss the subject include: Anthony Buzzard, *What Happens When We Die?* (Atlanta Bible College, Morrow, GA, 1986); Oscar Cullmann, *Immortality of the Soul or Resurrection of the Dead?* (The Epworth Press, London, 1958); LeRoy E. Froom, *The Conditionalist Faith of Our Fathers* (Review and Herald Publishing Assn., Washington DC, 1966); Sidney Hatch, *Daring to Differ: Adventures in Conditional Immortality* (Brief Bible Studies, Sherwood, OR, 1991); Percy E. White, *The Doctrine of the Immortality of the Soul* (Christadelphian Scripture Study Service, Torrens Park, South Africa); Victor Paul Wierwille, *Are the Dead Alive Now?* (American Christian Press, New Knoxville, OH, 1973).

[3] It is interesting to note that while the Old Testament has the concept of a kind of human soul, the soul is never pre-existent or immortal but, instead, the result of the creative activity of God (Gen. 2:7). Only under Persian and Greek influence was the Platonic notion of the divine pre-existence of the soul, its imprisonment in the human body, and its immortality taken up in Judaism. This occurred at a late stage and on

(continued)

The belief in being alive in some form after death is contrary to the revelation of the Bible. According to the Bible, a person who dies is dead until he or she is raised to life by the Lord Jesus and made to stand at one of the judgments. That is why the Bible speaks of a "day," or time, of judgment rather than an ongoing judgment occurring when people die. Revelation 20:4–6 speaks of some of the dead "coming to life" to reign with Christ, while others do not yet come to life. Revelation 20:13 states that the sea and the grave will give up the "dead" who are in them so they can be judged. If people are judged when they die and consigned either to heaven or hell, then there is no reason to get them up from the dead for "a day of judgment." Why drag someone out of heaven or hell and judge him again if he had already been judged at the time of his death?

Once the religions of the world accepted the idea that the "soul" or "spirit" did not die when the body died, the next step was to determine its post-mortem address, in other words, where does the soul live after the body dies? The answers vary from religion to religion, but there are some similarities. A study of the various religions of the world shows that it was, and still is, very common to believe that "good" people go either to the abode of the gods (sometimes called "heaven"), or to some wonderful place on earth, while evil people go to a place of punishment or torment. These beliefs eventually found their way into both Judaism and Christianity. In *The Early History of Heaven*, J. Edward Wright addresses the biblical conception of what happens to the dead:

> Two verses from the Book of Psalms summarize the biblical conceptions of the afterlife and of humans' place in the heavenly realm: "Heaven is Yahweh's heaven, but the earth he has given to humans. The dead do not praise Yahweh, nor all those who go down to silence"

---

the periphery of Judaism. Karl-Josef Kuschel, *Born Before All Time? The Dispute over Christ's Origin* (Crossroads, New York, 1992), p. 184.

(Psalm 115:16,17). These verses pointedly indicate what the biblical tradents thought about humanity's place in the heavenly realm—they have no place there![4]

Wright goes on to point out that both Judaism and Christianity adopted ideas of the afterlife from the culture surrounding them:

In the fifth century BCE, belief in a **heavenly** afterlife developed and spread across the Mediterranean world and the ancient Near East [emphasis added]. Segments in Judaism and Christianity eventually adopted the belief that humans could have a place in the heavenly realm...The emerging Jewish conceptions of the universe and the ideas about what happens to a person after death were not the natural outgrowth of biblical religiosity but were the product of the fruitful interaction of the ancient biblical traditions with new trends in religion and science during the Greco-Roman period. Early Christianity...inherited aspects of both the biblical traditions and the newer Hellenistic expressions of Judaism.[5]

It is noteworthy that belief in a "heavenly" afterlife, as opposed to an "earthly" or "nether-worldly" afterlife, spread after the death of Malachi, the last of the writing prophets. After his death, there were few people left who could oppose the incursion of false doctrine into Judaism. Josephus, a writer and historian who lived in the first century, wrote about the Essenes. They were one of the Jewish sects of his time and the authors of many of the Dead Sea Scrolls. From Josephus' writing it is clear that they believed, as did the Greeks, that the physical body was not a blessing at all but rather more like a prison and that the

---

[4] J. Edward Wright, *The Early History of Heaven* (Oxford University Press, New York, 2000), p. 85. "Tradent" is a very rare word, not found in most dictionaries. A tradent is a person who delivers property of any kind, physical or intellectual, from one person to another.

[5] Ibid., pp. 117–18. "BCE" means "Before the Common Era" and is a secularized way of expressing "BC," which means "Before Christ."

The Christian's Hope

soul rejoiced when it was freed by the death of the body. Furthermore, after being freed, the soul went up to heaven.

> For their doctrine is this: that bodies are corruptible and that the matter they are made of is not permanent; but that the souls are immortal and continue forever; and that they come out of the most subtle air, and are united to their bodies as in prisons, into which they are drawn by a certain natural enticement; but that when they are set free from the bonds of flesh, they then, as released from a long bondage, rejoice and mount upward.[6]

Historical texts reveal that this type of misinformation about the Hope and everlasting life circulating in the culture of biblical times influenced both the Jews and the early Christians. Historical texts reveal that both the Jews and the early Christians had various ideas about the eternal future. Unfortunately, the biblical texts were often misunderstood and also often ignored as the source of ultimate authority, just as they are today.

The impact of Greek religion and the Greek language on the doctrine of life after death among the Jews cannot be overstated. Alexander the Great conquered Israel in 332 BC. As a result, by about 250 BC there were so many Jews speaking Greek (many of whom could not read Hebrew) that it became necessary to develop a Greek translation of the Old Testament. This translation is called the Septuagint. It is significant that the translators chose the Greek word *"Hades"* to translate the Hebrew word *"Sheol"* in the Hebrew text. This choice had a very powerful impact because the souls in *Sheol,* according to Scripture, are all dead, but the souls in *Hades,* according to Homer and other Greek and Roman writers, are all alive. Thus, by the stroke of a translator's pen, everyone throughout the Old Testament who had died was granted life in the grave. The linguist and scholar E. W. Bullinger

---

[6] William Whiston, *The Works of Josephus* (Baker Book House, Grand Rapids, 1974), Vol. 1, p. 149.

writes about *Sheol*, which is a place for the dead, not the living. After listing every single occurrence of *Sheol* in the Bible, he concludes:

(a) That as to *direction* it is down.

(b) That as to *place* it is in the earth.

(c) That as to *nature* it is put for the state of the dead. Not the act of dying, for which we have no English word, but the state or duration of death.

Sheol therefore means *the state of death*; or *the state of the dead*, of which *the grave* is tangible evidence. It has to do only with the dead. It may be represented by a coined word, Grave-dom, as meaning the dominion or power of *the grave*.

(d) As to *relation* it stands in contrast to the state of the living, see Deut. 30:15,19, and 1 Sam. 2:6–8. It is never once connected with the living except by contrast.

(e) As to *association* it is used in connection with: mourning (Gen. 37:34,35); sorrow (Gen. 42:38; 2 Sam. 22:6; Ps. 18:5; 116:3); fright and terror (Num. 16:27,34); weeping (Isa. 38:3,10,15,20); silence (Ps. 31:17; 6:5; Eccles. 9:10); no knowledge (Eccles. 9:5,6,10); punishment (Num. 16:27,34; 1 Kings 2:6,9; Job 24:19; Ps 9:17, Revised Version, RE-turned, as before their resurrection).

(f) And, finally, as to *duration*, the dominion of *Sheol* or the grave will continue until, and end only with, *resurrection*, which is the only exit from it.[7]

Many linguists and scholars have noticed that *Sheol* is a place where people are dead. Alice Turner writes:

The Jews, judged solely by the evidence of the Old Testament, were either the least morbid or the least imaginative of the Mediterranean peoples. Unlike their neighbors, they had no relationship with the dead; they did not worship them, sacrifice to them, visit them, hope to reunite with

---

[7] Bullinger, op. cit. *Lexicon*, p. 369.

The Christian's Hope

them in the afterlife, nor anticipate any kind of interaction with Yahweh after death—quite the contrary.[8]

The Old Testament was not written by "the least imaginative" Jews. It was inspired by God and penned by men who knew that the dead were actually dead. Lifeless. Not "alive" in any form. And the reason that they knew they would not "reunite" after their death with others who had died before them was that God had revealed that no one is alive in the grave. There will be a reunion, but only *after the resurrection*.

In stark contrast to the Hebrew *Sheol,* where everyone is dead, in the Greek *Hades,* everyone is alive. The myths and legends about *Hades* in Greek literature and poetry vary greatly, but everyone agreed that the dead are definitely alive. People's beliefs about the dead differed in their details, such as whether or not they remembered their first life or were tortured by various imps and demons, but in each and every case they were alive.[9] Because the Greeks believed that people stayed alive in some form after they died, they scoffed at the idea of a resurrection and mocked Paul when he spoke of it (Acts 17:32).

The translation of *Sheol* as *Hades* in the Septuagint, which brought all the dead back to life, so to speak, occurred more than two hundred years before Christ. Therefore, there was plenty of time for the Jewish world to become confused about the state of the dead by the time Christ died and the Christian Church started. For many Jews, the Septuagint was the only Scripture available to them because they could not read the Hebrew text. Reading it in the context of the Greco-Roman world around them contributed to the establishment and continuance of the erroneous belief that the dead were alive. This confusion made its way into Christianity as people with differing beliefs about the state of the dead became Christians.

The confusion about the state of the dead also came directly into the New Testament because the word *Hades* is used in the Greek texts of

---

[8] Alice K. Turner, *The History of Hell* (Harcourt and Brace, New York, 1993), p. 40.
[9] Ibid., pp. 20–29.

the New Testament for the place of the dead. Even though Christ would have spoken Hebrew and Aramaic, and thus used *Sheol* and its Aramaic equivalent, his words are written in the Greek text as if he used the word *Hades*. Acts 2:31 refers to the resurrection of Christ by saying, "his soul was not left in hell *[Hades]*" (KJV).[10] The use of *Hades* in the Greek New Testament, especially in light of the Greco-Roman culture in which it was circulating, contributed to the erroneous belief that people continued to live after the body died.

The Church Reinforces the Doctrine about Heaven

Although the early Christian belief in the soul going immediately to heaven or hell was the result of the influence of other religions and mistranslations, in time the idea was reinforced within the Church. Asceticism made its way into the Christian Church and promulgated the idea that earthly pleasures had no value and were even harmful. The Church Fathers Clement of Alexandria (c. 150–215) and Origen (c. 185–254) seem to be the first who studied the theoretical roots of asceticism, a concept borrowed from the Greek Stoics as a way to purify the soul from its passions.[11]

Christian ascetics renounced earthly things and endeavors and attempted to cleanse their souls by strict discipline and denial of worldly pleasures. By the third century, Christian asceticism was catching on, and out of that movement grew both the age of the Desert Fathers and Monasticism, including all the strict disciplines that the monks endured. Christian ascetics renounced worldly wealth and took vows of poverty, renounced the taste of fine foods and had plain diets with much fasting, renounced the companionship of women and took vows of chastity, renounced the comfort of fine clothing and wore

---

[10] The confusion about the proper translation and understanding of *Hades* is still ongoing. For example, in Acts 2:31 quoted above, the KJV uses "hell," while the NIV uses "grave."

[11] Cross and Livingstone, op. cit., *Dictionary of the Christian Church*, p. 95.

rough robes, renounced regular sleep and performed long vigils, and so forth. During this time it was common for Christians to believe that anything associated with the earth, especially if it was pleasurable, was evil and even demonic. At this time in history, the idea that the everlasting home of the believer was "heaven," a spiritual place devoid of earthly influences, became firmly entrenched. To an ascetic, the idea that eternity would be spent on a recreated earth complete with fine food, wine, and music would have been preposterous.

Orthodox Christianity has never recaptured the great truth in Scripture that God's people will live on a recreated earth and not in heaven. Erroneously explaining many verses in light of an everlasting home in heaven bolstered the increasingly entrenched tradition. Also, many verses that clearly speak about the earth were "spiritualized" to fit the idea either of an everlasting home in heaven or applied to the earth now. In fairness to the average Christian, it is no real surprise that the erroneous belief that the saved will live forever in heaven continues unabated. Few Christians have ever been taught the clear verses about the saved inheriting a recreated earth, but rather they have been inundated with other verses mishandled and taught as if they were the final word on the subject. These "unclear" verses that seem to support the idea that believers will spend eternity in heaven are the subject of Appendix B.

CHAPTER 8   *Rebuilding the Hope*

The Sermon on the Mount

Life can be very challenging at times, but having a clear view of the Hope to "anchor" our souls makes living a godly life a little easier. Unfortunately, very few Christians today have a clear picture of the future because the Hope of everlasting life on a restored earth has been replaced with the unbiblical teaching of "eternity in heaven." This is not the only time in history when the truth concerning the Hope has been lost or badly distorted. At the time of Christ, the Sadducees, who controlled the Temple in Jerusalem, taught that there was no resurrection at all (Matt. 22:23; Acts 23:8). The Pharisees, the other powerful religious body, were also confused about the Hope. In John 3, Jesus had a conversation about the Hope with the Pharisee Nicodemus who was a member of the Jewish ruling council and a teacher, and he was very confused. At one point in the conversation, Jesus reprimanded Nicodemus saying, "You are Israel's teacher and do you not understand these things?" (John 3:10).[1] What the Pharisees, and hence Nicodemus, believed can be traced to a concept common among both the Greeks and the Romans of this period. They believed that the soul was the "real you" and that at death it left the body and went to the "netherworld," which could be a better place somewhere on earth or

---

[1] The record of Jesus and Nicodemus in John 3 confuses most Christians because, like Nicodemus, they do not understand the Hope of Israel about which Jesus was speaking. He was referring to the Resurrection of the Just, when Jewish believers will be raised to life in the Kingdom. See Appendix H.

perhaps where their gods lived. Many Jews, including the sect of the Essenes, adopted this belief. By the time Christ started his ministry, there was massive confusion about what happened after death and apparently very little clear, Scripture-based teaching on the subject.

It is evident from Jesus' teachings that he understood the importance of having a clear understanding of the Hope. Both he and John the Baptist traveled the countryside proclaiming, "Repent, for the Kingdom of heaven is near" (Matt. 3:2; 4:17). In fact, the "good news" that Christ preached was the "good news" about the Kingdom, that is, the coming Kingdom on earth. The Greek word *euaggelion* (good news) is often translated by the Middle English word "gospel," which means "good news" and comes from the Old English "godspel." The NIV uses the phrase, the "gospel of the Kingdom" in Matthew 24:14, while in Matthew 4:23; 9:35; Luke 4:43; 8:1, and 16:16, it uses the phrase "good news of the Kingdom." It is very important to realize that Jesus taught the good news about "the Kingdom." No single verse mentions the good news about "heaven." In fact, a study of all the teachings of Christ shows that much of what he taught was either directly speaking about the Kingdom or telling people what they should do to get into it. Many Christians today use the phrase "the Kingdom" to refer to those who are saved and have heaven as their destiny, but there is no actual scriptural support for such an interpretation. "The Kingdom" refers to the Kingdom that Christ will establish on earth and rule as King.

Jesus knew the value of having a true hope, as opposed to a false hope, and that is exemplified in his teaching ministry. He spent the opening part of his first major teaching recorded in the Word of God, the Sermon on the Mount, rebuilding the Hope for Israel. Most Christians do not know that everything Jesus said in the Beatitudes, the first part of the Sermon on the Mount, relates primarily to the future hope.[2] Most Christians also do not know that what he taught was not "new revelation." It had already been stated in the Old Testament but had been almost forgotten by his time. What is commonly taught by Christians is that the Beatitudes refer to *this life*. For example, under "Beatitudes" in the *Mercer Dictionary of the Bible,* the following definition is provided:

> Beatitudes. The term is used to designate the condition of individuals or groups who are faithful or righteous and who may therefore expect to enjoy the favor of God. *Such blessings were expected to be realized in this life...*"[3] [emphasis added].

It is a distortion of the text to interpret the Beatitudes as referring to this life. Although there are certain aspects that do apply today, such as a pure-hearted person seeing God more clearly than someone with an impure heart, the primary emphasis is on the future.[4] How can "Blessed are the poor in spirit, for theirs is the Kingdom of Heaven" be applied to this life? It cannot, because the Kingdom of Heaven will not be in place until Christ comes to earth again. How can "Blessed are those who mourn, for they will be comforted" be accurately applied to this life when many people who mourn die without ever being comforted? How can "Blessed are the meek, for they will inherit the earth"

---

[2] "Beatitude" means "supreme blessedness or happiness, perfect bliss." Hence, theologians have named the first nine verses in the Sermon on the Mount, "The Beatitudes." They each start with the phrase, "Blessed are."

[3] Watson Mills, ed., *Mercer Dictionary of the Bible* (Mercer University Press, Macon, GA, 1990) pp. 92–93.

[4] Students of the Bible must understand the difference between "interpretation" and "application." "Interpretation" is what the verse is actually saying—what it means. "Application" is how a person can apply the verse or an insinuation from the verse in his own life. Someone may say he is "blessed" by God because he is "poor in spirit" (i.e., humble) and refer to Matthew 5:3. However, that is not the primary meaning of the verse, even though the person applies it to his life. A more accurate application (and interpretation) would come from his using 1 Peter 5:5.

be applied to this life? Many meek people never own land and most never "inherit" any land at all. These blessings relate to *the future,* and Christ was simply teaching what the prophets of long ago had taught. He was rebuilding the walls of doctrine that had been torn down by years of unbelief.

Some Christians try to apply the Beatitudes to this life by spiritualizing them, i.e., by making them something other than literal. For example, *The New International Commentary* expounds on the phrase "the meek shall inherit the earth" by saying that greedy, aggressive people are not able to enjoy what they have in this life, but the meek "have the capacity to enjoy in life all those things that provide genuine and lasting satisfaction."[5] The first and most obvious problem with this interpretation is that it does not deal with what the verse actually says. There is a world of difference between "inheriting the earth" and "enjoying what one has." No wonder there is so much confusion regarding Scripture. It will be impossible to arrive at truth if teachers arbitrarily substitute words that do not reflect what is actually written.[6] It is safe to assume that if Christ had wanted to communicate to his

---

[5] Mounce, op. cit., *Matthew*, p. 39.

[6] Very few Christians are taught how to read and properly interpret Scripture. Most biblical education in churches consists of simply saying, "This is what this verse means," rather than showing people how to use the exegetical tools available to them, such as concordances, lexicons, Bible dictionaries, customs books, etc., so they can arrive at a proper understanding by themselves. If Christians were educated in how to interpret Scripture, perhaps there would not be as many denominations as there are today. Certainly God never meant for each Christian to have his or her own interpretation. Although Christians often act as if having one's own opinion of the meaning of Scripture is perfectly fine with the Lord, there is no biblical support for this belief. The Bible speaks of "the" truth, not many truths, "one faith," not many faiths, and Scripture exhorts Christians to be "perfectly united in mind and thought" (1 Cor. 1:10). When the Church at Corinth was divided, Paul wrote and scolded them with, "Is Christ divided?" (1 Cor. 1:13). Some basics of how to interpret the Bible are given in the pamphlet, *22 Principles of Bible Interpretation,* (Christian Educational Services, Indianapolis, IN).

audience that only meek people can enjoy what they have, he would have said just that.

A second problem with the idea that the verse refers to enjoying things now is that such an interpretation does not provide the comfort and hope that many people need. Many of those in Christ's audience were poor, hungry, sick, had lost children or relatives to premature death, and were terribly oppressed by the Romans and even their fellow Jews who had rulership over them. They owned little and life was very, very difficult. Would it really have comforted them if what Christ said had meant, "Don't worry, those greedy people cannot really enjoy all the wealth they have, but you can enjoy what you have"? It would not have comforted them any more than it would comfort people who are poor, sick, and oppressed today. But having hope that things in the future will be better than they are now can be very comforting and encouraging. Furthermore, experience teaches that hope in a wonderful future is more important to people who are having difficulties in life than to those who are having an easy life.

I have ministered to impoverished people in Haiti and the slums of the Philippines. Those people have an idea of what "the good life" is because they can see the wealth around them, wealth to which they have no access. It does not comfort or encourage them to hear, "Be content, because those greedy, wealthy people cannot enjoy what they have, but you can enjoy what you have." What comforts people and gives them the strength to endure is *hope*—knowing that all the effort it takes to stay meek and loving when life is so tough will be worth it someday. William Shakespeare, a brilliant writer and keen observer of human life, wrote, "The miserable have no other medicine, but only hope." Thankfully, a hope that is alive and vital in the heart of a person is indeed good medicine. In this life, although there are some wealthy people who are very meek, it is often the greedy and ruthless people who get rich, live in plush houses, take long vacations, eat the best food, and wear the nicest clothes. They are enjoying their "reward" now, but there is a day coming when evil people will be gone and the earth, a wonderful recreated earth that is much better than this one, will belong to the meek.

The Beauty of the Beatitudes

When a person understands that the subject of the Beatitudes is the future life, not this one, they are easy to understand, profound in their meaning, and powerful in their impact. Christ, the master teacher, garnered truth from the Old Testament and taught it, and as long as the Beatitudes are taken literally and applied to his future Kingdom, what is taught is simple and clear. The Beatitudes are recorded in both Matthew and Luke. There are significant differences between the two Gospels, so both should be examined carefully. In Matthew, Jesus was teaching to a crowd (Matt. 5:1), some of whom were his disciples, but many were not. Not everyone in the crowd was saved. Since he was teaching from a mountainside, the teaching is called, "The Sermon on the Mount." In Luke, Christ was teaching on a plain (Luke 6:17) and although a crowd was listening, he spoke specifically to his disciples (Luke 6:20). Each of the Beatitudes is identified below along with Old Testament references that teach the same truth and short commentaries.

Matthew 5:3
Blessed are the poor in spirit, for theirs is the kingdom of heaven.

Psalm 149:4; Isaiah 29:19; 66:2; Zephaniah 3:12. "Poor in spirit" means poor or humble in their attitude.[7] Those who are humble will inherit the future Kingdom of Heaven, so they are blessed.

Matthew 5:4
Blessed are those who mourn, for they will be comforted.

---

[7] One of the meanings of "spirit" in both the Bible and the English language today is "attitude." We commonly say a happy person is "in good spirits." Graeser, Lynn, and Schoenheit, op. cit., *The Gift of Holy Spirit*, p. 104. Thayer, op. cit., *Lexicon*, p. 523.

Isaiah 61:3. There will be comfort in the future Kingdom for all those righteous people who mourn now.

Matthew 5:5
Blessed are the meek, for they will inherit the earth.

Psalm 37:9–11; Isaiah 57:13; Ezekiel 37:12; Zephaniah 3:8–12. The meek will inherit the physical earth. Those who are self-righteous and never come to God for salvation will not have everlasting life and thus will not inherit anything. In the graphic words of Malachi, "not a root or a branch will be left to them" (Mal. 4:1).

Matthew 5:6
Blessed are those who hunger and thirst for righteousness, for they will be filled.

Psalm 37:28,29; Isaiah 1:26; 11:4; Daniel 9:24. A person who thirsts for righteousness will not have that thirst quenched in this life because the corruption and unrighteousness that exists on earth will continue until Christ finally defeats the Devil and his minions. Also, although personal righteousness is available in a spiritual sense to the Christian, it is not attainable in a practical sense because we all give in regularly to temptation and sin because of our sin nature. All this will change in the Millennial Kingdom, where righteousness, both personal and interpersonal, will reign supreme.

Matthew 5:7
Blessed are the merciful, for they will be shown mercy.

Hosea 6:6; Micah 6:8; Zechariah 7:9. The merciful may not receive mercy in this life, but they will definitely be shown mercy by God at the Judgment and afterwards. In Matthew 25:31–46, Christ said that those who had fed the hungry, given drink to the thirsty, sheltered the outcast, clothed the naked, and visited those who were sick or in prison would be shown mercy at the Judgment and allowed into the Kingdom, while those who had not would be excluded.

Matthew 5:8

Blessed are the pure in heart, for they will see God.

Psalm 1; Psalm 73, especially vs. 13 and 24; Malachi 3:16–18. The pure in heart will enter the Kingdom where they will see God in ways not available to people today. The impure will not enter, so they will not see God. The fact that God will be known in ways not available now is shown in such verses as Revelation 21:3: "Now [in the Everlasting Kingdom] the dwelling of God is with men and He will live with them. They will be His people and God Himself will be with them".

Matthew 5:9

Blessed are the peacemakers, for they will be called sons of God.

Psalm 37:37. This clearly refers to the future because the peacemakers on the earth today are often scoffed at and discounted as cowards and compromisers. This is the case whether the conflicts are inter-family, inter-racial, or international. Nevertheless, the Lord recognizes their efforts and they will be called "the sons of God" in the Kingdom, where they will live forever.

Matthew 5:10–12

(10) Blessed are those who are persecuted because of righteousness, for theirs is the kingdom of heaven.
(11) Blessed are you when people insult you, persecute you and falsely say all kinds of evil against you because of me.
(12) Rejoice and be glad, because great is your reward in heaven, for in the same way they persecuted the prophets who were before you.

The records of the persecution of righteous people in the Old Testament are very well known and far too many to list. This cannot be speaking of blessings in this life, because many people were greatly persecuted and some were even martyred. Hebrews 11 has a short summary of such cases, including Abel, Enoch, Noah, Joseph, Moses, as well as others, and states that they endured trial and persecution "so that they might gain a better resurrection" (Heb. 11:35), that which the Bible calls "the first resurrection" (Rev. 20:5,6) and "the resurrection of the righteous" (Luke 14:14, sometimes translated, "the Resurrection of the Just"). Those who are persecuted because of righteousness will attain the Resurrection of the Righteous, a resurrection into the Kingdom of Heaven.

The Gospel of Matthew records Christ teaching the crowds, but the Gospel of Luke records him speaking specifically to his disciples, so in Luke he was speaking to people who were being instructed in righteousness. Also, since he was speaking to his disciples, he was addressing people who were living in such a way that they would receive significant rewards when he came as King and set up his Kingdom.

Luke 6:20
Blessed are you who are poor, for yours is the kingdom of God.

Christ said, "Blessed are you [disciples] who are poor." It is very important to understand that Christ was addressing those of his disciples who were poor and not all poor people in general. Poverty is not a ticket to everlasting life, but discipleship is. These poor disciples were not blessed because they were poor, but blessed in spite of their poverty because they would inherit the Kingdom. These disciples feared the Lord and thus, besides being meek, righteous, peacemakers, etc., they are those of whom God spoke when He said:

Malachi 3:16–18

(16) Then those who feared the LORD talked with each other, and the LORD listened and heard. A scroll of remembrance was written in his presence concerning those who feared the LORD and honored his name.

(17) "They will be mine," says the LORD Almighty, "in the day when I make up my treasured possession. I will spare them, just as in compassion a man spares his son who serves him.

(18) And you will again see the distinction between the righteous and the wicked, between those who serve God and those who do not."

The poor disciples who feared God will indeed be His when he makes up his treasured possession.

Luke 6:21

Blessed are you who hunger now, for you will be satisfied.

Isaiah 25:6; 30:23–26; 32:15; 35:1,6,7; 51:3; Jerermiah 31:5,11–14; Ezekiel 47:7–12; Joel 2:18–26; 3:18; Amos 9:13. That there will be an abundance of food in the Millennial Kingdom has already been established in this book. These disciples may have been poor and hungry, but when the Kingdom comes they will feast on "the best of meats and the finest of wines".

Luke 6:21

Blessed are you who weep now, for you will laugh.

Many verses attest to the joy that will be in the future Kingdom. When the Messiah comes, he will "heal the brokenhearted" (Isa. 61:1, New American Bible). He will "comfort all who mourn" (Isa. 61:2). There will be great comfort for those people who are weeping and crying now. One of the verses describing this is in Isaiah:

Isaiah 61:3

[The Messiah will] provide for those who grieve in Zion—to bestow on them a crown of beauty instead of ashes, the oil of gladness instead of mourning, and a garment of praise instead of a spirit of despair.

It was a common custom for the brokenhearted and repentant to sit in ashes or put ashes on themselves (2 Sam. 13:19; Esther 4:1; Job 2:8; Jon. 3:6), and this verse describes ashes being replaced by beauty.[8] It was common to use oil to make yourself look and feel healthy and radiant when you were doing well but not to use oil when things were going badly in your life (Ps. 45:7; 92:10; 104:15). These people who grieved and were mourning will be given the oil of gladness. Their despair will be turned into praise. Isaiah 65:17–19 says that the sound of weeping and crying will be heard no more, but instead, people will be glad and will rejoice forevermore.

Luke 6:22,23

(22) Blessed are you when men hate you, when they exclude you and insult you and reject your name as evil, because of the Son of Man.
(23) Rejoice in that day and leap for joy, because great is your reward in heaven. For that is how their fathers treated the prophets.

For an explanation of these verses refer to Matthew 5:10–12 above.

Jesus Christ set a wonderful example for Christian teachers in making the Hope a priority and teaching it clearly to both his disciples and to the crowds. Jesus was aware of the fact that the people he was teaching lived difficult lives and that a clear teaching on the Hope would help them make commitments and stay anchored to the

---

[8] Jonah 3:6 has "dust" in the NIV instead of ashes but the Hebrew text is "ashes."

Heavenly Father and to the Word. He knew that this would position them for blessings in this life and great rewards in the next. He also knew that his audience had not been taught much accurate information about the Hope so, gleaning information from the Old Testament, he presented it in a clear and dynamic fashion. Today, thousands of years later, his wonderful words still give hope to those with ears to hear.

CHAPTER 9 *Sin, Forgiveness, and Holiness*

Sin and Forgiveness

Like an undetected cancer, sin can have horrible effects that are invisible to the eye. The effects of sin can and do occur in this life, but more significantly they can reach into everlasting life in the form of lost rewards. Understanding what God says about rewards and loss of rewards in the future Kingdom reveals the truly horrible effects of sinful behavior. An unfortunate part of much Christian belief is that "getting to heaven" is the only really important objective for anyone. The result of such thinking is that sinful behavior becomes tolerable, worse yet, even acceptable. After all, according to common belief, a little sin will not keep anyone from being saved. While this is true, it does not negate the fact that sinful behavior will result in the loss of rewards in the future. In addition, sinful behavior negatively impacts a person's relationship with the Lord in this life. Therefore, godly behavior is very important, both now and for the future.

It is clear from Scripture that it is impossible to live without sinning, but this does not justify sinful behavior. Many times people want to ignore sin because it is painful to confront, particularly if it is deeply rooted. This results in Christians "making peace" with the sin entrenched in their lives rather than "making war" on it. They give up trying and think that if they rely on the mercy of the Lord at the Judgment "things will all work out." However, Scripture clearly states that the Lord is just and that "Anyone who does wrong will be repaid for his wrong, and there is no favoritism" (Col. 3:25). As previously noted, Christ will be ashamed of "carnal Christians" when he comes (Mark 8:38; Luke 9:26; 1 John 2:28), and they may "lose" what they have worked for (2 John 8) or even be punished (1 Thess. 4:6). God is merciful, but His mercy is expressed in this life by His forgiveness of sins when people genuinely ask for forgiveness. There is no indication in Scripture that at the Judgment Seat the Lord will ignore people's sin and be merciful by withholding consequences. In fact, it would not be just for the Lord to give "carnal Christians" the same reward as Christians who had struggled and labored to be godly, and even endured persecution for the cause of Christ.

Christians with habitual sin in their lives should not "gamble" that they will receive mercy at the Judgment. Scripture openly indicates this will not happen, but they do not need to appear before the Lord ashamed and with unconfessed sin. If any Christian has habitual sin in his life, if he is a liar, thief, idolater, drunkard, is angry and bitter, is entangled in sexual sin, or whatever, rather than give up the fight against sin, he needs to boldly wade into it. God wants each Christian to win his war against sin, and He will help anyone who calls on Him to live a holy life. Many verses make it clear that God wants people to turn from sin. For example:

Ezekiel 33:11

Say to them, "As surely as I live, declares the Sovereign LORD, I take no pleasure in the death of the wicked, but rather that they turn from their ways and live. Turn! Turn from your evil ways! Why will you die, O house of Israel?"

The great beauty of this verse, and others like it, is that it shows God is not nearly as concerned about noticing people's sin and waiting for the Judgment as He is with people turning from their sin and being forgiven. God loves every person and greatly desires him or her to "turn from evil and live." He faithfully forgives all those who ask to be forgiven.

The Call to Holiness

Throughout the Scriptures, God commands personal holiness, which means to stop participating in sinful behavior and live in obedience to the Lord.

> **Leviticus 11:44**
> I am the LORD your God; consecrate yourselves and be holy, because I am holy.

> **1 Peter 1:15**
> But just as he who called you is holy, so be holy in all you do.

The seven Church Epistles (Romans through Thessalonians) are the specific revelation from God and the Lord Jesus Christ to the Christian Church, which began on the Day of Pentecost and will end with the Rapture. Although other parts of the Bible may apply to Christians, the Church Epistles are specifically to be applied by the Church of the Body of Christ.[1] This is why each epistle opens with, "To the Church of God in…" or "To the saints in…." Therefore, what the epistles make known about turning from sin and walking holy and blameless before God is particularly important for and applicable to Christians. Personal holiness is one of the doctrines specifically mentioned in every Church Epistle. Below is a verse or section of verses from each of the Epistles clearly showing God's desire for each and every Christian to be holy before Him. There are many such verses in the Church Epistles, so it was not challenging to find verses on personal holiness, but it was difficult to choose just one representative verse from each epistle.

---

[1] See footnote 10 on page 25 for more information.

Romans 12:1

Therefore, I urge you, brothers, in view of God's mercy, to **offer your bodies as living sacrifices**, **holy and pleasing to God**—this is your spiritual act of worship.

1 Corinthians 15:34a

Come back to your senses as you ought, and **stop sinning**.

2 Corinthians 7:1

Since we have these promises, dear friends, let us purify ourselves from everything that contaminates body and spirit, **perfecting holiness** out of reverence for God.

Galatians 5:24

Those who belong to Christ Jesus have **crucified the sinful nature** with its passions and desires.

Ephesians 4:17,22–24

(17) So I tell you this, and insist on it in the Lord, that you **must no longer live as the Gentiles do**, in the futility of their thinking.

(22) You were taught, with regard to your former way of life, to **put off your old self**, which is being corrupted by its deceitful desires;

(23) to be **made new** in the attitude of your minds;

(24) and to put on the **new self**, created to be like God in **true righteousness and holiness**.

Philippians 1:9,10

(9) And this is my prayer: that your love may abound more and more in knowledge and depth of insight,

(10) so that you may be able to discern what is best and **may be pure and blameless** until the day of Christ.

Colossians 3:5–10

(5) **Put to death, therefore, whatever belongs to your earthly nature**: sexual immorality, impurity, lust, evil desires and greed, which is idolatry.

(6) Because of these, the wrath of God is coming.

(7) You used to walk in these ways, in the life you once lived.

(8) But now you must **rid yourselves of all such things as these**: anger, rage, malice, slander, and filthy language from your lips.

(9) Do not lie to each other, since you have taken off your old self with its practices

(10) and have **put on the new self**, which is being renewed in knowledge in the image of its Creator.

1 Thessalonians 4:4

Each of you should **learn to control his own body** in a way that is **holy and honorable**.

2 Thessalonians 3:11–13

(11) We hear that some among you are idle. They are not busy; they are busybodies.

(12) Such people we command and urge in the Lord Jesus Christ to settle down and earn the bread they eat.

(13) And as for you, brothers, **never tire of doing what is right**.

Is there any doubt that the will of God is that Christians stop sinning and walk holy before Him? Of course, to stop sinning can be very difficult, but a major key is not to give up the struggle, having faith that our efforts will have everlasting value.

"Repent" is a word familiar to most Christians. The essence of "repentance" is "change," namely, to stop sinning and ask forgiveness of God. Asking forgiveness is essential to the process of being cleansed of sin and being reconciled to Him. This makes perfect sense, even in the natural world. If you have been sinning against someone, and he knows about it, there cannot be a complete reconciliation between the two of you until you ask to be forgiven. Just stopping the sin is not enough. The same is true with God. He wants you to confess your sin to Him in order to completely restore the relationship. When you confess your sins, He "cleans the slate," so to speak. He literally cleanses you from your sin. The Bible is very clear on this.

2 Chronicles 7:14
If my people, who are called by my name, will humble themselves and pray and seek my face and turn from their wicked ways, then will I hear from heaven and will forgive their sin...."

Proverbs 28:13
He who conceals his sins does not prosper, but whoever confesses and renounces them finds mercy.

Isaiah 55:7
Let the wicked forsake his way and the evil man his thoughts. Let him turn to the LORD, and he will have mercy on him, and to our God, for he will freely pardon.

Jeremiah 3:12,13a
(12) Go, proclaim this message toward the north: "Return, faithless Israel, declares the LORD, I will frown on you no longer, for I am merciful, declares the LORD, I will not be angry forever.
(13a) Only acknowledge your guilt—you have rebelled against the LORD your God."

Ezekiel 18:21,22a
(21) But if a wicked man turns away from all the sins he has committed and keeps all my decrees and does what is just and right, he will surely live; he will not die.

(22a) None of the offenses he has committed will be remembered against him.

1 John 1:9

If we confess our sins, he is faithful and just and will forgive us our sins and purify us from all unrighteousness.

The above verses testify that God has always been willing to forgive sin and pardon the sinner. Therefore, Christians should never "make peace" with sin, but should continue to battle against it, confess it, and ask for forgiveness if they falter.[2]

It is wonderful for Christians to know that God has clearly marked the way to walk and that He is also loving and forgiving. His desire is for every person to turn from evil and walk obediently before Him, and He will help with that task, while still honoring freewill decisions. At the same time, God is just. Scripture says:

2 Corinthians 6:2

"In the time of my favor I heard you, and in the day of salvation I helped you." I tell you, now is the time of God's favor, now is the day of salvation.

---

[2] The Greek word "confess" is *homologeo*, which is comprised of *homo*, "the same," and *lego*, "to speak" or "to say." It is "to say the same thing" (Vine, op. cit., *Lexicon*, "confess," p. 216). It can be difficult to accurately translate *homologeo* because the usual connotation of "confess" is that a person has done something wrong. There is no *necessary* implication of wrongdoing in the Greek word. When there is no wrongdoing, "assert," "declare," or "profess" would be better than "confess." Thus, one would "profess" that Jesus is Lord (Rom. 10:9) but "confess" his sins (1 John 1:9). In order to *homologeo* (confess or profess), one must believe what he is saying and be convinced it is true (Thayer, op. cit., *Lexicon*, p. 446). If a person does not believe that Jesus is Lord, he cannot "confess" that. If a person is not genuinely repentant about his sin and does not think he needs to be forgiven, then he cannot genuinely "confess" (*homologeo*) his sin. A person who just mouths the words, "I'm sorry God," when in his heart he is not sorry at all, is not actually "confessing" his sin the way the Bible says to.

These words should ring loudly in the ears of every Christian. *Now* is the time for mercy, forgiveness, and God's favor. The Judgment will be a time for justice; at that time God will give every person what he deserves. *Now* is the time to stop sinning. *Now* is the time for every Christian to live obediently so that he can look forward to a rich reward at the Judgment.

Fighting Fear, Discouragement, and Condemnation

It has been almost a dozen years now since I have come to realize that it is possible to be punished and suffer loss at the Judgment. When I first came to realize the seriousness of my own upcoming Judgment, I had emotional reactions that ran the gamut from concern to fear. The Judgment is not an easy thing to face up to. There are times in my life when I feel very "on top of things." At those times I feel very comfortable with my approaching Judgment, and sometimes even have a "Bring it on" attitude. However, I am "on top of life" less than I sometimes care to admit. I often feel like the psalmist:

> **Psalm 51:3**
> For I know my transgressions, and my sin is always before me.

Oh, how well I know my transgressions, and how clearly my own sin is before me. Many times I feel worry or anxiety about my own future Judgment. Am I doing as well as I think I am? Have I really messed up somewhere and do not know it? Will I get there expecting rewards only to find that I missed "the big picture" of Christianity and was not pleasing to Christ? These thoughts go through my head, and one blessing I get from them is that they keep me searching my soul and the Word, and they keep me open to advice from other Christians.

Thankfully, most of the time I have a peaceful feeling about my coming Judgment. I try to remember that my walk with the Lord is a never-ending balancing act. Indeed, it seems God designed life so that everything needs balancing. For example, the Lord wants me to give financially, but not to the point I need others to support me. He wants me to pray, but not so much that I do not do any actual work. He wants me to share my faith with those who do not yet believe, but not so much that I have no fellowship with other members of the Body of Christ. Because life is a balancing act and we Christians are constantly making decisions about what to do, we must come to the point that we are not constantly tormenting ourselves about the decisions we make and the times we do not achieve perfection.

In spite of trying to be content with my efforts, I sometimes condemn myself for falling short of the perfection set forth in the Word. I want to be holy and obedient, but like the apostles on the night of Christ's arrest, my spirit is willing but my flesh is weak. And I am not the only one who experiences this. As I said, I have been teaching this for almost 12 years now, and often in my audiences there are people who are shocked and frightened by the verses I share about the Judgment. Some of them have told me about their struggle with whether or not they will be accepted or receive any rewards. This is especially true for people who already have a low opinion of themselves or who feel they have ignored the commands of God and instead done what they wanted to in life. I have met many people whom I consider obedient Christians, but who feel they are not very good Christians at all.

God did not tell us about Judgment Day so we would be overcome with worry. In His grace and mercy, He told us about the Judgment so we will take life seriously, obey Him, and be rewarded. Knowing about my coming Judgment has helped me in my walk with the Lord. I have already covered how knowledge of the coming Judgment can be a motivator for godliness, and that has been the case both for me and for other Christians I have spoken with. Nevertheless, if I looked at my life and compared it to "perfection," I could be frightened about the coming Judgment. However, as I have prayed for understanding, spoken with wise and insightful Christians, and studied the Bible, I have been able to control my thoughts and stay positive and blessed. God knows about my sin nature and He knows about the spiritual battle I live in daily. No man with a sin nature has ever achieved perfection in his walk. In fact, even Adam and Eve, who did not have sin natures, did not achieve perfection. The Bible says that "all" have sinned and fallen short of the glory of God. That is why God always accepts anyone's sincere prayer for forgiveness. Although I know it is not good to sin, I accept my fallibility, and I am thankful for my Savior.

It is a fact that most people do not think of themselves as highly as they ought. Very often other people see our good qualities much more clearly than we ourselves do. Many godly Christians I have met are acutely aware of their own sin, but not so acutely aware of their own goodness. In those situations it is easy to become discouraged by the influence that the sin nature sometimes seems to have in day-to-day life. Even Paul was moved by the Lord to write about its strong influence:

Romans 7:15,18–20

(15) I do not understand what I do. For what I want to do I do not do, but what I hate I do.

(18) I know that nothing good lives in me, that is, in my sinful nature. For I have the desire to do what is good, but I cannot carry it out.

(19) For what I do is not the good I want to do; no, the evil I do not want to do—this I keep on doing.

(20) Now if I do what I do not want to do, it is no longer I who do it, but it is sin living in me that does it.

I certainly do not compare my life and ministry to the greatness and fruitfulness of that of the apostle Paul, yet even he felt the effects of the battle raging within him between the old nature and the new nature. This is the powerful effect of the sin nature that works inside each of us Christians. But praise God, Paul's solution, and yours and mine also, is to have faith in the person and work of Jesus Christ:

Romans 7:24,25

(24) What a wretched man I am! Who will rescue me from this body of death?

(25) Thanks be to God—through Jesus Christ our Lord!

Amen. Thanks be to God through Christ. How do we balance our fallibility with God's high standards? Rather than be disheartened and defeated when we sin, we need to pick ourselves up and make war on our sins and personal weaknesses. After all, we have a God who not only forgives our sins, but who, when we confess them, forgets them. Our heavenly Father, like any parent, is not blessed when His children wallow in their own defeat, misery, and condemnation. He rejoices when we pick ourselves up from failure and defeat. Proverbs tells about the behavior of the righteous: "For though a righteous man falls seven times, he rises again" (Prov. 24:16). The Bible affirms that righteous people fail and sin daily—but they pick themselves back up.

Another important thing to realize is that when verses such as 2 John 8 speak of losing rewards, they do not necessarily mean losing *all* rewards for all the good things that we have ever done. For example, if I share my faith in Jesus Christ with someone who becomes born again, nothing can take that fact away. The Lord is just, and he highly values the efforts we make on his behalf.

Christians are God's beloved children. He knows we have a sin nature, and He knows that sometimes our flesh gets the better of us. As Christians, we must learn to balance our desire to live without sinning with the reality that we will sin. Wallowing in guilt, shame, and condemnation does not bless God, Christ, or other Christians. Nor do we want to make light of sin or give in to it simply because we can be forgiven for it. Rather, we must honestly confess our sin and forgive ourselves when we fall short—like God does.

CHAPTER 10   *Valuing This Life*

How We Picture the Next Life Affects What We Think About This One

A person's perception of the next life has a significant impact on his or her view of this life. People who believe there is no future life are likely to live in excess in this life, exhibiting attitudes like "get it while I can" or "do unto others before they do unto me." The Bible points out this attitude in Isaiah.

> **Isaiah 22:13**
> But see, there is joy and revelry, slaughtering of cattle and killing of sheep, eating of meat and drinking of wine! "Let us eat and drink," you say, "for tomorrow we die!"

In such people's minds there is no ultimate punishment for wicked behavior or ultimate reward for good behavior, so this life and what they can get from it is all that matters. Then there are people who do believe there is a next life but view it as completely disconnected from this life because it takes place in some kind of vaporous, cloud-filled, angels-with-wings kind of world. These people tend to discount this world and may even be repelled by it. It is this latter viewpoint that will be the starting point of this chapter because it raises the issue of what "spiritual" is. The importance of having an accurate understanding of what is spiritual cannot be overstated because it dramatically impacts a person's view of the next life and, in turn, dramatically impacts the person's view of this life.

Attempting to determine what is "spiritual" has led to much confusion in the religious world. When someone believes something is or is not "spiritual" it has a great impact on his life. It shapes his values, and therefore defines what he feels comfortable doing. Many Christians base their definition of "spiritual" on their concept of heaven. Traditionally, heaven is a place where the souls of the saved reside in sublime bliss, fulfilled just by being in the presence of God. The result of this perception is that many Christians think there is very little about this life that is spiritual.

In an effort to clarify the word "spiritual," it is important to first dismiss the common misconception that there is a direct conflict between that which is spiritual and that which is physical. Based on this misconception, spiritual is "good" and physical is "bad" and the Christian must choose between them. The Bible, however, indicates that the opposite of "spiritual" is not "physical" but "fleshly" or "worldly."

God created people with physical bodies. People then decide whether they will focus on that which is spiritual or on that which is fleshly. People can be very spiritual and yet enjoy the physical things in life at the same time. One of the reasons God created the heavens and earth the way He did was for man to enjoy all its physical beauty. He created the sun and moon and hung them in the sky knowing that, besides being functional, they would be enjoyable. He created domestic animals, such as dogs and cats, knowing that they would be more than just "work animals," but friends and companions as well (Gen. 1:24,25).[1] God created plants that are both "pleasing to the eye and good for food" (Gen. 2:9). He put Adam and Eve in "the Garden

---

[1] The Hebrew word translated "livestock" in the NIV and "cattle" in the KJV can refer to wild animals in some contexts, but when it is placed in contrast with words that refer to wild animals, it means domestic animals (cp. Gen. 1:24, where "livestock" is contrasted with "wild animals"). R. Laird Harris, Gleason L. Archer, and Bruce K. Waltke, *Theological Wordbook of the Old Testament* (Moody Press, Chicago, IL, 1980), pp. 92, 279–81.

of Eden," which in Hebrew means "the garden of delights" or "the delightful garden."

There is no question that God intended man to enjoy life in a physical environment. However, because many Christians are taught that this world is physical and therefore "bad" compared to "heaven," which is spiritual and therefore "good," the real value and enjoyment of the earthly life God has provided is lost. In fact, most Christians assume that when they die, their lives will change drastically and all the things they now know and enjoy will pass away. Such a mindset often dilutes the fulfillment available in many daily activities. After all, what is the real value of something that will pass away into oblivion? But what if the activities of this life will not pass away? What if they continue on into the next life? Would it not be easier to see the value in them, and would it not be easier to relate to the future life?

In orthodox Christian teaching, there is almost no relation between this world and the next. The way some Christians disdain this life and look forward to being in "heaven" almost makes it seem as if God made a gigantic mistake when He created this earth for mankind. A good question to ask is what would have happened had Adam and Eve never sinned? They would have lived on earth forever. Was it God's will for them to sin? Of course not. The only logical conclusion is that God's will for mankind is to live on the earth forever—not in a corrupted world like this one, but in a perfect world like that which He originally created. If God made Adam and Eve to live on earth forever, it just cannot be true that "the earth is evil but heaven is wonderful."

The point is this: just because something is related to earthly life or is "fun" does not mean it is not spiritual or valuable. Are there things about this life that are not spiritual? Certainly, and we are not to be so invested in this life that we forget about the work of the Lord and get lost in earthly pursuits alone. However, there is a great difference between realizing that we are to seek first the Kingdom of God and believing that nothing in this life is of any real value because it will all pass away and thus has no relation to our "real" life in the next world.

There is also a great difference between realizing that we must be about the Father's business and thinking that having fun is somehow innately ungodly or unspiritual. Though we live in physical bodies on a physical earth, there is much about earthly life that is wonderful, godly, and "spiritual."

The somewhat ironic truth is that because God designed life to be lived by those who believe in Him, Christians should be the ones who most enjoy the things God placed on the earth. It is unfortunate that the misconception of heaven and what is truly spiritual has caused some people to withdraw from many of the activities that God intended for people to enjoy. God knew Adam would have to focus much of his time and energy on keeping the Garden. He also knew that when He told Adam and Eve to be fruitful and multiply and fill the earth that they, just like any other couple raising children, would have their hands full. Much of the work of parenting is due to the fact that children require a lot of time and energy, not because of the fallen nature of man. Surely no one believes that had Adam not sinned, all those children would have raised themselves. God planned work for man, including parenting. Not only do these activities not hinder salvation and holiness when they are carried out with dependence upon God and obedience to His Word, but they even contribute to man's spiritual growth and wholeness.

Don't Retreat—Relish!

In contrast to having a godly attitude about work and family, the belief that this world is somehow inherently ungodly can cause people to retreat and withdraw from much of life and even their God-given responsibilities. It is often taught that personal holiness is to be obtained by withdrawing from the pleasures of the world. Unfortunately, it is even occasionally taught that it is also necessary to withdraw from the responsibilities of this life. The well-known historian Will Durant writes of early Christians who, to be acceptable in the eyes of God, withdrew from daily life to pursue their individual salvation, perhaps in a monastery, the desert, or elsewhere.

> Too many Christians of these early centuries thought they could serve God best—or rather, most easily escape hell—by abandoning their parents, mates, or children, and fleeing from the responsibilities of life in the frightened pursuit of a selfishly individual salvation.[2]

It is hard to comprehend how anyone could believe that abandoning parents, wife, and children would be pleasing to God, but "holiness" was perceived as being something "other worldly," something "heavenly" that was apart from the necessary activities of this life. According to this belief, having to take care of a family infringed upon one's personal holiness. To these people, the daily tasks of life seemed far removed from their perception of "heaven" and "real spirituality." This viewpoint highlights just how important it is to have an accurate understanding of the future life on earth. Knowing what life will be like in the future provides a context in which to understand the value of this present life.

There are other people whose concept of heaven and what is truly spiritual has caused them to pull away from what most people consider to be fun activities because they believe that those activities will somehow contaminate them. Often, out of a pure motive, they separate themselves because they want to live a "holy" life. It is important to be holy, but it is vital to understand that enjoying what God has made available does not make one unholy. Dancing and drinking wine were part of life for the Old Testament believers. Why then do so many Christians consider these to be categorically ungodly or "unholy"? Some say, "Well, those things can lead to worldliness and sin." If this is the case, why was it acceptable behavior for the Old Testament believers? Why did the psalmist say to praise God with music, singing, and dancing (Ps. 150, etc.)? Why is there a promise that in the Millennial

---

[2] Will Durant, *The Age of Faith* (Simon and Schuster, New York, 1950), p. 76.

Kingdom people will enjoy "the best of meats and the finest of wines" (Isa. 25:6)? Would Jesus Christ have turned more than one hundred and twenty gallons of water into wine (John 2:5–10) if drinking wine was ungodly or a sure path to worldliness? Hardly. Anything can be done to excess or done in a sinful manner, but that is hardly a reason to stop doing things that God allows. It is significant that hundreds of years ago, when the concept of the true Christian hope of a wonderful life in a flesh-and-bone body on this physical earth was exchanged for a concept of a life without a physical body in heaven, the belief that there was real godly value in enjoying life on this earth was seriously curtailed.

There is a profound change that occurs in the way you think about the physical activities of life when you realize that many of them will go on almost unchanged in the next life. Do you enjoy a good meal with fine meat and vegetables and a glass of wine? If you are saved, you can relish that wonderful meal you are eating and look forward to plenty more. You can think of what you enjoy now as part of the love God has for you now and a "foretaste" of what life in the Kingdom will be like. Do you enjoy sitting in your back yard, enjoying the fresh air and scenery? There will be plenty of that. Do you enjoy physical activity and working on worthwhile projects such as farming or grow- ing a garden? All that will continue. Do you enjoy walking in the woods or down a country road in the springtime when the flowers are in bloom and the birds are singing? There will be wonderful flowers and birds on the recreated earth, and you will be able to enjoy the walk without worrying about dangerous people or animals, mosquitoes, poison ivy, or thorns. The hurtful things like poison ivy and thorns are here as a result of Adam's sin and the curse on the ground (Gen. 3:17,18), and they will not be present on the next earth.

God originally created the earth for mankind. When Adam sinned, the ground was cursed, the human body was given over to both decay and a sin nature, and much of life became difficult and painful. In spite of all that, however, it is still possible to find great joy in life today.

Christians need to enjoy the things that God, in His love, placed on earth to enrich their lives. Furthermore, Christians need to reflect on how much more they will enjoy each other, good food, productive work, holidays and festivals, and that "feeling good" feeling they will get from a healthy and energized new body on God's recreated earth.

CHAPTER 11   *Concentrate on the Here and Now*

Don't Watch the Anchor—There Is Work To Do on Board

God calls the Hope "the anchor of the soul." As an anchor keeps a boat from being blown away in a storm or drifting away with the currents, the Hope keeps Christians from being blown away from God by the storms of life or drifting from Him through the ebb and flow of everyday life. This chapter will focus on the fact that when the anchor is working properly, it does not require constant attention. No modern ship has a camera focused on the anchor so that the people on board can watch it hour after hour. When the anchor is holding firm, the people on the ship forget about it and get busy doing their shipboard duties. So too, Christians who have built an accurate knowledge and understanding of the Hope in their lives can apply themselves to the work of God at hand in this life with single-minded focus.

As shown in the previous chapter, it is possible for Christians to become so focused on the future that they become detached from this life. They pray about heaven, sing about heaven, think and talk about heaven. They concentrate on heaven and pull away from the world as if the things of this life are just wasted time. They do not enjoy this life or see any value in it. Therefore, they do not apply themselves seriously to any "worldly" task. Perhaps this accounts for the origin of the saying that someone "is so spiritual he's no earthly good." Unfortunately, for some of these people the words from the old hymn, "This world is not my home, I'm just a-passin' through" are all too descriptive. They are so focused on "passin' through" that they fail to grasp the intrinsic value of this life. This is especially tragic when it results in a failure to get involved in the lives of others. Even more damaging is the impact this attitude has on those who then disdainfully view Christians as being "too spiritual" or "good-for-nothings;" people who pray and go to church all the time but who will not do any real work or get involved in the community. [1]

In contrast to devaluing this life and pulling away from it, the Bible makes it clear that the way to ensure a wonderful welcome into the Kingdom and to receive rich rewards is to obey the practical directives of God's Word, working to improve the world, and seeking to bless all people. Jesus was without doubt the most spiritual person to ever walk the planet, yet before he started his ministry he worked as a carpenter. It would not be a "stretch" to assume that he was one of the best (if not the best) carpenters who ever lived. Based on everything that can be known of him through Scripture, it would be hard to imagine that he ever did a shoddy job on a piece of furniture and then said, "It doesn't really matter. After all, I'll be in heaven in a few years." Or that he sat around all day and complained about not being able to get on with the "really important" things. It would be safe to assume that while he was a carpenter, he put his whole heart into his responsibilities and did the best work possible. It is evident in Scripture that when he ministered to people, he ministered to them at the level of their need. He got involved in peoples' lives. Christians should seek to emulate Jesus—to try to be like him in every way. With a secure "anchor," Christians can concentrate on this life and put single-minded focus into the task at hand, whatever it might be. They can invest themselves into the building and maintaining of family relationships, and they can seek to help others around them. When a child of God lives this kind of lifestyle, it brings honor to the Father.

---

[1] This attitude tends to surface at certain times and places. However, non-Christians really cannot deny the extensive involvement of Christians in charity work, community activities, local government, etc.

On Being a "Do-Gooder"

The Bible is clear that we Christians are to be "do-gooders." We are to do good works. Sometimes that fact gets distorted, as if the only good work God expects from us is to pray, go to church, give money, and keep ourselves physically separate from the world. That, however, is clearly not what Scripture says, and it is not the will of God. When God mentions not being "polluted by the world," He is speaking of being influenced to the point that we become "conformed" to the world in our minds and hearts (Rom. 12:2). We are to do good works in the world without becoming "worldly."

Christians are familiar with the commandment, "Love your neighbor as yourself," and even many non-Christians are familiar with "the Golden Rule," which is "Do to others what you would have them do to you" (Matt. 7:12). Besides these two commandments, there are many other verses about doing good works. These include:

Proverbs 3:27
Do not withhold good from those who deserve it, when it is in your power to act.

Ephesians 2:10a
For we are God's workmanship, created in Christ Jesus to do good works.

Colossians 1:10
And we pray this in order that you may live a life worthy of the Lord and may please him in every way: bearing fruit in every good work.

Some more specific examples of good works identified in Scripture are provided below.

Matthew 10:42
And if anyone gives even a cup of cold water to one of these little ones because he is my disciple, I tell you the truth, he will certainly not lose his reward.

Since most houses today have running water, the ease with which most Americans can give water to a guest obscures the point that everyone in the biblical culture understood: "cold water" came only from the town well or cistern because water in jars at home warmed up very quickly in the heat. Giving a cup of cold water meant inconveniencing yourself and walking to the town well carrying a container, perhaps waiting in line to draw the water, lifting the water up out of the ground, and then carrying the water back to the house—all so someone could quench his thirst. The fact that Christ connects giving cold water with rewards to be received in the future is a powerful testimony to the value of even the most seemingly mundane good works in the eyes of God.

Wealthy people are commanded to be rich in good works and willing to share.

1 Timothy 6:18

Command them [rich people] to do good, to be rich in good deeds, and to be generous and willing to share.

This verse often gets "watered down" in the minds of most Americans because the United States is a country in which so many people are rich that typically only the "super-rich" are considered actually rich. Using biblical standards, however, the average family in America is truly wealthy. Most Americans eat well three times a day and many have snacks in between. This was not the standard of life in biblical times and it has not been the standard for most people throughout history. Even today it is not the standard for millions of people in the world. Most Americans are never in danger of freezing to death because they lack clothing and shelter, but historically, having an abundance of clothing and reliable shelter is rare.

Many Americans who seem to have no money and live "from paycheck to paycheck" are in that position because they live beyond their means rather than because they actually cannot afford food and shelter. The Bible makes it clear that some people live in such a way that they are receiving their reward now, in this life, and will not receive a reward in the future (Matt. 6:1–6,16–18). Each and every person needs to evaluate his or her life and decide whether it is deserving of rewards in the future or if he or she is living to be rewarded now by the things of this world. Everyone should take seriously the Lord's command to be "rich in good deeds" and "generous and willing to share."

Taking care of one's family is also a godly priority.

1 Timothy 5:8
If anyone does not provide for his relatives, and especially for his immediate family, he has denied the faith and is worse than an unbeliever.

These strong words make it clear that God places a high value on family and taking care of one's family. Believers should take heed and align their values with God's values. There is an unfortunate tendency among those who are committed to God to put the work of the ministry ahead of caring for their families. Many Christians deceive themselves into thinking that God would have them take care of "His people" rather than their own families. When the Bible is examined honestly, it is evident that the flesh-and-blood family should take precedence over church work. This is not to say that the two are mutually exclusive, only that it requires vigilance to maintain priorities based on God's Word.

Perhaps one of the clearest sections of Scripture that connects good works now with the future life in the Kingdom is in Matthew. At "the Sheep and Goat Judgment" Christ will separate those who lived through the Tribulation and the battle of Armageddon into two groups—those who will enter his Kingdom and those who will not. Even though the Christian's salvation is not based on good works

(Eph. 2:8), this section in Matthew, written to Jews, emphasizes to all believers the importance of good works.[2]

Matthew 25:34–45

(34) Then the King [the Messiah, Jesus Christ] will say to those on his right, "Come, you who are blessed by my Father; take your inheritance, the kingdom prepared for you since the creation of the world.

(35) For I was hungry and you gave me something to eat, I was thirsty and you gave me something to drink, I was a stranger and you invited me in,

(36) I needed clothes and you clothed me, I was sick and you looked after me, I was in prison and you came to visit me."

(37) Then the righteous will answer him, "Lord, when did we see you hungry and feed you, or thirsty and give you something to drink?

(38) When did we see you a stranger and invite you in, or needing clothes and clothe you?

(39) When did we see you sick or in prison and go to visit you?"

(40) The King will reply, "I tell you the truth, whatever you did for one of the least of these brothers of mine, you did for me."

(41) Then he will say to those on his left, "Depart from me, you who are cursed, into the eternal fire prepared for the Devil and his angels.

(42) For I was hungry and you gave me nothing to eat, I was thirsty and you gave me nothing to drink,

---

[2] That the Christian Church is separate from Israel and is governed by different laws and regulations is covered in Appendix C.

(43) I was a stranger and you did not invite me in, I needed clothes and you did not clothe me, I was sick and in prison and you did not look after me."

(44) They also will answer, "Lord, when did we see you hungry or thirsty or a stranger or needing clothes or sick or in prison, and did not help you?"

(45) He will reply, "I tell you the truth, whatever you did not do for one of the least of these, you did not do for me."

These verses could not be written any more plainly. Feeding the hungry, giving clothing and shelter, and comforting those who are sick, in prison, and in need are very important to the Lord. He has some very stern words for those who enjoy their bounty without having compassion for the poor and needy around them:

Luke 6:24,25

(24) But woe to you who are rich, for you have already received your comfort.

(25) Woe to you who are well fed now, for you will go hungry. Woe to you who laugh now, for you will mourn and weep.

The message is not, as some would propound, that Christians need to take a vow of poverty. Rather, God is sounding an alert concerning the potential pitfalls of being wealthy. Wealth makes it all too easy to trust in riches rather than God and to indulge oneself rather than seeking to help others. God's message is to take heed to being charitable to those in need. Christians are surrounded by misery and should make a serious effort to do whatever possible to alleviate people's suffering. It is impossible to completely eradicate suffering and pain in this fallen world, but that does not justify a lack of effort. Christians with an accurate understanding of the Hope can remain anchored and focus their energies on good works knowing that there is a Paradise coming in which there will be justice on the earth and no sickness or hunger. That Hope anchors our soul.

CHAPTER 12   *Coming Full Circle*

From Paradise to Paradise

God originally planned for mankind to live forever on a wonderful earth, enjoying life in peace and safety and without pain and death. God initiated His plan by putting Adam and Eve in a magnificent garden, which is called "Paradise" in the Greek Old Testament. That plan seemed to fall apart when Adam sinned and man was driven out of Paradise. Nevertheless, God never changed His mind, and His original plan will eventually come to pass. The things of God will eventually come "full circle." Mankind will forever enjoy a wonderful earth with good food and healthy bodies. In addition, Jesus Christ will rule as King on this wonderful earth. This is the Kingdom so often spoken of in the Bible.

When Christ conquers the earth and establishes his Kingdom, Paradise will be re-established. Christians and those in the First Resurrection will be blessed to live in a Kingdom ruled by a just king, Jesus Christ. There will be meaningful and fulfilling work to do, and the assignment that each person receives will be in accordance with what he or she has done for the Lord in this life on earth. That fact is a major reason why the Hope is called the "anchor of the soul." Knowing that rewards in the future Paradise can be earned or lost based on today's behavior helps to anchor people to their Christian commitment and motivates them to watch their lives very closely.

What a wonderful Hope God has set forth in His Word to anyone who cares to accept it. No wonder Peter wrote: "In keeping with his promise, **we are looking forward to a new heaven and a new earth**, the home of righteousness" (2 Pet. 3:13). Every Christian should obey the Lord and walk in such a way that, just as Peter did, he or she can "look forward" to the Rapture and the Kingdom coming to earth. Peter also said, "Always be prepared to give an answer to everyone who asks you to give the reason **for the Hope that you have**" (1 Pet. 3:15).

As Christians, we should be excited about our Hope. It should be a source of great joy, because no matter how challenging this life might be, we always have the Hope to look forward to. We should be enthusiastic about our wonderful future life and our new, glorious bodies, and we should speak to others about it. Excitement and joy should show on our faces and in our lives. When it does, and someone asks us about it, or when our way of life opens a door of utterance for us, we should be able to "give the reason" for the Hope we have. In His grace and kindness, God has told us wonderful things about our future, and we need to be able to articulate them so that His love and kindness can bring others to repentance and salvation also.

Events Important to Understanding the Hope

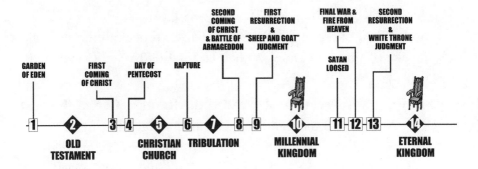

1 **The Garden of Eden**. The original Paradise (Genesis 1–3).

2 **The Old Testament**. During this time, God deals first with Gentiles, and then, after the inception of the nation of Israel via Jacob, with both Jews and Gentiles.

3 **The First Coming of Jesus Christ**. He was born, grew, ministered, was crucified, and then raised from the dead (The Four Gospels).

4 **The Day of Pentecost** (Acts 2). This event starts the Christian Church. From this point, those who believe, either Jew or Gentile, become "one new man" in Christ (Eph. 2:14–17).

5 **The Christian Church**. In Ephesians it is called "the Administration of God's Grace" and "the Administration of the Secret" (Eph. 3:2,9).

6 **The Rapture**. The Christian Church is taken off the earth and meets Christ in the air (Christ does not land on the earth) and is with him in heaven through the Tribulation (1 Cor. 15:51–54; 1 Thess. 4:13–18). Christians will stand before the Judgment Seat of Christ. With the Christian Church gone, Jews and Gentiles remain on earth and God deals with them as separate entities just as He did in the Old Testament and in the Gospels (Rev. 7, etc.).

7 **The Tribulation**. The period of intense trouble that is often spoken of in the Old Testament (Rev. 6–19).

8 **The Second Coming of Christ to the earth to Israel and the battle of Armageddon**. Christ comes down from heaven with his armies (his Second Coming) and fights the battle of Armageddon, which ends the Tribulation. He conquers the earth (Rev. 14:17–20; 16:16; 19:11–21) and the Beast and False Prophet are thrown into the lake of fire. The Devil is chained for 1,000 years (Rev. 19:20; 20:1–3).

9 **The First Resurrection, also called the Resurrection of the Just** (Rev. 20:4–6). All the righteous who died before the Day of Pentecost or during the Tribulation are raised from the dead and judged. Also at this time is the "Sheep and Goat Judgment" (Matt. 25). Those people who survive the Tribulation and are judged righteous are allowed into the Millennial Kingdom, while those who survive but are found unrighteous are thrown into the lake of fire.

10 **The Millennial Kingdom**. This lasts 1,000 years (Rev. 20:4–9).

11 **Satan loosed**. During this "short time" (Rev. 20:3), he deceives the nations of the world. These nations attack Jerusalem (Rev. 20:7–9).

12 **The Final War**. Fire comes from heaven and destroys the enemies of God. The Devil is thrown into the lake of fire (Rev. 20:9,10).

13 **The Second Resurrection (Resurrection of the Unjust) and White Throne Judgment**. The unrighteous of all time and all those who died during the Millennial Kingdom are raised and judged. The saved enter the Everlasting Kingdom while the unsaved are thrown into the lake of fire (Rev. 20:11–15).

14 **The Everlasting Kingdom**. God sets up His Kingdom on earth and it lasts forever (Rev. 21,22).

Verses Sometimes Used to Support the Idea that Our Everlasting Future is in Heaven

"Difficult" Verses

While many verses in the Bible are so plain that even a child can read and understand them, for instance, "You shall not steal," many other verses can be more difficult to grasp. This is attributed to several factors. For one thing, the Bible was originally written in another language (actually three other languages—Hebrew, Aramaic, and Greek) and the recorded events took place in another culture. This can sometimes result in an "outside looking in" perspective, not unlike someone visiting a "foreign" country. The country is "foreign" only to the visitor, not to the people who live there, and it is easy for the visitor to misinterpret what he sees and experiences. Although this can make the task of accurately understanding the Bible somewhat difficult, no one should believe that it is impossible. If it is not available to understand the Bible and the truths contained in it, then God is being disingenuous when He says that He wants all men to come to a knowledge of the truth (1 Tim. 2:4).[1]

To a large degree, it is the failure to understand the cultural context of the Bible, as well as the scope of Scripture and the context of specific verses, that has resulted in some verses being misinterpreted and

---

[1] Actually, according to the Greek text, God wants all people to come to a "full or complete knowledge" of the truth, not just "a knowledge" of it. The *Amplified Bible* expresses this very well, saying that it is God, "Who wishes all men to be saved and [increasingly] to perceive *and* recognize *and* discern *and* know precisely *and* correctly the [divine] Truth" [italics and brackets in original].

used to support the idea that heaven is the ultimate home of believers. The purpose of this chapter is to examine these "difficult" verses in the light of the scope of the entire Bible, the context of the verse in question, the translation of the Greek or Hebrew text, and the culture and customs of the time in order to bring their true meaning to light.

Elijah in Heaven

2 Kings 2:11 says, "Elijah went up by a whirlwind into heaven" (KJV). Most Christians immediately assume that Elijah went up to be with God, but that is not what the people who lived during Elijah's time thought. First of all, "heaven" refers to other things beside the place where God lives. It is the place where birds fly, rain and snow come from, etc. Scripture mentions, "the fowl of the heaven" (Gen. 7:23, KJV), "rain from heaven" (Acts 14:17), "snow from heaven" (Isa. 55:10, KJV), and clouds in heaven (1 Kings 18:45, KJV).[2] The prophets of Elijah's day did not believe that he was taken up to the place where God lives. They knew he was taken up into the air but believed he would eventually be set down somewhere. They thought if they looked hard enough, they would be able to find him (2 Kings 2:16).

While others wanted to search for Elijah, Elisha understood that if the Lord had wanted Elijah there, He would not have moved him. Understanding the customs of the time further helps to clarify this section of Scripture. God had told Elijah to anoint Elisha to succeed him (1 Kings 19:16). According to custom, Elisha could not assume leadership of the prophets as long as Elijah was present. Therefore, in order to allow Elisha to lead, God had to find a way to graciously remove Elijah. He chose to do it by a whirlwind. Elijah was not taken up to the place where God lives, but he was taken up into the air and placed somewhere else. God simply moved Elijah from one place to another and he lived out his days somewhere else. Elijah could not

---

[2] Although some translations use "air" or "sky" instead of "heaven," anyone who checks the Hebrew or Greek text will see immediately that the text reads "heaven."

have been taken to heaven to live with God because he lived before the time of Christ. It is Christ's shed blood that is the only valid payment for all men's sin, including Elijah's. If Elijah were already enjoying everlasting life in heaven, there was no need for Christ to come and to die for his sin.[3] The Gospel of John makes it clear that Elijah did not go to heaven. It says, "**No one** has ever gone into heaven except the one who came from heaven—the Son of Man" (John 3:13).

The Reward in Heaven

There are many verses that refer to reward, or treasures, or even a home in heaven. These include verses such as Matthew 5:12 ("Great is your reward in heaven"), Matthew 6:19,20 ("Do not store up for yourselves treasures on earth...but store up for yourselves treasures in heaven"), Colossians 1:5 ("The hope that is stored up for you in heaven") and 1 Peter 1:4 ("Kept in heaven for you"). It is understandable that these verses and others like them can be confusing and may lead one to believe that the righteous will go to heaven. However, Jesus was talking to Jews who knew (or should have known from the Old Testament scriptures) that they would inherit the earth. Therefore, their understanding of these concepts would not be based on a literal use of the word heaven in the sense that these physical things, namely, rewards, treasures, and homes, were actually in heaven, but rather, that God, who is in heaven, is "storing" them or keeping record of them. The actual receipt of these things will occur in the future on earth. The Old Testament made it clear that people would get what they deserved and that this would happen when the Kingdom was established. The idea of God keeping track of man's behavior is clearly recorded in the Old Testament.

---

[3] Graeser, Lynn, and Schoenheit, op. cit., *Is There Death After Life?*, p. 85.

Malachi 3:16

Then those who feared the LORD talked with each other, and the LORD listened and heard. A scroll of remembrance was written in his presence concerning those who feared the LORD and honored his name.

Ecclesiastes 12:14

For God will bring every deed into judgment, including every hidden thing, whether it is good or evil.

The Book of Revelation notes that at the Judgment, "The books were opened" and "The dead were judged according to what they had done as recorded in the books" (Rev. 20:12). That God was keeping a reward or treasure for them in heaven, and that they could add to that treasure by their good deeds, was a common concept in Judaism.

> The notion of a heavenly treasure, beyond the reach of corruption, was a common eschatological concept in Judaism. The righteous on earth do not yet possess it, for it belongs to the future; nevertheless they can now add to it.[4]
>
> An important concept in Jewish and Christian theology is the belief that sins and virtues accumulate and are "stored" the way money might be stored in a treasury. The Lord was believed to keep records of every sin and virtue and require the books be balanced from time to time.[5]

The Jews in Christ's audience knew that God was keeping track of their deeds with the intention of rewarding them. They will receive what is rightfully theirs when the Messiah returns and establishes his Kingdom on earth.

---

[4] J. Emerton, C. Cranfield, and G. Stanton, *The International Critical Commentary: Matthew* (T. & T. Clark, Ltd., Edinburg, 1988), p. 631.

[5] George Wesley Buchanan, *The Anchor Bible: To the Hebrews* (Doubleday & Company, Inc., Garden City, NY, 1972), p. xxv.

They Will Be Like the Angels in Heaven

Matthew 22 records that the Sadducees, who did not believe in the resurrection, came to Jesus and asked him a difficult question. They asked Jesus what would happen to a woman who had seven husbands in her first life. Whose wife would she be in the resurrection? Christ answered them by saying, "At the resurrection, people will neither marry nor be given in marriage; they will be like the angels in heaven" (Matt. 22:30). What is important for the discussion in this book is the fact that Christ was not speaking about being on earth or in heaven. He did not say, "In the resurrection, people will be like angels [and live in heaven]." Rather, he revealed two great truths: angels do not have husbands and wives, and, after the resurrection, the saved will not have husbands and wives. Thus, as far as marriage is concerned, the saved will be like the angels in heaven.

It is also important to understand that Jesus never said that after death or after the resurrection, people *become* angels. Although it is widely believed that when people die they become angels, this is not the testimony of Scripture. Believers' natural bodies will be changed and they will become immortal, but they will not become angels.

I Go to Prepare a Place for You

John 14:1–3 has often been used to teach that the saved will spend forever in heaven.

John 14:1–3
(1) Do not let your hearts be troubled. Trust in God; trust also in me.
(2) In my Father's house are many rooms; if it were not so, I would have told you. I am going there to prepare a place for you.
(3) And if I go and prepare a place for you, I will come back and take you to be with me that you also may be where I am.

The NIV translation of verse 3 is misleading. The phrase "take you to be with me" incorrectly implies that Jesus would take the disciples somewhere, presumably back to heaven. A literal and more accurate translation of this phrase would be "receive you unto myself." Christ was not going to "take" the disciples anywhere; he was going to "receive them unto himself." The King James Version handles this section well:

John 14:1–5 (KJV)

(1) Let not your heart be troubled: ye believe in God, believe also in me.

(2) In my Father's house are many mansions: if *it were* not *so*, I would have told you. I go to prepare a place for you.

(3) And if I go and prepare a place for you, I will come again, and receive you unto myself; that where I am, *there* ye may be also.

(4) And whither I go ye know, and the way ye know.

(5) Thomas saith unto him, Lord, we know not whither thou goest; and how can we know the way?

An examination of this section of Scripture should begin with a careful study of what it does *not* mean. It does not mean, "When you die, you go to heaven." Christ told his disciples they would be with him *when he came again for them.* He did not say they would be with him when they died. Even some orthodox Christians have noted that Christ must come for believers if they are going to be with him. On this basis they teach that he actually comes and retrieves each believer's soul at death and escorts it back into heaven. Besides the fact that this is an assumption unsupported by Scripture, it would seem to be very impractical. There are so many Christians dying every day that Christ would be doing nothing but commuting back and forth from heaven to earth—if indeed he ever got a chance to complete even one round trip without interruption. In any case, these verses clearly refute the idea that the "soul" goes to heaven or hell when a person dies.

There are other orthodox Christian theologians who acknowledge that Jesus' coming for the disciples refers to his coming from heaven to earth when he comes to fight at Armageddon. Yet these same theologians assert that, after gathering the disciples, Christ will take them back to heaven. One problem with this belief is that no verse states that once Christ conquers the earth he will go back to heaven. Scripture clearly portrays Christ ruling on earth, as we have seen throughout this book.

In order to see how the disciples would have understood what Christ was saying, the context of this section of Scripture must be examined very closely. Although the disciples did not fully understand what he was saying, they could have if they had carefully listened to, and believed, everything he had previously taught. Jesus' disciples knew about the Kingdom coming on earth. What they did not yet grasp was that the Messiah would have to suffer, die, be buried, be raised from the dead, and then ascend into heaven before it could come, and Jesus was preparing them for these events. Christ spoke with his disciples and said, "Let not your hearts be troubled." Why would he say that? He wanted to ease the terror that the disciples would naturally feel when he was arrested, tortured, and crucified.

Jesus went on to say that in his Father's "house" were many mansions. The "house" of the Father is the Kingdom that is to come. There is no reason to believe that the word "house" is literal. The Bible never speaks of God living in a "house" in heaven, and it never says that saved believers will live in separate rooms in God's house. The Bible states that there will be people living all over the world in the Millennial Kingdom, not just in one house. Also, since the Everlasting Kingdom has a city that is about 1,400 miles square, it certainly seems that people will not live in just one house at that time either. It was common in the biblical culture to use the word "house" to refer to a nation or kingdom, such as in the phrase, the "house of Israel."[6] Christ used the word "house" to mean a kingdom when he said, "Any kingdom divided against itself will be ruined, and a **house** divided against itself will fall" (Luke 11:17).

The "mansions" in the Kingdom are places to stay, rooms, or abiding places. The KJV translation of "mansions" is an old English usage. In 1611, when the King James Version was written, a "mansion" was a place of residence, no matter what size, and also the house of the lord of the manor. Over time, the word "mansion" came to be used only of large houses, as it is used today in common English. What Christ said in terms that were clear in his culture was, "In my Father's Kingdom are many places to live." This is certainly true, as is borne out by the many scriptures that refer to the Kingdom, including the one that says the people will live in "secure homes" (Isa. 32:18).

The truth being revealed in this verse is that there will be room for any and all who want to come. When Jesus said, "In my Father's house [Kingdom] are many places to stay," he was continuing to comfort his disciples. He was not leaving them behind because there was no room for them in the Kingdom; rather he was leaving to prepare "a place" for them there. The "preparation" that was necessary to bring the Kingdom included his torture, death, and resurrection. All of these events were necessary in order to complete mankind's salvation. Without the death, resurrection, and ascension of Christ, no man would ever be raised from the dead to enter the Kingdom. When the disciples heard what Jesus said, they would not have thought about a house "in the air." This would have been a totally foreign concept to them. They were, however, well aware that there was going to be a Kingdom on earth.

---

[6] This can be verified very quickly in any concordance. "House of Israel" is used 146 times in the KJV, the "house of Judah" is used 41 times, and "house of David" is used 26 times.

Verse 3 says, "And if I go and prepare a place for you, I will come again, and receive you unto myself; that where I am, *there* ye may be also." Bible commentators have had trouble explaining this verse and different commentaries have different explanations. Most orthodox explanations are incorrect because they involve mansions "in heaven" and living in the air forever. Even when one realizes that the Kingdom is on earth however, there are still several ways to understand the verse. Three possible interpretations will be examined. All of them are sensitive to the context of John 14, the time Christ was speaking (his last supper), and what the disciples would have been able to understand based on what they knew from the Old Testament and from what Jesus had taught them.

The "last supper" was no ordinary meal. When the Four Gospels are compared, we see that Jesus used the occasion to teach on a wide variety of subjects. He spoke about his betrayal; he instructed his disciples to serve one another and demonstrated his teaching by washing their feet; he taught about love and obedience; he spoke of the New Covenant and partook of the cup and bread; he taught about the vine and the branches; he forewarned the disciples that they would be hated by the world; he spoke of the coming holy spirit; he predicted Peter's denials; he taught about his ascension, which he called "going to my Father." With all this in mind, it is evident why the interpretation of John 14:3 is difficult. The three most likely interpretations are:

1) And if I go and prepare a place for you *[by my death and burial],* I will come again *[be resurrected],* and receive you unto myself *[welcome you back into my life even though you fled, and did not at first believe I was alive];* that where I am, *there* ye may be also *[in the Kingdom when it comes on earth].*

2) And if I go and prepare a place for you *[at my ascension],* I will come again *[at my Second Coming when I fight at Armageddon and conquer the earth],* and receive you unto myself *[welcome you into the Kingdom];* that where I am, *there* ye may be also *[in the Kingdom].*

3) And if I go and prepare a place for you *[by my death, resurrec-tion, and later my ascension],* I will come again *[first at my resurrection and later when I fight at Armageddon and con-quer the earth],* and receive you unto myself *[first when I wel-come you back into my life even though you fled and did not at first believe I was alive, and then later when I welcome you into my Kingdom];* that where I am, *there* ye may be also *[in the Kingdom].*

The third interpretation is actually a combination of the first two. People who argue for the first interpretation say that Jesus did not need to talk about his ascension at this time because his death was the more immediate event. He would have 40 days after his resurrection to teach about his Ascension. Those who argue for the second interpretation say that Christ had the ascension clearly in mind and that it was a major subject of discussion (it comes up after John 14:12 when he said he was going to the Father). Furthermore, they say, when he said later in his discourse that he was "going away," it was clearly "to the Father" (John 16:5ff) and not to the grave. People who say that the third inter-pretation is correct point out that Christ often communicated more than one meaning in a word or phrase and see no reason why he was not referring to both things—after all, both are true. This discussion over which interpretation is correct may never be settled, and, from the standpoint of this book, it is not necessary to speak definitively on which is correct. The purpose of this study is to show that the future home of the saved is on earth, not in heaven, and all three interpreta-tions support this truth.

Continuing in John 14, Jesus said to his disciples, *"Where* I go, you know, and *the way* you know" (John 14:4). These words are important. The disciples had been told both "where" and "the way" Christ was going. The "where" he was going was to the grave and eventually into heaven (at his ascension). The "way" was via his torture, death, burial, resurrection, and ascension. The disciples "knew" all these facts either because of Christ's teaching or because of Old Testament teaching.

Nevertheless, they did not fully believe, and so they were confused by what he said.

Thomas said, "Lord, we don't know where you are going, so how can we know the way?" (John 14:5). What apparently confused the disciples was that all of this was in the context of Christ's "going away" and then coming back. The disciples did not yet believe that Christ would have to suffer and die as a prerequisite to entering into his glory. From their point of view, Jesus did not need to "go" anywhere. They thought he was going to conquer the earth and set up his Kingdom right then and there.

One last point: It is evident that the disciples did not realize that Christ would be ascending into heaven. After his resurrection, they asked if he was going to establish his Kingdom (Acts 1:6). If the disciples were not expecting *Christ* to go to heaven, they certainly would not have thought that *they* were going.

My Kingdom is Not of This World

The fact that Christ said his Kingdom was "not of this world" has led people to believe that it must be somewhere else, namely "heaven."

John 18:36 (KJV)
Jesus answered, My kingdom is not of this world: if my kingdom were of this world, then would my servants fight, that I should not be delivered to the Jews: but now is my kingdom not from hence.

The key to properly understanding this verse is to know what Jesus meant by the phrase, "of this world." It is commonly assumed that he meant his Kingdom would not be on the physical earth, but the phrase is not a reference to the physical earth. He was referring to the world as it is today—fallen and under the influence of the Devil. It is used with the same force as "this age."[7] Christ's Kingdom is not of "this world" because it will not be under the influences of the evil that so characterizes today's world. His future Kingdom will not be of "this world" because "this world" is run by the Devil and it will have been judged (John 12:31).

Today's world, "this world," is going to pass away, even as 1 Corinthians 7:31 says: "For this world in its present form is passing away." It cannot be that the "world" as a physical reality is passing away because both the Old and New Testament testify that God will create a new earth. That the phrase "this world" means the fallen world is made clear in other scriptures. For example, Jesus spoke of his disciples not being "of the world" (John 15:19). It is clear that the disciples were "of the world" in the sense that they lived on the physical earth and were fully human. Yet it is also clear they were not "of the world" in the sense that they were not a part of the evil influences of the world.

In stark contrast to the disciples, Jesus referred to the Pharisees who opposed him as being "of this world" (John 8:23). Like the disciples, they were human beings who lived on the physical earth, but they were caught up in its evil. The contrast between the disciples, who were "not of this world," with the Pharisees, who were "of this world," shows clearly that the phrase has nothing to do with actually being on earth or being in a physical body. It speaks of involvement with evil and demonic influences. Christ said that his Kingdom was not of this world, but that it will come at the "renewal" of all things and be exempt from the evil influences of this world.

---

[7] C. K. Barrett, *The Gospel According to St. John* (The Westminster Press, Philadelphia, 1978), p. 536.

Flesh and Blood Cannot Inherit the Kingdom of God

1 Corinthians 15:50

I declare to you, brothers, that flesh and blood cannot inherit the kingdom of God, nor does the perishable inherit the imperishable.

Some people have used this verse to try to show that the new, immortal body each saved person will receive will be spirit instead of flesh, or that the saved will not be on earth in the future but in heaven. Both of these ideas are erroneous. Christians will be given a new body that is fashioned like Jesus' glorious body (Phil. 3:21), which was still flesh and bone even after his resurrection. When he appeared to his disciples after his resurrection, they said he was a spirit, but he refuted that idea.

Luke 24:36–39

(36) While they were still talking about this, Jesus himself stood among them and said to them, "Peace be with you."
(37) They were startled and frightened, thinking they saw a ghost.
(38) He said to them, "Why are you troubled, and why do doubts rise in your minds?
(39) Look at my hands and my feet. It is I myself! Touch me and see; a ghost [pneuma] does not have flesh and bones, as you see I have."

Although the NIV uses the word "ghost," the Greek word is *pneuma* and is more accurately translated as "spirit." In his glorified body, Christ had flesh and bones. He could be touched and felt. He even ate with the disciples (Luke 24:43). Therefore, if the King of the Kingdom has a physical body with flesh, flesh can most definitely enter the Kingdom. Then what is the meaning of this verse in Corinthians? The phrase "flesh and blood" is used five times in Scripture and it means "people" in the common sense of the word. Jesus told Peter that "flesh and blood" (i.e., people) had not revealed his identity, but his Father in heaven had (Matt. 16:17). Ephesians 6:12 states that Christians are not wrestling against "flesh and blood" (i.e., people) but against spiritual forces. 1 Corinthians 15:50 means that "natural" people cannot inherit the Kingdom of God because the present human body is not capable of everlasting life. It is corruptible. Therefore, it must be changed so that it becomes like Christ's.

There is more to it, however. At the "Sheep and Goat Judgment" (Matt. 25), the righteous people living on earth will be allowed to enter the Kingdom without their corruptible bodies being changed into immortal bodies. This is why there will be death in the Millennial Kingdom. However, these people do not, at the point of entry, "inherit" the Kingdom in the fullest sense. The key to understanding this is in 1 Corinthians 15:50 itself. The last phrase of the verse says, "nor does the perishable inherit the imperishable." This is true because "flesh and blood" is perishable. It must be made imperishable in order to "inherit" the Kingdom. Living in the Kingdom for a hundred years or so and then dying does not constitute "inheriting" the Kingdom—at best it is only visiting. The "flesh and blood" body must be made "imperishable" in order for it to actually inherit the Kingdom. This is exactly what Corinthians goes on to say:

1 Corinthians 15:51–53

(51) Listen, I tell you a mystery: We will not all sleep, but we will all be changed—

(52) in a flash, in the twinkling of an eye, at the last trumpet. For the trumpet will sound, the dead will be raised imperishable, and we will be changed.

(53) For the perishable must clothe itself with the imperishable, and the mortal with immortality.

The above verses say that Christians will be "changed," but not into "spirit beings." The change is from mortal to immortal and from perishable to imperishable. The new, imperishable body will enable each believer to "inherit" the Kingdom and enjoy its fullness forever.

Our House in Heaven

2 Corinthians 5:1
Now we know that if the earthly tent we live in is destroyed,
we have a building from God, an eternal house in heaven,
not built by human hands.

This verse apparently contradicts the position that the saved will live forever on earth. It seems to say that the saved will have an eternal house in heaven. However, when the keys to the proper interpretation of Scripture are applied, this difficult verse can be understood to fit with the many clear verses that say the earth will be the final habitation of man.

In 2 Corinthians 5:1, the word "eternal" describes the word "house," not the phrase, "in heaven." The verse does not say Christians have a house "eternally in heaven." It is the "house" that is eternal, and although it is "in heaven" now by promise, that will change. This verse is expressing the fact that is stated in other parts of Corinthians and the Church Epistles that each Christian's future heavenly body will be imperishable. What does it mean that the Christian's house is in heaven? It cannot mean that God already has a closet full of "lifeless new bodysuits" waiting in heaven that Christians will somehow slip into when they get there. Scripture is clear that Christians will get their new bodies by having their old ones changed (1 Cor. 15:51,52). When God is reserving something that is not presently accessible or available, it is said to be "in heaven," as if it already tangibly existed (see "The Reward in Heaven" above and Appendix E on the prophetic perfect). God will give each Christian a new body at the Rapture, so Paul could say that Christians have a house "in heaven."

Seated in Heaven

Ephesians 2:6 has caused confusion to some Christians because it speaks as if Christians were already in heaven with Christ.

Ephesians 2:6

And God raised us up with Christ and seated us with him
in the heavenly realms in Christ Jesus.

Since Christians are obviously living on the earth now, how can it
be that they are also "in heaven" at the same time? Some Christians
say that they are "physically" on earth but "spiritually" in heaven, but
that is inaccurate. It is not biblical to say that a Christian's "spirit" is in
heaven because the Bible says that holy spirit is "sealed" inside each
Christian and we are still on earth.[8]

The key to understanding Ephesians 2:6 is knowing a common
biblical idiom that uses the past tense when speaking of *a future event
that is certain to occur*. This idiom is very well known to biblical
scholars and is called by several different names, including, "the
prophetic perfect," "the historic sense of prophecy," and "the perfective
of confidence." It is also sometimes known as the concept of the "here
now, but not yet."

At the Rapture, Christians will be gathered together to be with
Christ in the heavenly realms. This future event is so certain that it is
spoken of as having already occurred. This is a clear example of the
prophetic perfect. This does not, however, mean that Christians will
continue to live in heaven forever. Christians will return to earth with
Christ at the battle of Armageddon and continue to be with him on
earth forever (refer to Chapter 3). The prophetic perfect idiom is
important to know in order to understand many biblical texts. The
subject is handled at length in Appendix E.

---

[8] Some Christians may be threatened by the thought that they are not "spiritually" in
heaven, as if the reason they can hear from the Lord is that they are in heaven with
him. God created mankind as earth dwellers. Christians can hear from the Lord
because each one has the gift of holy spirit within him. God has always spoken to
His people and the space between heaven and earth does not in any way hinder Him
from communicating with people.

They Were Longing for a Better Country—a Heavenly One

Hebrews 11:16 speaks of a "heavenly" country. This does not mean that the country is *in heaven*. Nor does it mean that there is a city in heaven to which people go when they die or after the resurrection. The word "heavenly" can describe the origin of something, the qualities of something, or something's position in space. In this case, the word "heavenly" refers to the origin and qualities of the country.

> The author of Hebrews called "the land of promise" (11:9) "a heavenly [one]." This does not mean it is not on earth any more than the "sharers in [the] heavenly calling" (3:1) who had "tasted the heavenly gift" (6:4) were not those who lived on earth. Indeed, it was the very land on which the patriarchs dwelt as "strangers and wanderers" (11:13), but the expression means that it is a divine land which God himself has promised (Brackets are his).[9]

Hebrews 13:14 sheds more light on the city and country referred to in Hebrews 11:16.

Hebrews 13:14
For here we do not have an enduring city, but we are looking for the city that is to come.

On earth today there are no "enduring" cities. The Amplified Bible reads "permanent," which is a good translation. All the cities of this world are temporary and will one day come to an end. Nevertheless, the Bible says that there will be a new heaven and a new earth. The new earth will be a glorious place and its capital will be Jerusalem. Eventually, God will bring "the heavenly Jerusalem" to earth (Rev. 21:2). It is very significant in Hebrews 13:14 that the people were looking forward to a city in the future. Believers do not go to the city when they die, as if it were already in existence. The city is "to come" in the future and it will be on the earth.

---

[9] Buchanan, op. cit., *Anchor Bible: Hebrews*, p. 192.

Hebrews has many references to the Old Testament, including references to promises concerning the land. When God fulfills His promises to Abraham and others who are saved and they receive the Promised Land, the Hope of the Old Testament believers will become reality. In that "promised land" they will finally "rest."

The author of Hebrews had basically one hope or aspiration: receiving the promised land in its full glory and prosperity, free from foreign rule or threat from enemies. This was called inheriting or acquiring the promises (6:11,15–17; 11:13,33,39) and entering into "rest" (3:11,18; 4:1,3,5,8,11). The promise is that which was given to Abraham that his seed should inherit the land and be blessed with power, wealth, and number (Gen. 15). This is also the "rest" (4:1), and the reception of the land was called an inheritance (11:8). The "rest" which the Israelites might have had if they had not rebelled in the wilderness is the very rest still available. The good news announced to the Israelites under Moses' leadership is the same good news related to Jesus (4:1,6). Moses and Jesus were related to the same "house"—Moses as a servant and Jesus as a Son (3:2–6). Since the term "rest" was so closely related to the acquisition of Canaan, the intended readers were expected to object that the Israelites had received their promised rest when Joshua led the conquest of Canaan after forty years in the wilderness. The author of Hebrews had two answers: (a) If Joshua had really given them rest, at a later time God would not have spoken through David of another day (4:8); and (b) whoever finds rest ceases from his labors (4:10). Since Israel had never had a continuing period of settlement free from threat or "labor," she had not received her full and final rest that had been promised. That did not mean the "rest" still expected was different from the one early Israelites expected, but only that it would at last be completely received. This promise of rest-inheritance was inextricably tied to the land of Canaan, which is the place where the patriarchs wandered as sojourners (11:13).[10]

The Book of Hebrews contains clear revelation about the Hope of the believer. Unfortunately, because the information has been expressed as a fulfillment of Old Testament promises related to life on this earth, most Christians cannot relate to it. The average Christian is looking for promises of "being in heaven," not promises of a "better country" (Heb. 11:16). However, the promise of a "better country" is the same promise Christ spoke when he said that the meek shall inherit the earth. Christians who have a clear understanding of this "better country" eagerly anticipate its coming.

---

[10] Ibid., p. 194.

The Christian's Hope

The Permanence of Christian Salvation

This appendix will show that salvation for the Christian is unique in that it is unconditional and permanent, while salvation of the believers who lived during the Old Testament and Gospels and those who will live during the Tribulation is conditional and not permanent.[1] Ever since Adam and Eve were expelled from Eden, God has offered everlasting life to people. It is not the purpose of this book to deal with the specifics of *how* people got "saved" in the various administrations, or ages, since the creation of man. Suffice it to say that the Bible reveals that God will judge the hearts and actions of all men, and some will be granted everlasting life and some will not.

To understand both this book and the Bible, it is important that the reader be aware that God has used the words "saved," "believer," "righteous," and "saint" in every administration and age. This fact can cause confusion because it is natural to believe that, because the *words* are the same, the *reality* associated with them is the same.[2] It is natural

---

[1] The Word of God is silent about the permanence of salvation in the Millennial Kingdom. However, there is no prophecy that indicates that when a natural person living in the Kingdom believes that he would at that time receive permanent salvation. It seems likely, based on what can be known from the Old Testament and Gospels, that it would be conditional, not based on permanent "birth."

[2] God authored the Bible in such a way that it takes diligent study, prayer, and "a heart for God" to understand it. Some Christians seem almost offended at this point, as if they know more than God about how it should have been written, and they are upset that it takes time and effort to understand Scripture. Our wise God has hidden the truth from those who are wise in their own eyes and thus believe they already know, and from those who are too lazy to devote the time and energy to learn. God says He "conceals" things (Prov. 25:2), and we must cry aloud for understanding and

(continued)

to think that if Abraham was a believer and the Apostle Paul was a believer, then their salvation was the same. That is not the case, however. Abraham was a believer and he was saved, but his salvation was conditional upon his faithfulness. Paul was a believer also, but, because of God's gracious dealings with the Church, his salvation was based on the New Birth and was not conditional. The Bible student must not let the fact that God uses a few of the same words in both the Old and New Testaments confuse him into thinking that salvation is the same in all administrations and ages.

The following words are used in the Bible to refer to those to whom God will grant everlasting life. As indicated by the Scripture references, these words are applicable in every administration.

> **"Saved"** (Ps. 33:16–19; Isa. 45:17,22; Matt. 10:22; 19:24,25; Rom. 10:9–13). God is the Savior who saves people from everlasting death. So, those to whom He grants everlasting life are called "saved," whether they lived during Old Testament or New Testament times.

> **"Believers"** (1 Kings 18:3; John 4:41; Acts 4:32). Abraham lived before Israel existed, yet he is the "father of all those who believe" (Rom. 4:11; Gal. 3:7).

> **"The righteous"** (Ps. 34:17; 52:6; Mal. 3:18; Matt. 13:43; Acts 24:15). God declared Abraham righteous when he believed (Gen. 15:6). When a person is righteous before God, He will grant him everlasting life.

> **"Saints"** or, as it is translated in some versions, **"the godly ones"** (Ps. 31:23; 34:9; 52:9; 85:8; 132:16; 149:5,9; Dan. 7:18,

---

look for it as diligently as we would look for hidden treasure if we want to find it (Prov. 2:3–5). Jesus followed his Father's example and spoke to the crowd in parables so that they would hear but not understand (Matt. 13:10–15). Later, he would explain the parables to his students (Mark 4:34). Although the some of the words referring to salvation are the same in every administration, the diligent student will come to see the different ways they are used.

22,27; 2 Cor. 1:1; Eph. 1:1). The Hebrew word means "holy, set apart, consecrated." The Greek word also means "holy."[3] Thus, "saints" are people who are holy or set apart and who will be granted everlasting life by God.

In contrast to the terms above, the word **"Christian"** is unique to the epistles written specifically to the Christian Church.[4] It refers to those saved during the Church Age, the Administration of Grace, which started on the Day of Pentecost and will end with the Rapture.[5] In order to fully understand the uniqueness of the word "Christian" and the Christians' permanent salvation, it is essential to understand the Age of Grace and, indeed, the concept of administrations in the Bible.

---

[3] F. Brown, S. Driver, C. Briggs, *The Brown-Driver-Briggs Hebrew and English Lexicon* (Hendrickson Publishers, Peabody, MA, reprinted 1996), pp. 872, 1110. Thayer, op. cit., *Lexicon*, pp. 40–41.

[4] Unfortunately, there is no single theological word for the books of the Bible specifically addressed to Christians. Theologically, and in this book, the phrase "Church Epistles" is used to refer to the seven letters of Paul (although actually there are nine): Romans, Corinthians (1 and 2), Galatians, Ephesians, Philippians, Colossians, and Thessalonians (1 and 2). There are other writings to the Christian Church, however. The other Scripture written *to* Christians is: Acts; 1 and 2 Timothy; Titus; Philemon; Hebrews; James; 1 and 2 Peter; 1, 2, and 3 John; and Jude. There has been controversy about some of these, but CES places them in the Scripture to the Christian Church. In this book, the entire group of letters that God wrote *to* Christians is referred to as "Scripture to Christians," or "letters (or epistles) to the Church," and similar phrases. While all Scripture is "God breathed" and all of it is "profitable" to know and understand (2 Tim. 3:16), not all of it is *addressed to* Christians (for example, the requirement to be circumcised). Many parts of Scripture are "for our learning" (Rom. 15:4, KJV) but are not specifically *addressed to* the Church.

[5] For more on the start of the Christian Church on Pentecost and on dispensations in general, see: Mark H. Graeser, *Defending Dispensationalism* (Christian Educational Services, Indianapolis, IN, 1999), pp. 34–35; Clarence Larkin, *The Greatest Book On Dispensationalism In The World* (Rev. Clarence Larkin Estate, Glenside, PA, 1920), pp. 12, 77, "The Church" chart; and Charles C. Ryrie, *Dispensationalism* (Moody Press, Chicago, 1995), pp. 124–27.

Administrations in the Bible

One of the great truths of Scripture is that God has dealt with people differently at various times through history. These times, or ages, are called "administrations" or "dispensations." Throughout history, God has righteously and resourcefully responded to man's obedience and disobedience by changing the "rules" by which He wants men to live. If one does not understand the administrations in the Bible, it becomes full of apparent contradictions. One example of this is that Christians do not circumcise their children today, even though God told Abraham if a male child was not circumcised, he was not part of the covenant.

Examples of God changing the rules from administration to administration abound. In the Garden of Eden, God told Adam and Eve to eat only plants (Gen. 1:29), but after the Flood, God changed the rules and allowed man to also eat meat (Gen. 9:3). Another clear example concerns the Sabbath. Before the Mosaic Law, there was no specific law concerning the Sabbath, but when God gave the Law to Moses, He stipulated that anyone who worked on the Sabbath should be put to death (Exod. 31:14). Today, in the Administration of Grace, God has changed the rules again and it is not a sin to work on the Sabbath (Rom. 14:5; Col. 2:16,17. Of course, it is still a good idea to take a day of rest).

Another clear example of God changing the rules from administration to administration involves marriage regulations. Before the Mosaic Law, Abraham could marry his half-sister, Sarah, and also have more than one wife. In the Law Administration, after the Mosaic Law was given, God forbade marrying a half-sister (Lev. 18:9) but still allowed a man to have more than one wife.[6] In the Church Age, God forbids polygamy saying that each man is to have his own wife and each woman her own husband (1 Cor. 7:2). Knowing that there are

---

[6] For more detail on the difference between the administrations regarding multiple wives, see, John Schoenheit, *Sex and Scripture: A Biblical Study of Proper Sexual Behavior* (Christian Educational Services, Indianapolis, IN, 2000), pp. 25–28.

different administrations, exactly when they begin and end, and the rules distinctly associated with each is indispensable in explaining many of the apparent contradictions in the Bible. Martin Anstey wrote: "In this matter the golden rule is, 'Distinguish the dispensations and the difficulties will disappear.'"[7]

In Acts 2, on the Jewish holiday of Pentecost, a new administration began when the Lord gave the gift of holy spirit to everyone who believed. This new administration is the Church Age, which is called by several names in the Bible. It is called "the Administration of God's Grace" (Eph. 3:2, sometimes shortened to "the Administration of Grace"); "the Administration of the mystery" (Eph. 3:9, NASB); and "the mystery" (Eph. 3:3,4,9).

It is unfortunate that so many translators used the word "mystery" in their translations because the Greek word *musterion* does not mean "mystery," it means "secret." A "mystery" is something that cannot be understood, while a "secret" is something that can be known when it is revealed.[8] The Administration of Grace is not "mysterious" in the

---

[7] Martin Anstey, *How to Master the Bible* (Pickering & Inglis, London), p. 23.

[8] The Greek word *musterion* means "secret," and a secret can be known if it is revealed (Vine, op. cit., *Expository Dictionary*, "Mystery," p. 769; Bullinger, op. cit. *Lexicon*, "Mystery," p. 515; Thayer, op. cit., *Lexicon*, "*musterion*," p. 420;). This fact can also be seen within Scripture itself. Ephesians 1:9 says that God "**made known** to us the *musterion* of His will." God made His "secret" known to us when He revealed it in His Word. Historically, since the Orthodox Church considered many of the things of God "mysterious," using "mystery" as the translation of *musterion* seemed like a good choice. It is not wise, however, to "hedge" on the translation of a word when the actual meaning is clear. Translating *musterion* as "mystery" has promoted the mostly unbiblical doctrine that God and the things of God are baffling, perplexing, and puzzling. Furthermore, and worse, the translation "mystery" has played into the hands of some of the less godly authorities in the Church. Power has been abused and illogical and unscriptural doctrines have been promoted and sustained because God and the things of God have been (and still are) considered "mysterious." Versions of the Bible that translate *musterion* as "secret" include The New English Bible, The International Standard Version, the Complete Jewish Bible by David Stern, The Bible by James Moffatt, J. B. Phillip's New Testament, The New Testament in the Language of the People by Charles Williams, The Better Version of the New Testament by Chester Estes, Young's Literal Translation, and The

(continued)

sense that it cannot be understood, but it certainly was a "secret" until God revealed it to the apostle Paul. The fact that the administration in which we live is called the "Administration of the Secret" must be taken at face value. God would not have called it, "The Administration of the Secret" if there were not something secret about it that was not known in earlier administrations.

Once we understand that the Administration of Grace was a "secret," certain questions immediately come to mind: Who knew it? From whom was it hidden? "Why did God hide it?" When and how was it revealed? "How can I learn it?" These are logical questions, and they are all answered in the Church Epistles, the letters from the Lord to his Church. In fact, most of them are answered simply by reading through Ephesians 3. God knew "the Secret" but kept it hidden during the Old Testament and Gospels, first revealing it to Paul and then, in the Church Epistles, to the world.

Ephesians 3:5
[The Secret] "which was **not made known** to men in other generations as it has **now been revealed** by the Spirit to God's holy apostles and prophets."

Because the "secret" things that are part of the Administration of the Secret cannot be found in the Old Testament, the Bible speaks of the "unsearchable riches of Christ."

Ephesians 3:8
Although I am less than the least of all God's people, this grace was given me: to preach to the Gentiles the **unsearchable** riches of Christ.

Emphasized Bible by Joseph Rotherham. For more information on the promulgation of the word "mystery" in spite of its biblical definition, see "A Mysterious and Unknowable God," Graeser, Lynn, and Schoenheit, op. cit., *One God and One Lord*, pp. 388–90, and for more information on the translation of *musterion* as "mystery" see Appendix A, Colossians 2:2, pp. 512–513. For more information on the Administration of the Secret see, Bullinger, op. cit., *How To Enjoy the Bible*, pp. 94–96, 141–44.

The word "unsearchable" makes it clear that an extensive "search" of the Old Testament will not reveal the riches of the Grace Administration. In verse 9, God reiterates that the Administration of Grace was hidden in ages past.

Ephesians 3:9

And to make plain to everyone the administration of this mystery [secret], which **for ages past was kept hidden in God**, who created all things.

Christians should pay careful attention to these verses because they show that we have riches that were not revealed in the Bible until the Administration of Grace. That means these riches are not revealed in either the Old Testament or in the Four Gospels. If Christians really want to know the great things God has made available especially to them, they must search the Church Epistles (the letters of Paul to the Church) and the other Scripture written to Christians. These reveal the "riches" God has conferred specifically upon Christians.

Since this secret, the Grace Administration, was "hidden in God" and "not made known to men in other generations," it is a fair question to ask exactly how the apostle Paul came to know it. Paul wrote that the secret was "made known to me by revelation" (Eph. 3:3). In other words, the Lord Jesus Christ directly revealed the secret to Paul.

Galatians 1:11,12

(11) I want you to know, brothers, that the gospel I preached is not something that man made up.

(12) I did not receive it from any man, nor was I taught it; rather, I received it by revelation from Jesus Christ.

The Administration of the Secret was not revealed to men before the Lord revealed it to the apostle Paul. If it had been, there would have been no reason for Jesus to reveal it to Paul by revelation and no reason for Paul to make the point that he got his knowledge directly from Christ. If the information had been revealed before the Lord gave it in the seven Church Epistles, then someone could have taught it to

Paul, or he could have learned it from reading the Old Testament. Instead, Paul learned it directly from Christ because it was a secret before then.

Why did God not reveal the *musterion* until after Christ was cruci-fied? The answer to that question is given in Ephesians and Corin-thians. Ephesians says that God wanted to make his wisdom known by means of the Church to all the principalities and powers, which includes the Devil and all his demons.

Ephesians 3:10
His intent was that now, through the church, the manifold wisdom of God should be made known to the rulers and authorities in the heavenly realms.

What God gave the Christian Church is magnificent, and it is the Church that is to reveal the manifold wisdom of God. The book of Corinthians gives even more understanding as to why God hid the administration of Grace and that it absolutely was not revealed before Christ's crucifixion. The Administration of the Secret is so wonderful, and what Christians have in Christ is so magnificent, that had the Devil and his demons known it, they would not have crucified the Lord Jesus. Christians have permanent salvation by birth and the full-ness of holy spirit within them. Colossians says that each Christian has "Christ in you, the hope of glory" (Col. 1:27). What Christians have is so glorious and powerful that Satan would rather have had Jesus Christ remain alive than have thousands of Christians alive, each with the fullness of Christ within. Corinthians says this very clearly:

1 Corinthians 2:7,8
(7) No, we speak of God's secret *[musterion]* wisdom, a wisdom that has been hidden and that God destined for our glory before time began.
(8) None of the rulers of this age understood it, for if they had, they would not have crucified the Lord of glory.

Satan did not find out about the greatness of the Christian Church until after he had crucified the Lord. As we just stated, the secret that was "destined for our glory before time began" was first revealed to Paul and then to the world when it was written down in the Church Epistles. 1 Corinthians 2 goes on to say the same thing that Ephesians says about the secret not being known before the Grace Administration.

1 Corinthians 2:9,10a
(9) However, as it is written: "No eye has seen, no ear has heard, no mind has conceived what God has prepared for those who love him"—
(10a) but God **has revealed it to us** by his Spirit.

Using, "as it is written," Paul refers to the Old Testament to prove that no human had even conceived the things of the Administration of the Secret, which God has now "revealed" to the Church. Sadly, these verses often get quoted out of context. It is not uncommon to hear a preacher read these verses and then teach that God has things in store in the future that no eye has seen or ear heard. While that may be the case, it is certainly not what these verses are saying. These verses quote the Old Testament and say that what was not known or even thought about back then has now been revealed to the Christian Church.

In spite of such clear teaching about the secret, most Christians interpret certain verses in the Gospels as if the secret were already known at that time. This produces two unfortunate results. First, the wonderful uniqueness of the Christian Church is lost, and the things that God did especially for the Church, and not for any other administration, become hazy and confused. Second, the true meaning of some verses in the Gospels is lost. For example, if someone says that John 3:3, "Verily, verily, I tell you, no one can see the kingdom of God without being born from above" (NRSV), applies to the Christian New Birth, he totally misses the fact that Christ was actually speaking of the First Resurrection.[9]

The Uniqueness and Permanence of Christian Salvation

As we stated earlier, Christian salvation is unconditional and permanent, whereas the salvation God made available in other administrations is conditional and not permanent. While a person who lived and died in the Old Testament, Gospels or during the Tribulation could lose his salvation by turning his heart from the Lord, salvation is "born" into the Christian and, like any other birth, is permanent.[10]

That God changed salvation from being conditional to being unconditional was a great outpouring of grace, and it is one reason that the Church Age is called "the Administration of God's Grace" (Eph. 3:2). The Church Age is compared to the Law Administration in 2 Corinthians 3. The Law was good but compared to the Administration of Grace, it is called "the ministry that brought death" (v. 7) and "the ministry that condemns men" (v. 9). In fact, even though the Law Administration was "glorious," the Bible says that it "has no glory now in comparison with the surpassing glory" that has been given to the Church (v. 10). We Christians have something that is so glorious that in comparison with it the Law had "no glory." We have something considerably different from what the believer's had who lived under the Law. The fact that salvation is now permanent for the believer is

---

[9] John 3 is covered in Appendix H.

[10] It would be moving away from the subject of this appendix if we expound upon the conditional nature of salvation in the Old Testament, Gospels, and Tribulation. However, it should at least be noted that no verse in that body of literature indicates that salvation is permanent. There are no words such as "sealed," "guarantee," or "New Birth." Moreover, the conditional nature of salvation is set forth clearly in verses such as Deuteronomy 6:30; Ezekiel 33:11–16; Matthew 10:22; 24:13; and Revelation 2:10,11. For more information on the permanence of Christian salvation and of the holy spirit being given permanently to Christians, see, Graeser, Lynn, and Schoenheit, op. cit., *The Gift of Holy Spirit*, pp. 13–16, 24–25, 74–80.

one major reason that God would say that the Law had "no glory" in comparison to the Age of Grace.

Once it is understood that the permanence of salvation actually changed in the Age of Grace, the reason for the debate that has raged about the permanence of salvation can be understood as well. Many Bible teachers say salvation is permanent and quote verses that reinforce their position. Other teachers say that a person can lose his salvation and quote verses to support that position. Why is there such a problem? The answer is in large part due to the fact that in the Church Age salvation is "birth" and is permanent, but in the Old Testament, Gospels, and Book of Revelation salvation can be lost if one is not faithful. People who try to integrate the Bible into a "whole" rather than seeing God's gracious dealings in individual administrations have to choose sides about the permanence of salvation and find that there are verses that they cannot reconcile with their position, hence the debate over the subject. Once it is understood that Scripture must be examined with the individual administrations or dispensations in mind, the entire subject of salvation fits together.[11]

The Lord went to great lengths to reveal the permanence of salvation in his words to the Church. In contrast to the other terms that were covered earlier in this appendix, such as "saved" and "saint," etc., the word "Christian" (Acts 11:26; 26:28; 1 Pet. 4:16) refers to a person who has been promised everlasting life in the Church Age by being born of God. The word "Christian" applies only to those people who are saved during the Administration of Grace and it is not used in the Old Testament, Gospels, or the Book of Revelation.

A "Christian" is specifically and uniquely someone who has been "born again" (also translated as the "New Birth"). God chose the

---

[11] There are a few difficult verses in the Scripture written to the Church that have been occasionally used to show that Christians can lose their salvation. However, studying them reveals that in fact they are consistent with the truth that a Christian cannot lose his salvation. It would be off the subject of this book to do explanations of the difficult verses related to permanent salvation.

words "born again" very carefully. For a human baby to be born, the father contributes "seed" (sperm). Once the child is born, he cannot become "unborn." That is exactly the case with the Christian. A Christian has the "seed" (Greek: *sperma*, "seed, sperm, offspring") of the Father in him (1 Pet. 1:23; 1 John 3:9). The seed of God is as permanent as the seed of any human father. This "seed" and the "New Birth" are unique to the Christian Church.

Christians are "born again" when they confess that Jesus is Lord and believe God raised him from the dead (Rom. 10:9). At that time they receive the gift of holy spirit that is "sealed" inside them (Eph. 1:13). Before we develop this truth from Scripture, it is important to realize that the gift of holy spirit was not even given in its fullness until the Day of Pentecost in Acts 2. Before then, very few believers had holy spirit. For example, at the time of the Exodus, God placed holy spirit on seventy men so Moses would have help from others who had the spirit of God (Num. 11:16–30). It is significant that only seventy men had holy spirit when there were millions of Israelites who left Egypt. Moses wished that God would place his spirit on more people. He said to Joshua, "I wish that all the Lord's people were prophets and the Lord would put His spirit on them" (Num. 11:29b). Anyone who reads the Old Testament realizes that only a select few people had God's gift of holy spirit upon them. Furthermore, if someone was blessed enough to have holy spirit, he could lose it by disobedience. Saul and Samson lost it, although it was given back to Samson when he prayed to God: "Strengthen me just once more" (Judg. 16:28). David, after committing adultery with Bathsheba, prayed to God, "Do not cast me from your presence or take your Holy Spirit from me" (Ps. 51:11).

Although very few people throughout the Old Testament had holy spirit, the prophets foretold of a time when God's gift of holy spirit would be poured out on "all people" (Joel 2:28). Isaiah wrote, "I will pour out my spirit on your offspring, and my blessing on your descendants" (Isa. 44:3b). These prophecies of the coming of holy spirit were not spoken to the Christian Church, however. For one thing, it was never stated that holy spirit would come by "birth" and be permanently sealed inside those who believed. For another, all the Old Testament prophecies of the coming holy spirit referred to its coming *after* Armageddon as part of the Kingdom. The way it has been given by the Lord to his Church was hidden in the Old Testament.

Not only was the gift of holy spirit not poured out during the Old Testament, it was not given during the Gospel period. Even after his death and resurrection, Jesus told the disciples they would have to "wait" for it to come (Acts 1:4). On the Day of Pentecost, ten days after his ascension into heaven, Christ poured out the gift of holy spirit (Acts 2:4,33). Peter made it plain to the crowd that starting that day "every one" of them could receive this gift (Acts 2:38). This was very different from the Old Testament and Gospels and a dramatic change in its availability.

Christians must realize that the way God communicates truth to us in Scripture is by words, by vocabulary. Therefore, we must read very carefully and pay attention to what God says and where He says it. We must pay particular attention to the literature in the New Testament addressed to Christians if we are going to understand the unique truth that God has made available to the Church. When it comes to salvation, God's Word is very specific, and it makes a clear distinction between the salvation that Christians have and the salvation that people had in other administrations.

As stated above, Christians are "born" of God and birth is permanent. Any parent knows that once a baby is born, the child is a permanent addition to the family. God uses the word "birth" to make the point that our salvation is permanent. In fact, He uses several words for birth just so that the point is very clear. Christians are **"born again"** (1 Pet. 1:3,23). The Greek word used in these verses is ***anagennao***, which is built from the prefix *ana*, "again," and the word *gennao*, "to be born." *Anagennao* literally means "born again," and it is used specifically of Christians. Another word that reveals the Christian's experience of birth is ***paliggenesia***, which appears in Titus 3:5 as "**rebirth**." This word is from *palin*, "again, anew" and *genesis*, "origin, beginning, birth." It literally means a "new origin" or "rebirth." A third word that reveals the Christian's birth into the family of God is in James 1:18, which reads that God "chose to give us **birth** through the Word." The Greek word translated "birth" is ***apokueo*** and means "to bring forth from the womb, to give birth to."

The three separate and distinct words for "birth" used in reference to the individual's salvation by New Birth are used *only in letters written to the Christian Church*. These words are not used of an individual New Birth before the Day of Pentecost, nor are they used in the Book of Revelation, which concerns those on earth after the Rapture. Adding to the evidence are 1 John 2:29, 1 John 4:7, and other scriptures stating that Christians are "**born**" *[gennao]* of God. These verses use the standard word for birth that is used throughout the New Testament for the birth of human babies, but only in the letters to the Church is *gennao* used of the spiritual birth of an individual.[12] Of course, to say that one is "born of God," reinforces the truth that the Christian has had a "New Birth." Thus, as 1 John 3:1 states, Christians are "children" of God and we call God, "Abba, Father" (Rom. 8:15).

---

[12] John 1:13 needs to be clarified. John 1:13 has been used to show the New Birth was available before the Day of Pentecost. However, there is good evidence that the opening of the verse is singular and refers to Jesus Christ. Although the evidence of the Greek text favors the plural reading, there are very competent scholars who, for textual, contextual, and logical reasons, make the case that the opening words refer to Christ, not believers. Using the KJV, which much more literally follows the Greek text, the proper reading should be, "(12b) who believe on his name, (13) who [Jesus, referring back to "his name"] was born, not of blood, nor of the will of the flesh, nor of the will of man, but of God." This verse is not referring to the New Birth that Christians have, it is referring to the birth of Jesus Christ, and verse 14 continues the theme and says that the *logos* "became flesh." For more information see R. C. H. Lenski, *The Interpretation of St. John's Gospel* (Augsburg Publishing House, Minneapolis, MN, 1961), pp. 63–70, and Bullinger, op. cit., *Companion Bible*, marginal note on John 1:13.

Another word that indicates the permanence of Christian salvation, and one that occurs only in the Church Epistles, is *huiothesia*, which means "adoption." Vine notes that *huiothesia* means, "the place and condition of a son given to one to whom it does not naturally belong."[13] Because other verses say that Christians are "born" as children of God, one naturally wonders why Romans, Ephesians, and Galatians mention adoption. Is not birth preferable to adoption? Interestingly, in the Roman world, it was not. Romans recognized that when a child was born "you get what you got" whether you liked it or not, and if a Roman father did not like his children, he could disown them. On the other hand, according to Roman law, if a family adopted a child, that was their choice, so the adoption was permanent. Thus, in the Epistles written to churches that were heavily influenced by Roman culture and keenly aware of Roman law, the Lord indicated the permanence of Christian salvation by using the word "adoption" (Rom. 8:15,23; 9:4; Gal. 4:5; Eph. 1:5).[14]

Other verses in the epistles to the Church record what happens when a person becomes a child of God by birth. Note that most of these truths are recorded in the Church Epistles and none are written of people who lived outside of the Church Age. When God puts His incorruptible seed inside the Christian, he becomes "a new creation" (2 Cor. 5:17; Gal. 6:15). The Christian is literally "created" in Christ Jesus (Eph. 2:10). There is a "new man" created within (Eph. 4:24, KJV) that is called "the inward man" (Rom. 7:22; 2 Cor. 4:16, KJV). God's creation in each Christian is called, "Christ in you, the Hope of Glory" (Col. 1:27). As wonderful as Abraham was, he was never "a new creation" in Christ. As great a man as Daniel was, he never had a

---

[13] Vine, op. cit, *Lexicon*, p. 24.

[14] For an extensive and well-documented treatment of the subject of the permanence of adoption in the Roman world, see Charles Welch, *The Just and the Justifier* (The Berean Publishing Trust, London), pp. 208–13.

"new man," an inward man, created within him. As great a believer as Esther was, she never had "Christ in her."

In birth, the nature of the parents is conveyed to the children. Human parents give birth to human children with human natures and characteristics. When a Christian is "born" of God, he becomes a "partaker of the divine nature" (2 Pet. 1:4, KJV). This is uniquely stated about Christians. None of the great believers before the Church Age were partakers of the divine nature. That privilege came with the New Birth.

When God, who is "Holy" and "Spirit," gives birth in a Christian, that Christian permanently receives the nature of the Father, i.e., "holy spirit." We are "filled" (Acts 2:4) and "sealed" (2 Cor. 1:22; Eph. 1:13) with holy spirit. The significance of the word "sealed" should not be missed by the Bible student. There were people in the Old Testament and Gospels who had holy spirit upon them, but nowhere except in the Church Epistles does the Bible say that people are "sealed" with holy spirit. Before Pentecost, holy spirit was specifically *not* sealed in the believer. As we just saw above, at least two people in the Old Testament, King Saul and Samson, lost the spirit of God when they disobeyed Him. The word "sealed," in the Church Epistles, especially when it is contrasted with other parts of the Bible, is a strong proof of the permanence of salvation. Why say holy spirit is "sealed" inside each Christian if in actuality it is not?

Because holy spirit is sealed inside the believer, the Bible says it is the "guarantee" of our coming inheritance. "Guarantee" (*arrabon*) is another word that occurs only in the Church Epistles (2 Cor. 1:22; 5:5; Eph. 1:14). Zodhiates writes about *arrabon*, and says it is:

> "...earnest money, a pledge, something which stands for part of the price and paid beforehand to confirm the trans-action. Used in the NT only in a figurative sense and spoken of the Holy Spirit which God has given to believers

in this present life to assure them of their future and eternal inheritance."[15]

The word "guarantee" should assure us of our future salvation, and it is missing from the Old Testament, Gospels, and Book of Revelation because salvation was not guaranteed or assured in those administrations. The fact that holy spirit is called a "guarantee" of our salvation speaks for itself about the permanence of Christian salvation. What kind of guarantee would it be if it did not in fact guarantee anything?

Another truth hidden in the Old Testament and revealed in the Church Epistles is that the Christian Church is the "Body" of Christ (1 Cor. 12:27; Eph. 1:23; 4:12; 5:23,30; Col. 1:18; 2:19). There is no prophecy in the Old Testament or Gospels that the Church would be so intimately and permanently connected with Christ that we would be called "the Body of Christ." Body parts are permanent. Corinthians mentions feet, hands, eyes, and ears. Our hands are part of our bodies, and no one expects their hand to somehow "fall away" and become disconnected from the rest of the Body. So it is with the Body of Christ. In contrast with what we have today, Israel is never called "the Body of Christ." That privilege was reserved for the Church in the Administration of the Secret. The fact that we are the Body of Christ in part explains why the phrase "in Christ" is not used outside of the Scripture written to Christians. As part of the Body of Christ, each Christian is "in Christ."

It is not only individual words such as *anagennao* (born again), *arrabon* (guarantee), and "sealed" that reveal the permanent salvation that God has made available to Christians. There are many ways God expresses it. Chapter 6, Rewards in the Future Kingdom, showed that there are sections in the Epistles conveying the truth of the permanence of salvation. 1 Corinthians 3:10–17 was covered, which shows that even if one's works are burned and he suffers loss, "he himself will be saved." In contrast, in the Old Testament, there is no such

---

[15] Zodhiates, op. cit., *Word Study Dictionary*, p. 257.

promise. 2 Timothy 2:11–13 was also covered in Chapter 6, showing the permanence of salvation.

This appendix is not the place for a complete and exhaustive study, but another example that really stands out is in Romans. Romans 8:36 quotes Psalm 44:22 that we are considered as sheep for the slaughter, but 8:37 says, "No" (Wow! How about that for a change from the Old Testament), and then the text goes on to say that nothing in all of creation "will be able to separate us from the love of God that is in Christ Jesus our Lord" (Rom. 8:39b). This is a stark contrast to the teaching of the Old Testament. In Hosea's time, Israel had so disobeyed God that He said, "I will no longer show love to the house of Israel" (Hos. 1:6b). A short time later, when Israel would still not repent, God was even more forceful and said, "You are not my people and I am not your God" (Hos. 1:9). It should certainly be comforting to Christians to know that in this Age of Grace, we cannot be separated from God and His love.

When the Lord sealed holy spirit within Christians and gave them permanent salvation, he also gave them two new manifestations of holy spirit, which are speaking in tongues and the interpretation of tongues (1 Cor. 12:10). Speaking in tongues is a prayer and praise language that the person speaking does not understand but that is given to him by the Lord. It is a manifestation, an outward evidence, of the inner presence of holy spirit (1 Cor. 12:7); it is speaking to God (1 Cor. 14:2); it edifies the individual (1 Cor. 14:4); and it is giving thanks to God (1 Cor. 14:16,17). The other seven manifestations of holy spirit, which include prophecy, miracles, and healing, were available in the Old Testament and Gospels and were operated by those select people who had the spirit of God upon them. Speaking in tongues and interpretation of tongues, however, were not available before Acts 2, nor is there any prophecy about them until after Christ's resurrection.

Speaking in tongues was first manifested in Acts 2 on the day of Pentecost when the Church started, was practiced by the early Church in Acts (Acts 2:4; 10:46; 19:6), and is still available today (many

Christians speak in tongues). Among other things, speaking in tongues assures the speaker of the presence of holy spirit within. God wants every Christian to have that assurance as well as all the other blessings of tongues, so He says, "I want every one of you to speak in tongues" (1 Cor. 14:5a). It is noteworthy that Corinthians says that speaking in tongues will cease (1 Cor. 13:8), however, exactly when is not stated. It would seem logical that they would cease at the Rapture because there are no Old Testament prophecies about the Millennial Kingdom that mention tongues.

The fact that Christians do not have to stay faithful to God to maintain their salvation has been a point of contention for many people. A common rebuttal is, "Well, if that were true, then Christians could do anything they want and still be saved." While that may seem like a good argument, it is based on human feelings and not biblical evidence. Are we to be offended because God is good? The actual evidence in the text is quite clear: a Christian cannot lose his salvation. Nevertheless, there are good reasons a Christian should not sin even though his salvation is assured. As we have seen earlier in this book, sin affects one's future rewards. Furthermore, the Bible says that those who practice sin become slaves to sin—not a desirable thing. The fact that the Christian's salvation is assured allows each of us to let go of anxiety and concern about the future and concentrate fully on pleasing the Lord whether we succeed or fail in our endeavors.

In conclusion, although this appendix is not an exhaustive study of the topic, it shows that a careful reading of the letters to the Christian Church reveal that salvation for the Christian is permanent, unlike salvation for the people of the Old Testament, Gospels, and Tribulation, when salvation was conditional. The Administration of Grace is unique because although God uses many of the same words for Christian salvation as are used in the Bible for salvation in other ages, salvation in the Church Age is based upon the one-time experience of the New Birth.[16]

---

[16] The permanence of salvation in this Grace Administration is taught by several denominations besides CES and there are many books on the subject, including: Joseph C. Dillow, *The Reign of the Servant Kings* (Schoettle Publishing Co., Hayesville, NC, 1992) and Charles Stanley, *Eternal Security* (Thomas Nelson Publishers, Nashville, TN, 1990). For even more background on why CES teaches the permanence of a Christian's salvation, refer to the booklets: *24 Reasons Why Salvation is Permanent for Christians* (Christian Educational Services, Indianapolis, IN) and *Becoming a Christian: Why? What? How?* (Christian Educational Services, Indianapolis, IN).

Areas Assigned to the Tribes of Israel

A comparison of the areas assigned to the tribes of Israel as divided by Joshua (Joshua 13–21) and as they will be divided in the Millennial Kingdom according to Ezekiel 45, 47, and 48.

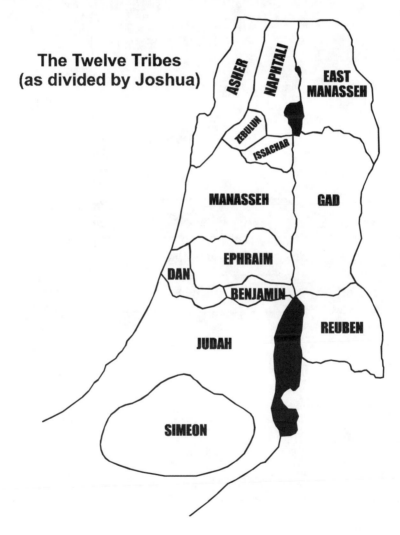

The Twelve Tribes (as divided by Joshua)

ASHER

NAPHTALI

EAST MANASSEH

ZEBULUN

ISSACHAR

MANASSEH

GAD

EPHRAIM

DAN

BENJAMIN

REUBEN

JUDAH

SIMEON

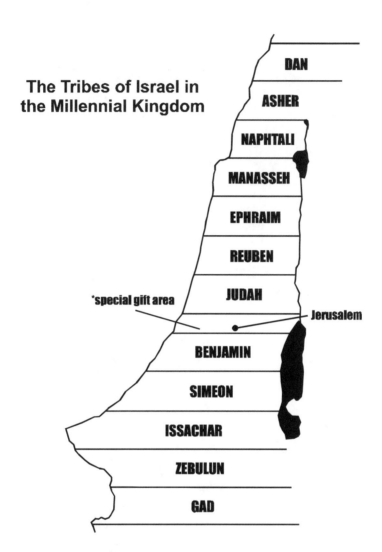

The Tribes of Israel in the Millennial Kingdom

DAN

ASHER

NAPHTALI

MANASSEH

EPHRAIM

REUBEN

JUDAH

*special gift area

Jerusalem

BENJAMIN

SIMEON

ISSACHAR

ZEBULUN

GAD

The Christian's Hope

The Prophetic Perfect

In the Hebrew and Aramaic idiom in which the Bible was written, when something was absolutely going to happen in the future, it is often spoken of as if it had already occurred in the past. Hebrew scholars are familiar with this idiom and refer to it as "the prophetic perfect," "the historic sense of prophecy," and the "perfective of confidence."[1] Students studying Semitic language and thought sometimes call this idiom "here now, but not yet" or "already—not yet."[2] Unfortunately, the average Christian has no knowledge of the idiom. This is due to the fact that in the vast majority of the cases in which it appears in the Hebrew, Greek, and Aramaic texts the translators have not done a literal translation into English but have actually changed the tense. Thus, the "prophetic perfect" is rarely apparent in English Bibles.

In fairness to the translators, because the English language seldom uses anything like the prophetic perfect, most Christians would only be

---

[1] The fact that scholars do not agree on one name for the idiom should not confuse anyone. Idioms typically do not have names. An idiom will be assigned a designation only if it is grammatically important enough to receive attention and it needs name recognition to facilitate discussion. If a non-English speaker heard someone say, "stop on a dime," and asked the name of the idiom, the answer would be that it really does not have a name. So it is with most idioms. They are not individually named. For two of the names assigned to the prophetic perfect, see Bruce Waltke and M. O'Connor, *An Introduction to Biblical Hebrew Syntax* (Eisenbrauns, Winona Lake, IN, 1990), p. 490.

[2] Dean and Susan Wheelock, "Here Now, But Not Yet," *Hebrew Roots*, Issue 00-1; Vol. 4, No. 4 (January, February, March, 1999), pp. 3–8. James D. G. Dunn, *Jesus and the Spirit* (William B. Eerdmans Publishing Company, Grand Rapids, MI, 1975), p. 309.

confused if it were left in the text.[3] For example, the Greek text of Jude 14 says that the Lord "came" with thousands of his saints. Scholars of the biblical languages recognize that Jude was simply using the prophetic perfect to indicate the certainty of the Lord's coming in the future with thousands of saints. But if they translated the verse literally, the average Christian would probably become confused and wonder, "When did the Lord come with thousands of his saints? The first and only time he came he had only a relatively small band of followers."

In his magnificent work *Figures of Speech Used in the Bible*, E. W. Bullinger says that the switch from the literal future tense to the past tense is technically the figure of speech *Heterosis*. He wrote that the past is used instead of the future to emphasize the certainty of an event.

> [The past tense is used instead of the future tense] when the speaker views the action as being as good as done. This is very common in the Divine prophetic utterances where, though the sense is literally future, it is regarded and spoken of as though it were already accomplished in the Divine purpose and determination. The figure is to show the absolute certainty of the things spoken of.[4]

Perhaps the most recognized Hebrew scholar of modern times is Friedrich Gesenius (1786–1842). He wrote about the perfect tense and its various uses (the "perfect" is sometimes called the "past tense," but the Hebrew and English do not look at verbs in quite the same way).[5]

---

[3] I say "seldom" because English does have something akin to the prophetic perfect. If a mother asks her son to take out the garbage, he may respond, "Done." Of course the job is not done yet, but the point is clear—he will do it in the future. The prophetic perfect works the same way; it speaks of the future as if it were already "done."

[4] Bullinger, op. cit., *Figures of Speech*, p. 518.

[5] The fact that the Hebrew and English treat verbs differently accounts for some of the differences in the English translations. For example, the Hebrew "perfect" tense refers to an action already completed, while the imperfect is not yet completed. Thus an "imperfect" can sometimes be equivalent to the English present tense, sometimes

(continued)

Although normally associated with action that has already occurred, Gesenius wrote that the perfect is used in some cases when the event is still actually future. He noted that the perfect was used:

> 3. To express *future* actions, when the speaker intends by an express assurance to represent them as finished, or as equivalent to accomplished facts:

> (b) To express facts which are undoubtedly immanent, and, therefore, in the imagination of the speaker, already accomplished. This use of the perfect occurs most frequently in prophetic language (*perfectum propheticum* [Latin for "prophetic perfect"]). The prophet so transports himself in imagination into the future that he describes the future event as if it had been already seen or heard by him, e.g., Isa. 5:13, *therefore my people are gone into captivity*; 9:1; 10:23; 11:9; 19:7; Job 5:20; 2 Chronicles 20:37. Not infrequently the imperfect [i.e., the actual future tense] interchanges with such perfects either in the parallel member or further on in the narrative.[6]

The last sentence is very important. Anyone studying the Hebrew text will notice that there are many times when ideas are expressed in couplets or parallel expressions.[7] It is often the case when one of the

---

to the future, and sometimes an exact equivalent cannot be determined because there is not enough information given.

[6] E. Kautzsch, ed., *Gesenius' Hebrew Grammar* (Clarendon Press, Oxford, 1910), pp. 312–13.

[7] Psalms and Proverbs are not the only Hebrew poetry in the Old Testament. Job and many of the prophetic books contain large amounts of poetry. "Unlike much Western poetry, Hebrew poetry is not based on rhyme or meter but on rhythm and parallelism. The *rhythm* is not achieved by balanced numbers of accented and unaccented syllables but by tonal stress or accent on important words. In *parallelism*, the poet states an idea in the first line, then reinforces it by various means in the succeeding line or lines. The most common type is synonymous parallelism, in which the second line essentially repeats the idea of the first (Ps. 3:1). In antithetic parallelism, the second line contains an idea opposite to that in the first (Ps. 1:6). In synthetic parallelism, the second or succeeding lines add to or develop the idea of the first (Ps. 1:1,2). In emblematic parallelism, the second line elevates the thought of the first, often by using a simile (Ps. 42:1)." *Ryrie Study Bible, Expanded Edition,*

(continued)

couplets is the prophetic perfect that the other is the literal imperfect or future tense. Coupling the perfect with the imperfect alerts the reader to the use of the prophetic perfect idiom because an event cannot be both past and future. If there is no couplet, the context and the subject matter are usually enough to allow the reader to determine whether or not the prophetic perfect is being used. In the above example of Jude 14, the reader is able to identify the use of the prophetic perfect because although this verse indicates the action occurred in the past, there are other verses which indicate that the Lord will come with thousands of his saints in the future.

The distinguished scholar and author of the very well known *Young's Concordance*, Robert Young, agrees with Bullinger and Gesenius. He wrote: "The past is frequently used to express the certainty of a future action."[8] The Hebrew grammarian C. L. Seow also writes:

> In some instances, the certainty of an immanent event in the mind of the speaker is enough to justify the use of the perfect. This usage of the perfect is especially common in prophecies, promises, and threats. In such cases, one should render the Hebrew perfect by the English present or even future.[9]

Often the only translation that accurately translates the prophetic perfect as a past tense is Young's Literal Translation of the Holy Bible (YLT). Robert Young was very interested in preserving the literal meaning of the Hebrew and Greek in his translation. That made his translation very different from the common translations of his day (the late 1800's), and he was questioned about why he put a past tense where the other versions usually had a future tense. This led to his

---

New International Version (Moody Bible Institute, Chicago, 1994), Introduction to Psalms, p. 801.

[8] Robert Young, *Young's Concordance*, (Wm. B. Eerdmans Publishing Company, Grand Rapids, MI, reprinted 1964), Hint #60 in "Hints and Helps."

[9] C. L. Seow, *A Grammar for Biblical Hebrew* (Abingdon Press, Nashville, TN, 1987), p. 93.

writing some prefaces to his version, one of which is entitled, "The Battle of the Hebrew Tenses." In that preface he writes:

> The *past* is either perfect or imperfect, *e.g.,* 'I *lived* in this house five years,' *or* 'I *have lived* in this house five years;' this distinction may and can only be known by the context, which must in all cases be viewed from the writer's standing point.
>
> In *every* other instance of its occurrence, it points out either—
>
> 1) A *gentle imperative, e.g.,* "Lo, I have sent unto thee Naaman my servant, and thou *hast* recovered him from his leprosy," [2 Kings 5:6]; see also Zech. 1:3, etc.; or
>
> 2) A *fixed determination* that a certain thing shall be done, *e.g.,* "Nay, my lord, hear me, the field I *have given* to thee, and the cave that is in it; to thee I *have given* it; before the eyes of the sons of my people I *have given* it to thee, bury thy dead," [Gen. 23:11]; and in the answer; "Only—if thou wouldst hear me—I *have given* the money of the field" [Gen. 23:13].[10]

There are many examples of the prophetic perfect in the Bible, far too many to list in this appendix. Nevertheless, the following references should be sufficient to make the point that the idiom is quite common. This is especially true in prophetic utterances where God is assuring people that some future event will absolutely occur.

Genesis 6:18. In Genesis 6, God told Noah to build the ark. After telling him how to build it, the Hebrew text reads that God said, "And you **have come** into the ark." The ark was not even built at that time, and when it was built God told Noah, "Go into the ark" (Gen. 7:1). The prophetic perfect in Genesis 6:18 makes it clear that Noah would absolutely enter the ark. Most English versions, not wanting to confuse

---

[10] Robert Young, *Young's Literal Translation of the Holy Bible* (Baker Book House, Grand Rapids, MI), preface, "The Battle of the Hebrew Tenses."

the reader, read something like, "And you will enter the ark." The YLT reads, "and thou hast come in unto the ark."

Genesis 15:18. The Hebrew text reads, "To your descendants I **have given** this land." This promise was made to Abraham before he even had any descendants to give the land to. Nevertheless, God states His promise in the past tense to emphasize the certainty of the event. The KJV, ARV (American Revised Version of 1901), YLT, and NASB all have the past tense in their versions.

Genesis 18:26. Abraham was bargaining with God to save Sodom. God told Abraham that if fifty righteous people could be found in the city, He would spare it. To make His point clear, God used the prophetic perfect. He literally said, "If I find at Sodom fifty righteous people, I **have spared** the whole place." The YLT accurately reflects the use of the past tense in the Hebrew text. The force of the prophetic perfect as a promise can be seen in the context. For example, in 18:28, God does not use the prophetic perfect but uses the literal future and says He "will not" destroy it if there are forty-five righteous people there.

Genesis 41:30. Joseph interpreted Pharaoh's dream and foretold that there would be seven years of plenty and seven years of famine. When mentioning the seven years of famine, he speaks of them in the perfect tense, using the prophetic perfect for emphasis. Literally, Joseph said, "And there **have arisen** seven years of famine." To avoid confusing the reader, almost every English version says that the famine "will arise." The YLT accurately reflects the past tense in the Hebrew text. It is obvious from the context that the seven years of plenty are yet to come and that the famine will follow the years of plenty. But, in the text, it sounds like the famine has already occurred. The coupling of the past and future in the context lets the reader know that the prophetic perfect idiom is being used and emphasizes the fact that there absolutely will be a famine.

Numbers 21:34. When Israel was coming out of the wilderness, Og, the king of Bashan, and his army came out to fight them. God wanted to assure Moses that Israel would win the battle so He said, "Do not be afraid of him, for I **have handed him over** to you" (NIV). Interestingly, almost every English version deviates from the usual practice and translates the verb in the literal past tense instead of translating it in the future tense. Thus, even in the NIV, it seems that the battle is over even though it had not yet been fought.

Numbers 24:17. The prophecy of the coming Messiah given by the prophet Balaam is placed in the prophetic perfect for emphasis. Although it would be more than 1,400 years before the Messiah would come, the Hebrew text has, "A star **has come forth** out of Jacob and a scepter **has arisen** out of Israel." English readers might be confused by the perfect tense so the translators use the future tense in most English versions. The YLT accurately reflects the use of the past tense in the Hebrew text.

1 Samuel 2:31. This verse is a prophetic announcement of what will occur to Eli, the High Priest. The Hebrew text is in the past tense and literally reads, "Lo, the days are coming, and I **have** cut off your arm [i.e., "your strength"]." Almost all modern versions translate this verse in the future tense so it makes sense to the modern reader. The NIV reads, "The time is coming when I **will** cut short your strength." The YLT follows the Hebrew text.

1 Samuel 10:2. The Hebrew text is in the past tense and says, "you **have found** two men." Most modern versions convert the past to the future so the reader is not confused. The NIV reads, "When you [Saul] leave me [Samuel] today, you **will meet** two men near Rachel's tomb." The YLT follows the Hebrew text.

Job 19:27. This verse contains one of the great statements of hope in the Bible. Job knew that sometime after he died he would be resurrected to life and be with the Messiah. The Hebrew text makes this future resurrection certain by portraying it as a past event. The NASB is similar to most English versions and reads, "Whom I myself **shall behold**, and whom my eyes **shall see**." In the Hebrew text, the first verb is imperfect (i.e., incomplete or future) but the second verb is in the past tense and literally reads, "My eyes **have seen** him [the Redeemer]." Thus, the Hebrew text couples the literal future with the prophetic perfect idiom making Job's declaration clear. He knew that his resurrection was future, but he was so confident of it that he spoke of it as being a past event. Most English versions (the YLT is an exception) have both verbs in the future so the reader will not be confused.

Psalm 45:7. Psalm 45 is known to refer to the coming Messiah. Verse 7 refers to the Messiah's love of righteousness and hatred of wickedness. In the Hebrew text, "love" is in the perfect (past) while "hate" is in the imperfect (not yet completed). The Hebrew would more naturally read, "You **have loved** righteousness, and hate wickedness." This is a good example of what Gesenius said when he noted that the prophetic perfect and imperfect are often coupled together and placed in parallel. It is noteworthy that the prophetic perfect places the emphasis on love, not on hatred. As much as it is important to mete out justice to enemies, it is essential for a ruler to love righteousness. The reader is assured of Christ's love of righteousness because it was put in the prophetic perfect 1,000 years before he was born. Interestingly, the modern versions vary in their handling of the verse. The NASB and the ASV put both verbs in the past, while the NIV and the RSV put them both in the present. The YLT closely follows the Hebrew text by putting "love" in the past and "hate" in the present.

Proverbs 11:7,21. These verses offer an interesting contrast between the futures of the unjust and the just. In verse 7 we read, "The hope of the unjust man **has** perished." The use of the past tense in the Hebrew text emphasizes the certainty of the future destruction of the wicked person. In verse 21, concerning the righteous man, we read, "the seed of the just **has** escaped." Again, the use of the past tense emphasizes the certainty of the future salvation of the righteous person. Because the actual judgment of the righteous and the wicked is still future, most modern versions read that the Hope of the wicked **will** perish and that the seed of the just **will** escape. God will mete out justice for both the righteous and the wicked. The use of the idiom absolutely emphasizes that God's coming Judgment is certain to occur and warns people to be careful how they live.

Isaiah 9:6. This verse speaks of the coming Messiah. To mark the certainty of the Messiah's future coming, the past tense is used in the Hebrew text. Although Isaiah wrote more than 700 years before the birth of Christ, the Hebrew text reads, "To us a child **has been** born, to us a son **has been** given, and the government **has been** on his shoulders, and he **has been** called Wonderful, Counselor..." Concerning this verse, the noted commentator Edward J. Young writes:

> We must note again how impressive this fact was to Isaiah. He speaks of the birth as though it had already occurred, even though from his standpoint it was future. We know that Isaiah is not speaking of a past occurrence, for the simple reason that to do so would not yield a good sense. Whose birth, prior to Isaiah's time, ever accomplished what is herein described? To ask that question is to answer it. Furthermore, we must note that the Child whose birth is here mentioned was also the One whose birth had been foretold in chapter 7.[11]

Isaiah 11:1,2. This is a wonderful prophecy concerning the coming Messiah, whom God foretold from the line of David. He used the prophetic perfect idiom to emphasize the certainty of the event. The Hebrew text couples the perfect with the imperfect and can be translated, "A shoot **has** come up from the stump of Jesse and a branch out of his roots **will bear fruit**." The Hebrew text of verse 2 also uses the prophetic perfect: "And the spirit of *Yahweh* **has rested** upon him...." Most of the modern versions use the future tense all the way through and read, "A shoot **will** come up from the stump of Jesse and a branch from his root **will bear** fruit. And the spirit of *Yahweh* shall rest on

---

[11] Edward J. Young, *The Book of Isaiah* (William B. Eerdmans Publishing Co., Grand Rapids. 1996), Vol. 1, p 329.

him...." The coming of the Messiah was absolutely certain and God represents that in the text by using the prophetic perfect.

Isaiah 52,53. These chapters contain what is referred to as one of the "Servant Songs" in Isaiah. It is a "song" about the coming Messiah. Interestingly, many of the verses in the perfect tense in the Hebrew text are not converted to the future tense in the English versions but are accurately translated in the past tense. Curiously, however, the translators chose to keep the prophetic perfect intact in some cases. Thus the English reader has no way to tell whether the Hebrew verb is perfect or imperfect because the translators were not consistent in how they translated the section. The section foretelling the Messiah's life and work starts in 52:13 and runs through Chapter 53. In the verses below, where the prophetic perfect is *not* already in the NIV, it will be in bold type. If the prophetic perfect is in the NIV, it will be in italics. Thus, the reader will be able to see at a glance how the translators have handled the text. There are also some imperfects in the Hebrew that were translated as perfects in English. These have been translated as imperfects, either present or future.

Isaiah 52:13–15 (Author's translation)

(13) Behold, My servant [the Messiah] acts wisely, He is high, and **hath been lifted up**, and **hath been exalted**.

(14) Just as many *have been astonished* at you—his appearance so disfigured more than man, and his form more than the sons of men.

(15) So he will sprinkle many nations. Kings shut their mouth on account of him, for that which was not told to them **they have seen**, and that which they have not heard they **have understood.**

Isaiah 53:1–12

(1) Who *has believed* our message? And the arm of Yahweh, to whom *has it been revealed*?

(2) For he grows up as a tender plant before Him, and as a root out of a dry ground. He has no form or majesty that we should look upon him, and no beauty that we should be attracted to him.

(3) He is despised, and rejected by men, a man of sorrows, and acquainted with sickness. And like one from whom men hide their faces, he is despised, and we *esteemed* him not.

(4) Surely our sicknesses he *has borne*, and our pains—he *has carried* them, and we *have esteemed* him plagued, smitten of God, and afflicted.

(5) Yet he *was pierced* for our transgressions, *bruised* for our iniquities. The punishment that made us whole *was* on him, and by his wounds there is healing to us.

(6) All of us like sheep have wandered, each has turned to his own way, and Yahweh *has laid* on him the iniquity of us all.

(7) He *was oppressed* and he *was afflicted*, yet he opens not his mouth. As a lamb to the slaughter he is brought, and as a sheep before its shearers is silent, so he opens not his mouth.

(8) By oppression and judgment he *was taken* away, and among his generation who considers that he *was cut off* out of the land of the living? For the transgression of My people—punishment to him.

(9) And they make his grave with the wicked, but with a rich man in his death, although he *had done* no violence, and no deceit in his mouth.

(10) Yet it *was* Yahweh's will to bruise him, He *has made* him sick. If his soul becomes an offering for guilt, he shall see his offspring, he shall prolong his days, and the purpose of Yahweh will prosper in his hand.

(11) Because of the anguish of his soul he will see—and be satisfied. By a knowledge of him, the righteous one, My servant, will justify many, and their iniquities he shall bear.

(12) Therefore I give to him a portion among the great, and he will divide the booty with the strong, because he *poured out* his soul to death, and he *was numbered* with the transgressors. For he bore the sin of many, and makes intercession for the transgressors.

This section of Isaiah contains many perfects and imperfects. No wonder the Ethiopian eunuch said to Philip, "Tell me, please, who is the prophet talking about, himself or someone else?" (Acts 8:34).[12] With 20/20 hindsight, Christians today all agree that this section of Isaiah is speaking of the Messiah. The use of the prophetic perfect in reference to the accomplishments of the Messiah emphasizes the certainty of his future actions.

Jeremiah 21:9. This verse speaks of the certain knowledge that those people who surrender to the Babylonians will have their lives spared. The Hebrew text reads, "Whoever goes out and **has** surrendered...will live." Of course, no one had yet surrendered, and so the modern versions read, "Whoever goes out and **surrenders**...will live." This is another good example of the coupling of the literal with the prophetic perfect idiom. "Surrendered" is in the perfect tense but "will live" is in the imperfect or future tense. Jeremiah was speaking inside the city, so no one he was talking to had gone out to the Babylonians or surrendered, yet the promise of God was that those who "had surrendered" would live.

Joel 2:21–24. These verses speak of the blessing of God upon the earth in the Millennial Kingdom, but the blessing is spoken of as if it already existed. God uses the prophetic perfect to assure Israel that His promises will not fail.

---

[12] The Septuagint also mixes the past with the present and future in this section, so even if the Ethiopian were reading the Greek Old Testament, he would still be confused about whether the person being referred to lived in Isaiah's past or future.

Joel 2:21–24

(21) Be not afraid, O land; be glad and rejoice. Surely the LORD has done great things.

(22) Be not afraid, O wild animals, for the open pastures are becoming (lit., **"have become"**) green. The trees are bearing (lit., **"have borne"**) their fruit; the fig tree and the vine yield (lit., **"have yielded"**) their riches.

(23) Be glad, O people of Zion, rejoice in the LORD your God, for he has given you the autumn [former] rains in righteousness. He sends you abundant showers, both autumn [former] and spring [latter] rains, as before.

(24) The threshing floors will be filled (lit., **"have been filled"**) with grain; the vats will overflow (lit., **"have over-flowed"**) with new wine and oil.

C. F. Keil, Hebrew scholar and co-author of the well-known *Commentary on the Old Testament in Ten Volumes*, writes on the use of the perfect (past) tense in these verses in Joel:

> The perfect is not only applied to actions which the speaker looks upon from his own standpoint as actually completed, as having taken place, or as things belonging to the past, but to actions which the will or the lively fancy of the speaker regards as being as good as completed, in other words, assumes as altogether unconditional and certain, and to which in modern language we should apply the present [or future]. The latter is the sense in which it is used here, since the prophet sets forth the divine promise as a fact, which is unquestionably certain and completed, even though its historical realization has only just begun, and extends into the nearer or more remote future.[13]

---

[13] C. F. Keil, *Commentary on the Old Testament in Ten Volumes, Vol. X, Minor Prophets* (William B. Eerdmans Publishing Company, Grand Rapids, MI, reprinted 1975), pp. 204–5.

Even though the promises being spoken of in Joel have not yet been fulfilled, God promises, by way of the perfect tense, that they absolutely will be fulfilled in the future.

Zechariah 12:10. In most English versions, the translators have brought some, but not all, of the occurrences of the past tense in the Hebrew text over into their English versions. The Hebrew text reads, "And I **have poured out** on the house of David, and on the inhabitants of Jerusalem, a spirit of grace and supplication, and they **have looked** upon him whom they **have pierced**, and they **have mourned** over him, as one mourns over an only child, and they weep bitterly for him, as one weeps over a first-born." This verse makes it seem as if the Messiah were already pierced, when in fact Zechariah was speaking five hundred years before the arrival of Christ. The prophetic perfect emphasized to the people that the sacrifice of Christ was a certainty.

Before moving on to the New Testament, it will be helpful to note that the idioms of the Hebrew language and culture come over into the New Testament text as well. E. W. Bullinger explains that the idioms of the Hebrew language and culture are reflected in the Greek text:

> The fact must ever be remembered that, while the language of the New Testament is Greek, the agents and instruments employed by the Holy Spirit were Hebrews. God spake "by the mouth of his holy prophets." Hence, while the "mouth" and the throat and vocal chords and breath were human, the *words* were Divine.
>
> No one is able to understand the phenomenon; or explain how it comes to pass: for Inspiration is a fact to be believed and received, and not a matter to be reasoned about. While therefore, the *words* are Greek, the *thoughts* and *idioms* are Hebrew.
>
> Some, on this account, have condemned the Greek of the New Testament, because it is not classical; while others, in their anxiety to defend it, have endeavored to find parallel usages in classical Greek authors. Both might have spared their pains by recognizing that the New Testament Greek

abounds with *Hebraisms*: i.e., expressions conveying Hebrew usages and thoughts in Greek words."[14]

Bullinger is correct about the Hebrew idiom coming into the Greek text, and although he says the New Testament text was originally Greek, there is evidence that there was an Aramaic original text underlying some of the Greek and giving it a Semitic flavor. Matthew and John almost certainly wrote in their native language, Aramaic. Later, these texts would have been translated into Greek. Following are some good examples of the prophetic perfect in the New Testament.[15]

Ephesians 2:6. The verse says, "And God **raised** us up with Christ and **seated** us with him in the heavenly realms in Christ Jesus." This verse is usually translated in modern versions just as it reads in the Greek—in the past tense. Such a rendering creates a problem. In the rest of the Bible, the translators have generally translated the "prophetic perfect" as a future tense so the reader will not be confused. The average Christian is not accustomed to seeing a future event described in the past tense. Thus, when he reads that Christians are "seated" (past tense) in the heavenly realms, he has no training to help him understand that this is a way of stating that Christians will absolutely be seated with Christ in heaven in the future.

F. F. Bruce, noted linguist and biblical scholar, writes specifically about Ephesians 2:6:

---

[14] Bullinger, op. cit. *Figures of Speech*, pp. 819–20.

[15] Two examples of a phrase using the prophetic perfect in the New Testament are John 4:23 and John 5:25. In both these verses Christ said, "A time is coming [literal future] and now has come [prophetic perfect]...." The John 4 reference is to the coming of the spirit, which, although it had not yet come, was certainly going to come in the future just as God promised. The John 5 reference is to the dead coming to life at the Resurrection, a point made clear in John 5:28. So, Jesus also used the same idiom as the writers of the Old Testament. He coupled the future tense, which is literal future, "a time is coming," with the non-literal, "and now has come." By using both phrases together, he made sure that the listener would not be confused and by using the idiom he emphasized the certainty of the events.

That God has already seated his people with Christ in the heavenly realm is an idea unparalleled elsewhere in the Pauline corpus. It can best be understood as a statement of God's purpose for his people—a purpose which is so sure of fulfillment that it can be spoken of as having already taken place.[16]

Christians are literally on earth, not in heaven. Therefore, we have to look up to heaven. As Colossians 3:1 says, "set your hearts on things **above**, where Christ is seated at the right hand of God." While Ephesians says that we are seated with Christ in heavenly realms, Colossians says that Christ is seated "above" us at the right hand of God. Obviously, both verses cannot be literal, and the Bible is not contradicting itself. Colossians is literal. We are on earth now and Christ is "above" us. Ephesians is using the prophetic perfect to say that we absolutely will be with Christ in heaven in the future.

Jude 14. This verse speaks of Enoch's prophecy and literally reads, "the Lord **came** with ten thousands of His holy ones." Of course, the Lord has not yet come, but his coming is so certain that the prophecy is written in the past tense. We can easily see how idioms like the "prophetic perfect" put translators in a tough position. If they translate the text literally, many Christians would be confused. If they do not, we lose a powerful vehicle for God to communicate the absolute certainty of future events.

There are many important examples of the "prophetic perfect" in the Bible and an exhaustive list would be difficult to compile. However, the examples listed above should be sufficient to document that a future event may be spoken of in the past tense in order to emphasize that it will absolutely come to pass.

---

[16] F. F. Bruce, *The New International Commentary on the New Testament, The Epistle to the Colossians, to Philemon, and to the Ephesians* (William B. Eerdmans Publishing Company, Grand Rapids, MI, 1984), p. 287.

The prophetic perfect also in large part explains why the New Testament sometimes says that "salvation," justification," "redemption," "glorification," and "adoption" are an accomplished reality and at other times says they are still future. Admittedly, this can make the New Testament difficult to understand and even occasionally results in arguments between Christians. There are verses stating that we Christians have already been saved (Eph. 2:8, "You have been saved through faith"), verses that state we are in the process of being saved now (1 Cor. 1:18, "But to us who are being saved, it [the cross] is the power of God"), and verses stating that our salvation is still future (Rom. 13:11, "Our salvation is nearer now than when we first believed" and 1 Thess. 5:8, which says that the "helmet" of the Christian is the "hope of salvation"). So, which is it? Are we saved now or is salvation something we have to wait and hope for? The prophetic perfect gives a window into understanding that question.

We Christians are not saved now in the sense that we are already rescued from death and the consequences of sin in this world. We still wrestle with sin and Christians die every day. Literally, although God is working out the process of our salvation now, our complete salvation is still future. We *will* have new bodies, we *will* be rescued from death, and we *will* be freed from sin and sickness. But right now, we have God's gift of holy spirit born inside us, which is "a deposit guaranteeing our inheritance until the redemption of those who are God's possession" (Eph. 1:13; 2 Cor. 1:22; 5:5). The fact that our future salvation is *guaranteed* means that, in the idiom of biblical language, it can be spoken of as if it were already accomplished. Thus, we Christians refer to ourselves as "saved" even though we struggle with sin, sickness, and death in our day-to-day lives.

There are other things that Christians will absolutely have in the future that are spoken of in the Bible in both the past and future tense. The Bible says the believer is already redeemed (Rom. 3:24; Eph. 1:7; Col. 1:14), but also awaiting redemption (Rom. 8:23; Eph. 1:14; 4:30). We are said to have been adopted into God's family (Rom. 8:15, translated "sonship" in the NIV), and yet we are still awaiting adoption (Rom. 8:23). We are said to be glorified (Rom. 8:30), but our glorification is also said to be future (Rom. 8:17 and Col. 1:27 say we have the "hope of glory"). We are spoken of as already justified (Rom. 5:1), but Galatians 5:5 says, "we eagerly await through the Spirit the righteousness for which we hope" ("justified" and "righteous" are from the same root word in Greek—one is a noun, the other a verb).

Christians who are not careful to rightly divide God's Word can end up like the six blind men arguing about what an elephant was like.[17] Each had grabbed a different part of the elephant and was vigorously defending his position. The man who had the leg declared he was like a tree, the one who had the ear said he was like a fan, the one who had the trunk asserted he was like a snake, and so forth. So too, Christians can grab different verses in the New Testament and begin arguing as if the Bible could contradict itself and one verse is literally true and the others literally false. That is not how to establish truth in the Christian world. The Bible is God-breathed and does not contradict itself. It uses words according to the language, culture, and idioms used in biblical times. Paul did not finish writing the Church Epistles and walk away saying, "Ha! They'll never figure *that* out." Certainly not. He wrote using words and phrases that reveal truth. The truth revealed by the prophetic perfect idiom is that the Christian does not need to worry about his salvation, redemption, or glorification. Although these things are not yet fully realized, the presence of the holy spirit in the Christian and the sure word of prophecy guarantees them when the Lord returns.

---

[17] Hazel Felleman, ed., *The Best Loved Poems of the American People*, "The Blind Men and the Elephant," John Saxe, (Doubleday & Company, Inc., Garden City, NY, 1936), pp. 521–22.

Understanding Difficult Proverbs

There are some verses in Proverbs, as well as other parts of the Bible, that do not seem to make sense if read without a knowledge of the future Judgment and rewards. In fact, the verses seem to contradict both common sense and other scriptures. A good example is Proverbs 15:10.

Proverbs 15:10 (NASB)
Grievous punishment is for him who forsakes the way; he who hates reproof will die.

Both statements in this proverb appear to miss the mark. The last is the more confusing so it will be dealt with first. It does not seem to make any sense for God to say, "he who hates reproof will die," because *everyone* will die whether they hate reproof or not.[1] Some Bible teachers, trying to rescue Scripture from seeming absurdity, argue that the verse is speaking of dying "before one's time," i.e., dying young.[2] That explanation cannot be correct, however, because it both violates common experience and contradicts other scriptures. Common experience is violated because wonderful, godly people often die young while many surly, mean-spirited, and ungodly people live to a ripe old age. Scripture is contradicted because it testifies to what common experience reveals. Many biblical writers noted that the wicked often lived long and prosperous lives, something that has always been a puzzle and even occasionally a thorn in the side to the righteous.

---

[1] The only exceptions to this are Christians who are alive at the time of the Rapture.

[2] Kathleen A. Farmer, *Who Knows What is Good?* (Wm. B. Eerdmans Publishing Co., Grand Rapids, MI, 1991), p. 79.

In spite of the testimony of the Bible, there are people who believe that if anything good or bad happens to anyone in this life, it is the will and justice of God.[3] Three of those people were Job's miserable comforters. Job had some very terrible things happen to him: his children died when a wind blew over the house they were in, enemies carried his herds away, and he became sick. The conclusion of his "miserable comforters" was that he had sinned and God was meting out deserved judgment. Eliphaz spoke first.

Job 4:7 (Eliphaz)
Consider now: Who, being innocent, has ever perished?
Where were the upright ever destroyed?

Job refuted Eliphaz and asserted that he had not sinned at all.

Job 6:24,29 (Job)
(24) Teach me, and I will be quiet; show me where I have
been wrong.
(29) Relent, do not be unjust; reconsider, for my integrity
is at stake.

Bildad was amazed that Job would defend his integrity when the physical "evidence" that he must have sinned was so strong. He spoke up:

Job 8:2–4,20 (Bildad)
(2) How long will you say such things? Your words are a
blustering wind.
(3) Does God pervert justice? Does the Almighty pervert
what is right?
(4) When your children sinned against him, he gave them
over to the penalty of their sin.

---

[3] The whole point of Graeser, Lynn, and Schoenheit, op. cit., *Don't Blame God!* is to show that this is not the case.

(20) Surely God does not reject a blameless man or strengthen the hands of evildoers.

The arguments went back and forth between Job and his "friends." Job gave what should have been the deciding argument in Chapter 21, an argument that agrees with human experience and the rest of Scripture.

Job 21:7–15 (Job)

(7) Why do the wicked live on, growing old and increasing in power?

(8) They see their children established around them, their offspring before their eyes.

(9) Their homes are safe and free from fear; the rod of God is not upon them.

(10) Their bulls never fail to breed; their cows calve and do not miscarry.

(11) They send forth their children as a flock; their little ones dance about.

(12) They sing to the music of tambourine and harp; they make merry to the sound of the flute.

(13) They spend their years in prosperity and go down to the grave in peace.

(14) Yet they say to God, "Leave us alone! We have no desire to know your ways.

(15) Who is the Almighty, that we should serve him? What would we gain by praying to him?"

Job was not the only one who had problems with the prosperity and longevity of the wicked. The prophet Jeremiah, who lived a very difficult life, also spoke with the Lord about why it was that the wicked prospered.

Jeremiah 12:1,2

(1) You are always righteous, O LORD, when I bring a case before you. Yet I would speak with you about your

justice: Why does the way of the wicked prosper? Why do all the faithless live at ease?

(2) You have planted them, and they have taken root; they grow and bear fruit. You are always on their lips but far from their hearts.

Habakkuk complained bitterly to the Lord about the injustice of this life and the fact that the wicked seemed to have the advantage over the righteous:

Habakkuk 1:2,3a,13

(2) How long, O LORD, must I call for help, but you do not listen? Or cry out to you, "Violence!" but you do not save?

(3a) Why do you make me look at injustice? Why do you tolerate wrong?

(13) Your eyes are too pure to look on evil; you cannot tolerate wrong. Why then do you tolerate the treacherous? Why are you silent while the wicked swallow up those more righteous than themselves?

Ecclesiastes states what many people have seen firsthand, that many times the wicked seem to do better than the righteous:

Ecclesiastes 7:15

In this meaningless life of mine I have seen both of these: a righteous man perishing in his righteousness, and a wicked man living long in his wickedness.

Asaph the psalmist was another biblical writer who had concerns about the injustice of this life—that the wicked are strong and prosperous.

Psalm 73:3–5,12

(3) For I envied the arrogant when I saw the prosperity of the wicked.

(4) They have no struggles; their bodies are healthy and strong.

(5) They are free from the burdens common to man; they are not plagued by human ills.

(12) This is what the wicked are like—always carefree, they increase in wealth.

The reality of what Asaph saw around him made him question his own commitment to godliness.

Psalm 73:13
Surely in vain have I kept my heart pure; in vain have I washed my hands in innocence.

Asaph was delivered from confusion and had renewed energy in his life when he came to understand the final end of the wicked and could compare it to his own hope of everlasting life.

Psalm 73:16,17
(16) When I tried to understand all this, it was oppressive to me
(17) till I entered the sanctuary of God; then I understood their **final destiny**.

Understanding the final destiny of man is an important key to living a godly and energetic life. It is also essential for understanding some otherwise difficult verses in the Bible. The wicked may prosper in this life, and even live to be old by human standards, but in the end they will be "ruined" (Ps. 73:18), "destroyed" (Ps. 73:19), and they will "perish" (John 3:16). Like the chaff when wheat is winnowed, they will be blown away by the wind (Ps. 1:4), or else they will be gathered and burned up (Matt. 3:12), incinerated so completely that not even a root or branch of them is left (Mal. 4:1). They will vanish like smoke (Ps. 37:20). They will exist "no more" (Ps. 37:10), and their lamp (life) will be "snuffed out" (Prov. 24:20). The wicked have no future hope (Prov. 24:20). When Proverbs 15:10 and other verses similar to it say that people who hate reproof, or are wicked, will "die," they are primarily referring to the final (or second) death in the lake of fire which occurs after the White Throne Judgment.

Once Proverbs 15:10 is understood in light of the Final Judgment, the first clause of the verse becomes clear. While it is true that those who "forsake the way" sometimes suffer "grievous punishment" in this life, it is also true that many hardened criminals and repeat offenders get away with their crimes all their lives.[4] Is the proverb untrue if the wicked go to their graves rich, powerful, and aged? No. Even though it may seem that these people have avoided "grievous punishment," the Christian knows that there is a day of reckoning coming when every thought and action of man will be revealed. Proverbs 15:10 and other similar verses are not "wrong," or even "general statements that are only sometimes true." They are profound messages and warnings and reveal that God looks at human life from the perspective of eternity.

---

[4] Proverbs 15:10 and other verses similar to it can often be applied to this life because God can and does bless the righteous in this life. However, blessings in this life are not its primary meaning.

Does the Lord Judge Now or at the Judgment?

It is commonly believed that God judges people "today" and that He does so by causing good things to happen to "good" people and bad things to happen to "bad" people. Some four thousand years ago Job's friends held this belief and it has continued through the ages.[1] In spite of its many supporters, Scripture indicates that this belief is erroneous. When something bad happens to a Christian, it is not God judging that person.[2] With rare exception, God does not judge people in this life, but awaits the Day of Judgment to execute justice. This appendix will make the point that God is not judging the sins of carnal Christians now, but that some Christians will indeed suffer loss, shame, and be "punished" at the Day of Judgment in the future. In the process of clarifying this subject, some apparent contradictions in Scripture will be resolved.

Some verses in the New Testament state that carnal Christians who die without repenting and confessing their sins will appear before the Judgment Seat of Christ, be judged, and suffer loss, punishment, and shame. Some of these verses were covered in Chapter 6, including 1 Corinthians 3:10–17; 2 Corinthians 5:10; Colossians 3:23–25; 1 Thessalonians 4:3–6; 2 Timothy 2:12; and 1 John 2:28. However, there are other verses that say Christians have been justified (Rom. 5:1; 1 Cor. 6:11), sanctified (1 Cor. 6:11), and accepted (Rom. 15:7). These verses have caused some people to conclude that

---

[1] See Appendix F for more specifics on Job's friends.

[2] Graeser, Lynn, and Schoenheit, op. cit., *Don't Blame God!*, pp. 95–116.

although Christians who have lived carnal lives will not receive any reward, neither will they suffer loss or be ashamed.

The Bible never contradicts itself. When verses seem to conflict, the wise Christian does not "choose sides" and play one verse against another, but works diligently to see how the seemingly contradictory verses can be reconciled. Knowing that difficult verses must be understood in light of clear verses is an important key to resolving apparent contradictions.[3] If there are nine clear verses and one unclear and seemingly contradictory verse on a subject, it is more honest and sensible to determine how the one unclear verse fits with the other nine, rather than to ignore the nine clear verses in favor of the one unclear verse. This appendix will reconcile these apparently conflicting scriptures. It will make the point that God is not judging the sins of carnal Christians now, but some Christians will indeed suffer loss, shame, and be "punished" on the Day of Judgment.

Whenever we discuss a subject, it is important to make sure that we are not just arguing over semantics. Saying that God will "punish" Christians who have been involved with sexual sin in their lives and have not confessed it, is using the language of Scripture (1 Thess. 4:6).[4] Exactly what the punishment will be in the Kingdom is not clear in Scripture, although it is obvious that some people will have less honorable positions than others. It is possible that when

---

[3] Christian Educational Services, op. cit., *22 Principles of Bible Interpretation*, pp. 2–3; Bullinger, op. cit., *How to Enjoy the Bible*, pp. 327–34; Panin, op. cit., *Bible Chronology*, pp. 19–21; Kay Arthur, *How to Study Your Bible* (Harvest House Publishers, Eugene, OR, 1994), pp. 73–76.

[4] Some versions use "avenger" instead of "punish" but the basic meaning is the same. The Greek word means "an avenger, a punisher." "Avenge" means "to inflict punishment on someone who has wronged oneself or another." It is used "when the motive is a desire to vindicate or to serve the ends of justice or when one visits just or merited punishment on the wrongdoer." The definition of "avenge," like the definition of "punish," does not include the concept of correction or modification of behavior. Vine, op. cit., *Lexicon*, p. 82; *Merriam Webster's Dictionary of Synonyms* (Miriam-Webster, Incorporated, Springfield, MA, 1984), p. 78.

Scripture uses the term "punish," it is equivalent to "suffering loss" and means that one will receive less reward than he could have received, or little reward, or no reward at all.[5] By definition, "suffering loss" is punishment. Scripture makes it clear that Christians will receive what they are due for the way they have lived. If they receive little or nothing as an inheritance, that is a punishment.

Some people believe that punishment would serve no purpose in the Kingdom because at that time there will be no ungodly behavior that needs to be modified or changed. This view misses the basic point of the concept of "punishment." Punishment is a penalty or a consequence for a sin or an offense. Punishment means, "a penalty imposed for wrongdoing." Punishment, by definition, is not something designed to change the behavior of a person; rather, it is a consequence for a sin, crime, or fault. Punishment is a vital part of justice, because without consequences there is no justice. While some punishments are used to motivate correct behavior, by definition, correction is not a part of punishment. For example, God is just, so the unsaved will be thrown into the lake of fire and consumed. There is no change of anyone's behavior. They simply suffer the consequence of their actions on earth. The death penalty was prescribed by God as a punishment for a number of crimes in the Old Testament and was not designed to reform the person's behavior.[6] At this point it is important to note that punishment does not necessarily mean beatings, whippings, inflicting pain, etc. Receiving no inheritance because of an ungodly lifestyle will be punishment, a penalty imposed for wrongdoing.

---

[5] The possible equivalence between suffering loss and being punished is made stronger in 1 Corinthians 3:15 where "suffer loss" could also be translated "suffer damage" or "suffer punishment." Vine, op. cit., p. 691; Louw and Nida, op. cit., *Lexicon*, p. 490.

[6] The death penalty was a vital part of God's system of justice in the Old Testament. See John W. Schoenheit, *The Death Penalty, An Affirmation of Life* (Christian Educational Services, Indianapolis, IN, 2000).

There are a number of words for consequences designed to modify behavior. "Chastise" usually means to inflict a punishment with a view to reforming or changing the person's behavior. "Chasten" usually means to correct by punishment. "Discipline" often implies punishment in order to bring or restore control. "Correct" often implies punishment for the purpose of improving or reforming.[7] So, "chastisement," "chastening," "discipline" and "correction" are punishments that are designed to correct or improve a person's behavior. However, none of these words are used in relation to the Judgment. No verse of Scripture says that what a person receives at the Judgment is "correction," "chastening," or "discipline." Each person will receive a reward or loss based on his works, and what he receives is a consequence of his actions in his past life.

The word "punish" in 1 Thessalonians 4:6 expresses what will happen at the Judgment to those who were involved with sexual sins and did not repent and confess those sins. In simple terms, God says that there are consequences for disobedience, and this is true for all people. When God speaks of the assignments in the Millennial Kingdom that will be given to the priests and Levites who were unfaithful to Him in their first life, He simply says they "must bear the consequences of their sin" and they "must bear the shame of their detestable practices" (Ezek. 44:10–13). They lived in sin in their first life and that sin will have a consequence. When He speaks of the Christian Judgment, He simply says some "will suffer loss" (1 Cor. 3:15). Each person will "receive what is due him for the things done while in the body" (2 Cor. 5:10). "Anyone who does wrong will be paid for his wrong" (Col. 3:25). Those who have denied him or marred the Christian Church will be denied (2 Tim. 2:12) or marred (1 Cor. 3:17).[8] The Bible does

---

[7] Definitions from *American Heritage Dictionary of the English Language* (Houghton Mifflin Company, Boston, Third Edition, 1996) and *Merriam Webster's Dictionary of Synonyms*, op. cit., p. 653.

[8] For the definition of "mar," see the explanation of 1 Corinthians 3:17 in Chapter 6.

not say that the consequences people receive for sin at the Judgment will be corrective. Consequences are a payment for the "job" that was done in the first life. A job well done merits a reward. A lousy job merits loss.

The carnal Christian who lives an ungodly lifestyle and never confesses his sin will be "punished" for wasting his life—a gift from God. Jesus wanted his disciples to understand this and expressed it through a parable (Matt. 25:14–30). He spoke of a servant who was given a talent and buried it in the ground so it did not even earn interest. When the servant did not take advantage of what was given him and lost the possible profit from his talent, the master called him "wicked," "lazy," and "worthless" (Matt. 25:26,30). Like the servant in the parable, each and every Christian is given "talents" to use for the Lord.[9] Will the Lord feel any differently toward those Christians who waste the life they have been given, especially since they have been saved by his own blood sacrifice, made powerful by holy spirit that he gave them, and given the very Word of God as a guide and reference, yet who bury their "talents"?

Some people believe that the verses saying we are "accepted" and "justified" mean that Christians cannot suffer loss, shame, or punishment at the Judgment, and therefore God must judge Christians in this life. This conclusion cannot be correct. First, many clear verses indicate that there will be loss and shame for some Christians at the Judgment. 1 John 2:28 says, "when he appears" we will not be ashamed if we have obeyed him. This implies that those who did not obey him will be ashamed. 2 Timothy 2:12 says that if we endure, we will reign with Christ in his Kingdom, but if we deny him, he will deny us. Obviously, if a Christian is denied, then he will suffer loss. These

---

[9] It is a "happy coincidence" of the languages that in Greek the "talent" was a unit of weight (some money was weighed out) and in English a "talent" is an innate ability given to a person by God. Thus the point of the parable is brought home clearly in the English because some people take the talents that God has given them and "bury" them, just as the servant buried the talent given to him.

verses are not talking about the present, but about the future. Colossians 3:24 says that the one who works for the Lord will receive an inheritance, meaning an inheritance in the future Kingdom. Then verse 25 says that those who do wrong will be "repaid" for their wrong. "Repayment" for doing wrong and "payment" for doing right will both occur at the Judgment in the future. Other clear scriptures outside the Epistles are Matthew 16:27, which says that Christ will reward people when he comes and Revelation 22:12 where Christ says he is coming "soon" and his reward is *with him*. The unclear or seemingly contradictory verses should be understood in light of these very clear verses.

The second reason to believe that God is not judging carnal Christians now but is waiting for the Day of Judgment is the prima facie evidence that disobedient Christians are not being "judged" in this life. If they were, there would be a noticeable difference between obedient Christians and disobedient Christians. There are Christians who openly worship the Lord, pray, go to church, give of their time and finances, share their faith with others, and in general live very obedient lives. There are also Christians who, even if they go to church, do not make a serious attempt to obey the Lord and instead are involved in various types of sin: they may lie and cheat in business, commit adultery, use illegal drugs, or participate in any number of ungodly activities. Can anyone honestly say that "carnal Christians" are being judged and disciplined by God in any way that clearly sets them apart from Christians who really try to walk godly before the Lord? Are they sick more often? Do they die younger? Do their businesses fail more often? Do their cars break down more frequently? Do they live in smaller houses and have fewer clothes? Do they lead more tragic lives? The answer is obviously, "No." In fact, many times innocent and godly Christians appear to be worse off than the carnal Christians.[10]

---

[10] There is more on the prosperity of the wicked and the suffering of the innocent in Appendix F.

Of course, it is true that there are carnal Christians who receive some consequences for their actions in this life. Some Christian drug users get AIDS from dirty needles; some Christians drive their automobiles at high speed and become crippled or die in car wrecks; some corrupt Christian politicians get caught and go to jail; and some Christian women "sleep around" and get pregnant.[11] But that does not prove that God is judging these Christians now.

God is no respecter of persons. When He does judge, He will not judge one person for his sin but overlook the sin of another. The fact that only some Christians who sin receive consequences for their actions is a clear indication that they are not coming under the judgment of God. It is more reasonable to conclude that they are receiving the natural consequences of their foolish behavior or that they are under attack from the Adversary. Also, many people do not receive what would be considered "fair judgment" for their sins. Some murderers get the death penalty while others get only a few years in prison. Some thieves spend years in jail while others get parole. When God's judgment does come, it will be equitable. Every person will get what he deserves, not just "some" people getting "a part" of what they deserve.

The reality is that this earth is a war zone. The forces of good are battling the forces of evil. Satan and his forces of evil come to "steal and kill and destroy" (John 10:10). He causes mental and physical disease (Luke 8:26–36; 13:10–13). He hinders and even occasionally stops the work of God (1 Thess. 2:18). He places thorns among God's people (2 Cor. 12:7). Both good and evil people alike are his victims. Meanwhile, God supports the people who love Him. Scripture says, "In all things God works for the good of those who love him" (Rom. 8:28a). He equips His people with "weapons of righteousness" (2 Cor. 6:7). Furthermore the Lord "opposes the proud but gives grace to the humble" (1 Pet. 5:5b). So God resists the ungodly and carnal

---

[11] These actions do not make a Christian unsaved. We have covered in other parts of this book that you can be a carnal Christian and still be saved.

and He works hard to bless those who love Him. The war rages and both the innocent and the wicked are casualties.[12] The fact that circumstances are not going well for a particular person is not evidence that God is judging that person.[13]

Both Scripture and life make it clear that God is not judging the sins of mankind now, but He is waiting for the Day of Judgment in the future. What about verses that say Christians are justified or accepted by God? If it means that they cannot be disciplined at the Judgment, it would also mean that they cannot be disciplined here and now. The New Testament is written from the viewpoint that each Christian has been judged in Christ and is justified in Christ. Romans 6:1–8 makes it clear that God identifies us with Jesus Christ and that when Christ died, we died with him. So, if a verse that says Christians are justified or accepted by the Lord means that they cannot suffer loss, shame, or punishment on the Day of Judgment, then those same verses would also mean that Christians cannot be punished *now*. Yet it is clear from previously cited scriptures that the carnal Christians will suffer loss, shame, or punishment at some time. The logical conclusion based on the clear scriptures is that it will occur at the Judgment in the future.

When the Bible speaks of the righteousness, justification, and acceptance of the Christian, it is speaking in relation to everlasting *life*, not everlasting *rewards*. Each Christian will stand before the Judgment Seat of Christ and be judged righteous and justified because of the work of Christ. But the fact that some people will receive a greater reward than others demonstrates that "justified" and "accepted" are not referring to rewards. Otherwise, because all Christians are justified, each and every Christian would get the same reward and that clearly is not the case. Salvation, justification, and acceptance before God are by

---

[12] The war between God and the Devil is not the only reason for the calamities on earth. Some are caused by the free will decisions of mankind.

[13] This point is greatly expanded in Graeser, Lynn, and Schoenheit, op. cit., *Don't Blame God!*, pp. 9–40, 107–30, 145–53.

grace and appropriated by faith. Rewards are earned; losses are also "earned."

It is the heart of the Lord Jesus Christ that each Christian appear blameless before him at the Judgment. Christians do not lack any spiritual gift or blessing that keeps them from living a godly lifestyle (1 Cor. 1:7; Eph. 1:3). They are fully equipped to be obedient and godly. Furthermore, the Lord will forgive any sin that is confessed. Christ died for us.

Colossians 1:22,23a

(22) But now he has reconciled you by Christ's physical body through death to present you holy in his sight, without blemish and free from accusation—

(23a) if you continue in your faith, established and firm, not moved from the Hope held out in the gospel.

Every Christian is responsible to live in a manner that is worthy of God's calling on his life and the gifts and abilities he has been given. Every Christian should strive to appear before the Lord at the Judgment Seat holy and blameless. This can be accomplished through a diligent effort to continue in the faith, unmoved from the Hope.

"You Must Be Born Again"

An Explanation of John 3:1–10 and Jesus' Statement about Being Born Again

John 3 contains a powerful teaching about the future hope of Israel. Unfortunately, poor translation and wrong teaching have obscured it so completely that the actual meaning of what Jesus said is unknown to most Christians. The purpose of this appendix is to clarify what Jesus meant when he said, "No one can see the Kingdom of God unless he is born again" (John 3:3). We will see that when Jesus spoke about being "born again," he was speaking about the First Resurrection, a subject clearly declared in the Old Testament. Jesus was not talking about being "born again" as this phrase has come into use in the Church Age and as it is commonly used by Christians today. He was not referring to being sealed with the gift of holy spirit and being "born" into the family of God. He was addressing Nicodemus, an Israelite, concerning the Hope of Israel, the First Resurrection.

The best way to begin this study is by reading from John 3.

John 3:1–10

(1) Now there was a man of the Pharisees named Nicodemus, a member of the Jewish ruling council.

(2) He came to Jesus at night and said, "Rabbi, we know you are a teacher who has come from God. For no one could perform the miraculous signs you are doing if God were not with him."

(3) In reply Jesus declared, "I tell you the truth, no one can see the kingdom of God unless he is born again."

(4) "How can a man be born when he is old?" Nicodemus asked. "Surely he cannot enter a second time into his mother's womb to be born!"

(5) Jesus answered, "I tell you the truth, no one can enter the kingdom of God unless he is born of water and the Spirit.

(6) Flesh gives birth to flesh, but the Spirit gives birth to spirit.

(7) You should not be surprised at my saying, 'You must be born again.'

(8) The wind blows wherever it pleases. You hear its sound, but you cannot tell where it comes from or where it is going. So it is with everyone born of the Spirit."

(9) "How can this be?" Nicodemus asked.

(10) "You are Israel's teacher," said Jesus, "and do you not understand these things?"

In this record, Nicodemus, a Pharisee, approached Jesus and engaged him in conversation. The Pharisees, like the Greeks, believed that when the body died the "soul" departed and continued living either in a good place or in a place of torment. Jesus was aware of their erroneous belief and took this opportunity to help Nicodemus understand the First Resurrection and entering the Kingdom of God. He spoke directly to Nicodemus' need, namely, correcting his misunderstanding about death, resurrection, and the future life.

In an effort to gain an accurate understanding of what Jesus said to Nicodemus, we must carefully consider each of the following points.

1) Nicodemus, an educated man and one of Israel's teachers, could and should have known what Jesus was speaking about because it is revealed in the Old Testament.

2) In John 3, the Greek words translated "born again" are not the same Greek words translated "born again" in the Church Epistles.

3) When Jesus spoke of "entering the Kingdom," he was not speaking of *Christian* "salvation," which is something entirely different.

4) Jesus was not offering the Christian New Birth to Nicodemus.

5) Jesus was making a statement of fact concerning the Hope of Israel, the First Resurrection. He was not prophesying to Nicodemus about the coming Church Age.

The first point to consider is that Nicodemus could and should have known what Jesus was talking about. In fact, Jesus mildly reproved him twice during the conversation. Jesus knew that Nicodemus was a Pharisee and did not know the truths that Jesus was teaching him. However, he also knew that Nicodemus should have known those truths because they are plainly set forth in the Old Testament. Jesus said, "You should not be surprised at my saying" (v. 7a). Nicodemus was surprised, but he should not have been. Jesus continued teaching Nicodemus, but when he still did not seem to understand, Jesus reproved him even more strongly and said, "You are Israel's teacher, and do you not understand these things?" (v. 10). These two statements of reproof show that Jesus expected Nicodemus to understand what he was saying.

Jesus would have never reproved Nicodemus for not knowing about the New Birth that is revealed in the Church Epistles because it is not foretold in the Old Testament.[1] There are prophecies in the Old Testament stating that in the Millennial Kingdom holy spirit will be poured out on all people, but that is not the same as the outpouring of holy spirit in Acts 2 that began the Christian Church. It is similar in many

---

[1] For documentation on this point, see Appendix C.

respects but it is not the same.[2] The Old Testament foretold that the outpouring would occur *after the Tribulation,* during the Kingdom of God, and therefore it cannot be a reference to the outpouring of holy spirit on the Christian Church, which is happening now, *before the Tribulation.*[3] Furthermore, there is no reference in the Old Testament to the fact that holy spirit would be "born" and "sealed" inside a person before his resurrection. The few believers in the Old Testament who were blessed with the spirit could lose it if they sinned (cp. King Saul and Samson). So, although the Old Testament foretold the coming of the gift of holy spirit, it *never* foretold the fullness of the New Birth as Christians experience it today. This means that Jesus could not have been talking to Nicodemus about the New Birth and reproving him for not grasping what he was saying.

Jesus could, however, rightly expect Nicodemus to know what the Old Testament said about the First Resurrection. The Old Testament reveals that the spirit of God will give life to dead believers who will

---

[2] The idea that they are the same comes from Peter's statement in Acts 2:16 (KJV), "This is that which was spoken by the prophet Joel." In the Companion Bible, E. W. Bullinger has an entire appendix on this subject and the phrase "This is that" used by Peter. He begins: "There is nothing in the words to tell us what is 'this' and what is 'that.' The word 'this' is emphatic, and the word 'But' with which Peter's argument begins, sets what follows in contrast. This shows that the quotation was used to rebut the charge of drunkenness (v. 13). So far from these signs and wonders being a proof that "these men" were drunken, 'this,' said the apostle, is 'that' (same kind of thing) which Joel prophesied would take place 'in the last days.' Peter does not say these *were* the last days, but that this (that follows) is what Joel says of those days. He does not say 'then was fulfilled,' nor 'as it is written,' but merely calls attention to what the prophet said of similar scenes yet future." Bullinger's assessment of the giving of holy spirit in Acts is correct: it is similar to, but not the same as, the giving of the spirit that will occur in the Millennial Kingdom. Bullinger, op. cit., *Companion Bible,* Appendix 183.

[3] Exactly when the Old Testament prophecies said that holy spirit would be poured out is very important and helps to differentiate between the giving of the spirit to the Church and the giving of the spirit to Israel. The Old Testament prophets with one voice said that the spirit would be poured out *after* the Tribulation and during the Kingdom. Isaiah 32:15; 44:3; 59:21; Ezek. 39:29, and Joel 2:28 all refer to after the Tribulation, in the Kingdom of God.

The Christian's Hope

then be "born" out of their graves (i.e., "birth from above"). Once they are out of their graves, these newly resurrected people will enter into the Kingdom the Lord has set up on earth.

The second point addresses the fact the Greek words translated "born again" in John 3 are not the same Greek words translated "born again" in the Epistles. It makes sense that if what Jesus is speaking of in John 3 is different from the New Birth, the vocabulary that describes it should be different, and it is. It is unfortunate that many translators used the phrase "born again" in both John and Peter because the Greek words used in these books are different. The mistranslation causes truth that is being revealed in the Gospel of John to be lost. In Peter, both "New Birth" (1 Pet. 1:3) and "born again" (1 Pet. 1:23) are translated from the Greek word *anagennao*, which is made up of the prefix *ana*, which means, "again" or "over again," and *gennao*, which means, "to beget" or "give birth." Translating *anagennao* as "born again" in Peter is correct. Christians can correctly speak of themselves as having been "born again."

In contrast with *anagennao*, the phrase "born again" in John 3 is translated from two Greek words: *gennao* and *anothen*. *Gennao* means, "to beget," and *anothen* means, "from above," "from the top," or "from the beginning." *Anothen* is first used in the New Testament in Matthew 27:51 when the curtain of the Temple was torn from the "top" *(anothen)* to the bottom. Another use is in John 3:31 when John the Baptist was testifying of Christ and said, "The one who comes from above *(anothen)* is above all." Here, the translators correctly translate *anothen* as "from above." James 1:17 reads, "Every good and perfect gift is from above *(anothen)*." These scriptures show that the word *anothen* means "from above." There are some well-respected translations that have "born from above" instead of "born again" in John 3:3 and 7, including: The Jerusalem Bible, New Jerusalem Bible, The Message, New Revised Standard Version, New American Bible, The International Standard Version, Young's Literal Translation, The Bible by James Moffatt, The Better Version of the New Testament by Chester

Estes, The New Testament in the Language of the People by Charles Williams, and The Emphasized Bible by Joseph Rotherham. In spite of these translations using "born from above" instead of "born again," the phrase is almost universally quoted in Christendom as "born again," which works against its being properly understood.

In John 3, Jesus was speaking about being born "from above," a truth revealed in the Old Testament, to correct Nicodemus' erroneous doctrine. Nicodemus was an educated and intelligent man, but his Pharisaic doctrine clouded the clear teaching of the Old Testament, namely, that in order for anyone to enter the future Kingdom, his dead body would have to be "born from above." The prophets of old said that the dead bodies of believers would be given life when spirit from above, that is, the animating life force of God, entered them. The spirit would give them life and so they would be "born" from God above and "born" from the grave. Having been born "from above," they could enter the Kingdom. Consider the following verse:

Isaiah 26:19

But your dead will live; their bodies will rise. You who dwell in the dust, wake up and shout for joy. Your dew is like the dew of the morning; **the earth will give birth to her dead.**[4]

---

[4] The NIV and NASB do an exceptionally good job of translating the difficult word, *napal*, which has a basic meaning of "to fall" and in this context refers to "dropping" children, i.e., giving birth. Brown, Driver, Briggs, op. cit., *The Brown-Driver-Briggs Hebrew and English Lexicon* p. 658. Isaiah 26:19 is referring to the First Resurrection. Delitzsch writes: "The dew from the glory of God falls like a heavenly seed into the bosom of the earth; and in consequence of this, the earth gives out from itself the shades which have hitherto been held fast beneath the ground, so that they appear alive again on the surface of the earth. ...When compared with the New Testament Apocalypse, it is "the first resurrection" which is here predicted by Isaiah." F. Delitzsch, *Commentary on the Old Testament in Ten Volumes, Vol. VII, Isaiah* (William B. Eerdmans Publishing Company, Grand Rapids, MI, reprinted 1975), pp. 451–52.

Isaiah not only said that people would be "born" out of the grave, he also wrote that the spirit would come "from above" or "from on high."

Isaiah 32:15–17

(15) Till the Spirit is **poured upon us from on high**, and the desert becomes a fertile field, and the fertile field seems like a forest.

(16) Justice will dwell in the desert and righteousness live in the fertile field.

(17) The fruit of righteousness will be peace; the effect of righteousness will be quietness and confidence forever.

That these verses in Isaiah refer to the Day of Judgment and the Millennial Kingdom is clear from their contexts. Ezekiel was another prophet who wrote about the spirit entering the dead bodies of believers and giving them life so that they can enter the Kingdom.

Ezekiel 37:12–14

(12) Therefore prophesy and say to them: "This is what the Sovereign LORD says: O my people, I am going to open your graves and bring you up from them; I will bring you back to the land of Israel.

(13) Then you, my people, will know that I am the LORD, when I open your graves and bring you up from them.

(14) I will put my Spirit in you and you will live, and I will settle you in your own land. Then you will know that I the LORD have spoken, and I have done it, declares the LORD."

In order to give life to the dead bodies of the believers, God will have to put His spirit in each one.[5] In Ezekiel's prophecy to the dead

---

[5] Unfortunately, this point is veiled in many English versions. The Hebrew word for "spirit" is *ruach*, which generally refers to an invisible force and is usually translated "spirit," "wind," or "breath." Many versions translate *ruach* as "breath" in

(continued)

bones of Israel, the Lord said he would make *ruach,* spirit, enter them and they would come to life (Ezek. 37:5,6,8–10,14). God, who is "the Spirit," will place His "spirit" in the dead bodies, which will give them life. This is why Jesus Christ said to Nicodemus, "The Spirit [God] gives birth to spirit" (John 3:6). The dead are literally "born from above" when God above raises up the Old Testament and Tribulation believers and animates them with His spirit. They will come to life and enter the Millennial Kingdom, which Christ will establish on earth.

The third point addresses the fact that when Jesus spoke of "entering the Kingdom," he was not speaking of Christian salvation. Many Bible teachers quote Jesus' words, i.e., that you must be born again to enter the Kingdom, as if "entering the Kingdom" were the same as "Christian salvation." It is not. When a Christian accepts Christ and is saved, he experiences the New Birth, but he does not enter the Kingdom, which is a place on earth and is not yet established. Christian salvation occurs in this life on this earth. In contrast, "entering the Kingdom" is available only when Jesus returns and sets up his Millennial Kingdom here on earth.

Unlike Christians who are "born again" but have not entered the Kingdom, Old Testament believers will enter the Kingdom without ever having experienced the Christian New Birth. It is important to realize that if Christ had said, "You must be born again [referring to the Christian New Birth] to enter the Kingdom," then Old Testament believers such as Abraham, Sarah, Moses, Miriam, David, Esther, etc., would not be allowed into the Kingdom because they never were

---

Ezekiel 37, but because of the scope of Scripture and the other prophecies relating to this subject, the chapter makes more sense if *ruach* is translated "spirit." The uses of *ruach,* spirit, in Ezekiel 37 that must be clearly understood include, "I will make *ruach,* [spirit], enter you" (v. 5); "I will put *ruach,* [spirit], in you" (v. 6); "there was no *ruach,* [spirit], in them" (v. 8); "prophesy to the *ruach,* [spirit]" (v. 9); "O *ruach,* [spirit]" (v. 9); and "and *ruach* [spirit], entered them" (v. 10). Interestingly, after translating *ruach* as "breath" through most of the chapter, in the final verse of this section (v. 14), the translators of the NIV do use the word "spirit" instead of "breath": "I will put my Spirit [spirit] in you and you will live."

"born again" in the Christian sense of the word. Surely Christ did not say anything that excluded Old Testament believers from the Kingdom! "Entering the Kingdom" and the New Birth must not be confused. Christians must understand the vocabulary God uses in Scripture to communicate truth and that is why having an accurate translation from the Hebrew and Greek texts is so vitally important.

The fourth point to understand is that Jesus was not offering the New Birth to Nicodemus as if he could have gotten born again in a Christian sense right then and there. The New Birth as Christians experience it was not available before the Day of Pentecost in Acts 2. It was then that for the very first time in history the gift of holy spirit was actually "born" inside a person. Even the apostles had to wait until the Day of Pentecost to be filled with holy spirit (Acts 1:8; 2:4), so Jesus could not have been offering the New Birth to Nicodemus.

The fifth point is that Jesus was not making a prophetic statement about the coming Church Age. The main reason Christians believe that Jesus was prophesying about holy spirit that came on Pentecost is that the words "born again" appear in the chapter and they think it refers to the Christians' New Birth. This reason is not valid however, because, as we have already shown, the phrase "born again" in John 3 is a mistranslation. Jesus Christ was speaking with Nicodemus about something of vital importance, namely, a proper understanding of the Old Testament prophecies and the First Resurrection. A plain reading of John 3 indicates that Jesus was talking to Nicodemus about a truth relevant to him at the time that he lived, not about a future reality that Nicodemus knew nothing about. Nicodemus could and should have known about the "birth from above," i.e., the First Resurrection, and this rules out the idea that Christ was prophesying about the future New Birth because the New Birth and the things that accompany it were so secret that had Satan known about them he would not have crucified the Lord Jesus.[6] Furthermore, Jesus mentioned entering the

---

[6] See Appendix C.

Kingdom, which is clearly *after* the Kingdom is made available— immediately after the First Resurrection.

In conclusion, in John 3 Jesus spoke about the First Resurrection. He wanted to clear up Nicodemus' theology about the First Resurrection because Jesus, more than anyone, knew the freeing value of truth. Jesus' statement that one cannot enter the Kingdom without being born from above was exactly what the Old Testament prophets had said hundreds of years earlier. The way to enter the Kingdom was to be born out of the grave by the spirit of God from above. Nicodemus misunderstood what Jesus said because, as a Pharisee, he was not aware of the clear teaching of Scripture about resurrection. Jesus' reproof of Nicodemus, including the fact that he pointed out that Nicodemus was a teacher but did not know the truth himself, fits the fact that the First Resurrection is part of the Old Testament prophecy. Jesus' statement that "the Spirit gives birth to spirit" is what happens according to Ezekiel 37 when the Spirit (God) gives His spirit from above and it then gives life to dead believers. The essence of what Christ said to Nicodemus in John 3 is: "Unless a dead person be given life by the spirit from above and come out of the grave (i.e., be "born from above"), he will not be able to enter the Millennial Kingdom when it comes—he will remain dead in the ground."

Bibliography

Abbott, T. K. The International Critical Commentary: The Epistles to the Ephesians and to the Colossians (T. & T. Clark, Edinburgh).

Alford, Henry. *The Greek Testament* (Moody Press, Chicago, 1968).

Anstey, Martin. *Chronology of the Old Testament* (Kregel Publications, Grand Rapids, MI, 1973).

Anstey, Martin. *How to Master the Bible* (Pickering & Inglis, London).

Arthur, Kay. *How to Study Your Bible* (Harvest House Publishers, Eugene, OR, 1994).

Barrett, C. K. *The Gospel According to St. John* (The Westminster Press, Philadelphia, 1978).

Blaiklock, E. M. and R. K. Harrison, eds. *The New International Dictionary of Biblical Archaeology* (Regency Reference Library, Grand Rapids, MI, 1983).

Bromiley, Geoffrey W., ed. *The International Standard Bible Encyclopedia* (William B. Eerdmans Publishing Company, Grand Rapids, MI, reprinted 1982).

Brown, F., S. Driver and C. Briggs. *The Brown-Driver-Briggs Hebrew and English Lexicon* (Hendrickson Publishers, Peabody, MA, reprinted 1996).

Bruce, F. F. *The New International Commentary on the New Testament, The Epistle to the Colossians, to Philemon, and to the Ephesians* (William B. Eerdmans Publishing Company, Grand Rapids, MI, 1984).

————. *Word Biblical Commentary: 1 & 2 Thessalonians* (Word Books Publisher, Dallas, TX, 1990).

Buchanan, George Wesley. *The Anchor Bible: To the Hebrews* (Doubleday & Company, Inc., Garden City, NY, 1972).

Bullinger, E. W. *A Critical Lexicon and Concordance of the New Testament* (Samuel Bagster and Sons, Ltd., London, 1969).

————. *Commentary on Revelation* (Kregel Publications, Grand Rapids, MI, 1984).

————. *Figures of Speech Used in the Bible* (Baker Book House, Grand Rapids, MI, reprinted 1968).

————. *How to Enjoy the Bible* (Samuel Bagster and Sons, Ltd., London, reprinted 1970).

————. *The Church Epistles* (Eyre and Spottiswoode, England, 1905).

———. *The Companion Bible* (Zondervan Bible Publishers, Grand Rapids, MI, reprinted 1964).

———. *The Giver and His Gifts* (Kregel Publications, Grand Rapids, MI, 1979) reprinted 1964).

Butler, Trent, ed. *Holman Bible Dictionary* (Holman Bible Publishers, Nashville, TN, 1991).

Buzzard, Anthony, W*hat Happens When We Die?* (Atlanta Bible College, Morrow, GA, 1986).

Carty, Jay. Counterattack, *Taking Back Ground Lost to Sin* (Multnomah, Portland, OR, 1988).

Christian Educational Services, *22 Principles of Bible Interpretation* (Christian Educational Services, Indianapolis, IN).

———. *23 Reasons to Believe in a Rapture Before the Great Tribulation* (Christian Educational Services, Indianapolis, IN).

———. *24 Reasons Why Salvation is Permanent for Christians* (Christian Educational Services, Indianapolis, IN).

———. *Becoming a Christian Why? What? How?* (Christian Educational Services, Indianapolis, IN).

Clouse, Robert, ed. *The Meaning of the Millennium* (InterVarsity Press, Downers Grove, IL, 1977).

Cross, F. L., and E. A. Livingstone, eds. *The Oxford Dictionary of the Christian Church* (Oxford University Press, New York, 1974).

Cullman, Oscar, *Immortality of the Soul or Resurrection of the Dead* (The Epworth Press, London, 1958).

Dillow, Joseph C. *The Reign of the Servant Kings* (Schoettle Publishing Co., Hayesville, NC, 1992).

Driver, S. R. *The Book of Genesis* (Methuen & Co., London, 1904).

Dunn, James D. G. *Jesus and the Spirit* (William B. Eerdmans Publishing Company, Grand Rapids, MI, 1975).

Durant, Will. *The Age of Faith* (Simon and Schuster, New York, 1950).

Emerton, J., C. Cranfield and G. Stanton. *The International Critical Commentary: Matthew* (T. & T. Clark, Ltd., Edinburg, 1988).

Ehrman, Bart D. *The Orthodox Corruption of Scripture* (Oxford University Press, New York, 1993).

Farmer, Kathleen A. *Who Knows What is Good?* (Wm. B. Eerdmans Publishing Co., Grand Rapids, MI, 1991).

Felleman, Hazel ed. *The Best Loved Poems of the American People*, "The Blind Men and the Elephant," by John Saxe, (Doubleday & Company, Inc., Garden City, NY, 1936).

Froom, LeRoy E., *The Conditionalist Faith of Our Fathers* (Review and Herald Publishing Assn., Washington DC, 1966).

Fruchtenbaum, Arnold. *In the Footsteps of the Messiah* (Ariel Ministries Press, Tustin, CA, 1982).

Fudge, Edward. *The Fire that Consumes* (Providential Press, Houston, TX, 1982).

Graeser, Mark H. *Defending Dispensationalism* (Christian Educational Services, Indianapolis, IN, 1999).

Graeser, Mark H., John S. Lynn and John W. Schoenheit. *Don't Blame God!* (Christian Educational Services, Indianapolis, IN, 4th ed, 1994).

———. *Is There Death After Life?* (Christian Educational Services, Indianapolis, IN, 1993).

———. *One God & One Lord, Reconsidering the Cornerstone of the Christian Faith* (Christian Educational Services, Indianapolis, IN, 2000).

———. *The Gift of Holy Spirit: Every Christian's Divine Deposit* (Christian Educational Services, Indianapolis, IN, 1995).

Hackett, H. B., ed. *Smith's Dictionary of the Bible* (Baker Book House, Grand Rapids, MI, reprinted 1981).

Harris, R. Laird, Gleason L. Archer and Bruce K. Waltke. *Theological Wordbook of the Old Testament* (Moody Press, Chicago, IL, 1980).

Hastings, James, *A Dictionary of the Bible* (Hendrickson Publishers, Peabody, MA, reprinted, 1988).

Hatch, Sidney. *Daring to Differ: Adventures in Conditional Immortality* (Brief Bible Studies, Sherwood, OR, 1991)

Howard, Rick C. *The Judgment Seat of Christ* (Naioth Sound and Publishing, Woodside, CA, 1990).

Kautzsch, E., ed. *Gesenius' Hebrew Grammar* (Clarendon Press, Oxford, 1910).

Keil, C. F. *Commentary on the Old Testament in Ten Volumes, Vol. X, Minor Prophets* (William B. Eerdmans Publishing Company, Grand Rapids, MI, reprinted 1975).

Kreeft, Peter. *Everything You Ever Wanted to Know About Heaven But Never Dreamed of Asking* (Ignatius Press, San Francisco, 1990).

Kuschel, Karl-Josef. *Born Before All Time? The Dispute over Christ's Origin* (Crossroads, New York, 1992).

Larkin, Clarence. *The Greatest Book On Dispensationalism In The World* (Rev. Clarence Larkin Estate, Glenside, PA, 1920).

Lenski, R. C. H. *The Interpretation of St. John's Gospel* (Augsburg Publishing House, Minneapolis, MN, 1961).

———. *The Interpretation of St. Luke's Gospel* (Augsburg Publishing House, Minneapolis, MN, 1961).

———. *The Interpretation of St. Paul's Epistles to the Colossians, to the Thessalonians, to Timothy, to Titus, and to Philemon* (Augsburg Publishing House, Minneapolis, MN, 1961).

———. *The Interpretation of St. Paul's Epistles to the Galatians, Ephesians and Philippians* (Augsburg Publishing House, Minneapolis, MN, 1961).

Lightfoot, John. *A Commentary on the New Testament from the Talmud and Hebraica* (Hendrickson Publishers, Peabody, MA, reprinted 1989).

Marshal, Howard, ed. *New Bible Dictionary* (Intervarsity Press, Downers Grove, IL, 3rd edition, 1996).

Metzger, Bruce. *A Textual Commentary on the Greek New Testament* (Deutsche Bibelgesellschaft/German Bible Society, Stuttgart, 1994).

———. *The Text of the New Testament: Its Transmission, Corruption and Restoration* (Oxford University Press, New York, 1992).

Mills, Watson, ed. *Mercer Dictionary of the* Bible (Mercer University Press, Macon, GA, 1990).

Morris, Leon. *The Gospel According to Matthew* (William B. Eerdmans Publishing Company, Grand Rapids, MI, 1992).

Mounce, Robert H. *New International Biblical Commentary: Matthew* (Hendrickson Publishers, Peabody, MA, 1985).

Nicoll, W. R. *The Expositor's Greek New Testament* (Wm. B. Eerdmans Publishing Company, Grand Rapids, MI, reprinted, 1990).

Panin, Ivan. *Bible Chronology* (The Association of the Covenant People, Vancouver, BC).

Plummer, Alfred. *The International Critical Commentary: The Gospel According to S. Luke* (T. & T. Clarke, Ltd., Edinburg).

Robertson, A. T. *Word Pictures in the New Testament* (Baker Book House, Grand Rapids, MI, 1930).

Ryken, Leland, James C. Wilhoit and Tremper Longman III, eds. *Dictionary of Biblical Imagery* (Intervarsity Press, Downers Grove, IL, 1998).

Ryrie, Charles C. *Dispensationalism* (Moody Press, Chicago, 1995).

Sarna, Nahum M. *The JPS Torah Commentary: Genesis* (The Jewish Publication Society, New York, 1989).

Schoenheit, John W. *Sex and Scripture: A Biblical Study of Proper Sexual Behavior* (Christian Educational Services, Indianapolis, IN, 2000).

———. *The Death Penalty, Godly or Ungodly?* (Christian Educational Services, Indianapolis, IN, 2000).

Seow, C. L. *A Grammar for Biblical Hebrew* (Abingdon Press, Nashville, TN, 1987).

Stanley, Charles. *Eternal Security* (Thomas Nelson Publishers, Nashville, TN, 1990).

Tan, Paul Lee. *A Pictorial Guide to Bible Prophecy* (Bible Communications, Inc., Garland, TX, 1991).

Thayer, Joseph. *Thayer's Greek-English Lexicon of the New Testament* (Hendrickson Publishers, Peabody, MA, reprinted 2000).

Trench, R. C. *Notes on the Parables of Our Lord* (Baker Book House, Grand Rapids, MI, 1981).

Turner, Alice K. *The History of Hell* (Harcourt and Brace, New York, 1993).

Vine, W. E. *The Expanded Vine's Expository Dictionary of New Testament Words* (Bethany House Publishers, Minneapolis, MN, 1984).

Waltke, Bruce and M. O'Connor. *An Introduction to Biblical Hebrew Syntax* (Eisenbrauns, Winona Lake, IN, 1990).

Welch, Charles. *In Heavenly Places* (The Berean Publishing Trust, London).

———. *The Just and the Justifier* (The Berean Publishing Trust, London).

Westermann, Claus. *The Parables of Jesus in the Light of the Old Testament* (Fortress Press, Minneapolis, MN, 1990).

Wheelock, Dean and Susan. *"Here Now, But Not Yet," Hebrew Roots*, Issue 00-1; Vol. 4, No. 4 (January, February, March, 1999).

Whiston, William. *The Works of Josephus* (Baker Book House, Grand Rapids, 1974).

White, Percy E. *The Doctrine of the Immortality of the Soul* (Christadelphian Scripture Study Service, Torrens Park, South Australia).

Wierwille, Victor Paul. *Are the Dead Alive Now?* (American Christian Press, New Knoxville, OH, 1973).

Wright, J. Edward. *The Early History of Heaven* (Oxford University Press, New York, 2000).

Young, Edward J. *The Book of Isaiah* (William B. Eerdmans Publishing Co., Grand Rapids, 1996), Vol. 1.

Young, Robert. *Young's Concordance* (Eerdmans, Grand Rapids, MI, 1964).

Zodhiates, Spiros. *The Complete Word Study Dictionary New Testament* (AMG Publishers, Chattanooga, TN, 1992).

Scripture Index

Topical Index

with Christ, 10, 21, 23, 29, 30, 32, 33, 41, 118, 122, 195, 196, 237, 238

Christian
unique to epistles, 203, 211

Christian Church, 21, 23, 24, 25, 26, 31, 40, 133, 134, 151, 179, 203, 208, 209, 212, 213, 214, 217, 219, 250, 259, 260

Christians
apantesis with the Lord, 30, 31
back to earth, 22, 24, 29, 32, 196
carnal, 99, 150, 247, 248, 251, 252, 253, 254
heirs together, 28
holy spirit in, 69
in the air, 23, 179
in the Millennial Kingdom, 120, 177
raptured, 22, 23, 29, 36, 37, 41, 62, 118
with Christ, 24

Church Age, 41, 79, 203, 204, 205, 210, 211, 215, 216, 220, 257, 259, 265

Church Epistle, 25, 26, 151, 195, 206, 207, 209, 215, 216, 217, 240, 259

Church of Body of Christ, 151

confess
Jesus is Lord, 91, 212
sin, 111, 154, 155, 159, 247, 248, 250, 251, 255

cook, 120

crown, 113, 114
incorruptible, 114
of glory, 114, 116
of life, 114, 116
of rejoicing, 114, 115
of righteousness, 114, 115

dancing, 165

David, 13, 39, 41, 60, 68, 74, 103, 212, 231, 236, 264

Dead Sea Scrolls, 130

death, 6, 127, 128, 185. *See also* second death

destroyed, 37, 38, 63, 76, 78, 81, 119
in the Millennial Kingdom, 37, 38, 81, 194
life after, 127, 128, 129, 131, 137
rescued from, 91, 202, 239

desert blooming, 19, 39, 54, 63, 64

Devil, 5, 73, 127, 128, 191, 192, 208
chained, 36, 45, 63, 81, 180
destroyed, 35, 36
in lake of fire, 77, 81, 180
loosed, 36, 73

Durant, Will, 164

Eden, 20, 78, 79, 80, 118, 119, 127, 163, 179, 201, 204

Elijah, 182, 183

Essenes, 130, 138

Esther 4:1, 146

Eve, 63, 78, 79, 89, 118, 119, 121, 127, 158, 162, 163, 164, 177, 201, 204

Everlasting Kingdom, 21, 29, 35, 36, 38, 46, 63, 75, 76, 77, 81, 180

fear God, 109, 110, 112, 113

Figure of Speech
Hendiadys, 77
Hyperbole, 61, 66, 67
Hypocatastasis, 50
Metaphor, 50, 51
Simile, 50

Final Judgment. *See* judgment

Final War, 74, 180

First Coming. *See* Christ

First Resurrection, 24, 25, 36, 37, 41, 83, 122, 124, 144, 177, 180, 210, 257, 258, 260, 265, 266

fishermen, 119

flesh and blood, 86, 193, 194

flesh and bones, 86, 193

food, 42, 53, 54, 64, 65, 90, 146, 162, 167, 177

forgiveness, 53, 111, 121, 149, 150, 153, 154, 155, 156, 158, 159, 255

fun, 65, 163, 164, 165

gather together, 23, 196

gaurantee, 92, 216, 217, 239, 240

Gentiles, 18, 22, 28, 32, 41, 74, 179, 206
ghost, 86, 128, 193
glorification, 239, 240
good news, 82, 83, 101, 115, 138
gospel, 2, 138
  of the Kingdom, 138
Gospels, 25, 69, 179, 189, 201, 206, 207, 209, 210, 211, 213, 216, 217, 218, 219
gravedigger, 119
Hades, 37, 131, 133, 134
Haiti, 141
health, 54, 62, 70
healthy, 63, 65, 84, 89, 167, 177
heirs together, 10, 28
hell, 71, 72, 127, 129, 134, 186
Hendiadys. See Figure of Speech
High Priest. *See* Christ
holiness, 113, 151, 164, 165
holy spirit, 66, 67, 68, 69, 79, 189, 196, 205, 208, 212, 213, 216, 217, 218, 219, 239, 240, 251, 257, 259, 260, 265
hope, 1, 2, 3, 4, 7, 71, 83, 102, 126, 131, 137, 138, 147, 169, 175, 177, 178, 198, 199, 230, 255
  of Christians, 4, 10, 21, 34, 166, 169, 178, 239
  of Glory, 215, 240
  of Israel, 9, 138, 257
  of resurrection, 4
  psychological value of, 5
hopeless, 5, 6
Hyperbole. See Figure of Speech
Hypocatastasis. See Figure of Speech
iron scepter, 42, 43
Jerusalem, 19, 29, 43, 47, 49, 54, 65, 70, 80, 81, 180, 197, 236
  New Jerusalem, 29, 75, 77, 78, 81, 88, 89
  other names for, 59
Jews, 17, 24, 28, 41, 67, 69, 131, 133, 138, 174, 179, 183, 184
jobs, 88, 92
John the Baptist, 103, 138, 261

Josephus, 130
Joshua, 15, 41, 46, 48, 68, 212, 221
judgment, 26, 27, 110, 113, 116, 124, 129, 143, 149, 150, 231, 242, 250, 253, 254
  day of, 124, 247, 248, 252, 254, 263
  Final/White Throne, 35, 36, 75, 76, 77, 83, 122, 124, 180, 246
  in the days of Noah, 27
  of Christians, 122
  reward/loss, 7, 89, 94, 96, 99, 101, 103, 104, 105, 107, 110, 111, 113, 118, 121, 156, 184, 247, 250, 251, 253, 255
  Sheep and Goat, 27, 120, 122, 123, 124, 173, 180, 194
  timing of, 122
Judgment Seat of Christ, 98, 99, 122, 150, 179, 247, 254, 255
justice, 10, 39, 54, 61, 70, 98, 110, 124, 156, 175, 230, 231, 242, 247, 249
King Saul, 68, 212, 216, 229, 260
kingdom. *See also* Everlasting Kingdom, Millennial Kingdom
  "flesh and blood cannot inherit", 193
  "in you", 55
  "not of this world", 191
  "prepare a place for you", 187
  "You must be born again", 257
  here now, 58
  in the Beatitudes, 142
  of Heaven, 139
  of Israel divided, 15, 17
  of Israel united, 15
  seek first, 163
lake of fire (burning sulfur), 76, 77, 81, 110, 115, 122, 124, 180, 246, 249
last supper, 189
Law, 204
Lazarus, 71
loss, 102, 250, 251
  of reward, 94, 99, 102, 149

suffer loss, 102, 110, 156, 217, 247, 248, 249, 250, 251, 254

meek, 10, 18, 34, 70, 139, 140, 141, 143, 145, 199

mercy, 110, 143, 149, 150, 156, 157

mercy seat, 53

Metaphor. See Figure of Speech

Millennial Kingdom, 15, 21, 27, 28, 29, 35, 36, 37, 38, 41, 54, 70, 72, 75, 81, 91, 118, 177, 180, 213, 219, 221, 234

    other names for, 59

mite, 108

moon, 80, 81, 162

Moses, 41, 74, 79, 109, 144, 204, 212, 229, 264

musician, 120

musterion, 205, 208

mystery, 25, 205

    Administration of, 205

New Birth, 104, 202, 210, 211, 214, 216, 220, 259, 261, 264, 265

new body, 41, 83, 84, 86, 87, 88, 89, 167, 193, 195

Nicodemus, 137

parable, 26, 31, 251

Paradise, 1, 3, 38, 42, 43, 60, 63, 72, 78, 79, 111, 118, 121, 126, 175, 177, 179

    malefactor in, 110

peace, 10, 42, 45, 54, 63, 90, 120, 177

peacemaker, 144

Pentecost, 26, 36, 41, 67, 123, 151, 179, 180, 203, 205, 212, 213, 214, 216, 218, 265

Peter, 24, 67, 87, 98, 178, 189, 193, 213

pneuma, 86, 193

prayer, 108, 158, 218

    house of, 69, 70

    Lord's Prayer, 54, 55

Promised Land, 12, 13, 18, 46, 198

prophetic perfect, 58, 195, 196, 223

prosperity, 42, 45, 46, 120

    of the wicked, 243

punishment, 94, 107, 129, 150, 156, 161, 246, 247, 248, 249, 250, 251, 254

quality, 62, 101, 103

Rapture, 1, 21, 22, 23, 24, 25, 29, 37, 75, 124, 151, 178, 179, 195, 196, 203, 214, 219

redemption, 239, 240

remember this life, 89, 90, 121, 133

repent, 98, 113, 153, 178, 218, 247, 250

resurrection, 4, 5, 13, 14, 15, 17, 18. *See also* First Resurrection, Second Resurrection, Resurrection of the Just, Resurrection of the Unjust, Resurrection of the Righteous

    of Jesus, 54, 85, 86, 88, 188, 190, 191, 193, 213, 218

Resurrection of the Just, 24, 67, 75, 144, 180

Resurrection of the Righteous, 122, 123, 144, 145

Resurrection of the Unjust, 75, 122, 124, 180

reward, 4, 7, 39, 82, 91, 92, 94, 96, 101, 102, 103, 104, 106, 108, 109, 111, 113, 115, 116, 118, 122, 125, 126, 145, 147, 149, 150, 156, 159, 170, 172, 173, 177, 248, 250, 251, 252, 254

    in heaven, 183

    loss of, 94, 249

rod of iron, 42, 68, 81

ruach, 264

sacred portion, 47, 48, 49, 54

safety, 42, 70, 90, 120, 177

salvation, 7, 53, 84, 91, 115, 164, 173, 178, 188, 201, 210, 230, 239, 240, 254, 259, 264

Samson, 212, 216, 260

Satan, 43, 73, 89, 180, 208, 209, 253, 265

Second Coming, 23, 25, 26, 27, 28, 41, 45, 70, 180

second death, 76, 115, 246